Planning on Uncertainty

PLANNING

ON

UNCERTAINTY

DECISION MAKING IN BUSINESS
AND GOVERNMENT ADMINISTRATION

Ruth P. Mack

The Institute of Public Administration
New York

WILEY-INTERSCIENCE

a Division of John Wiley & Sons, Inc.

New York • London • Sydney • Toronto

Library of Congress Catalogue Card Number: 79-155905

ISBN 0-471-56280-7

Printed in the United States of America.

10 9 8 7 6 5 4 3 2 1

*For seven
special
young men*

Acknowledgments

At the start of any serious investigation it is necessary to choose whether one intends to be the prey of answers or of questions. If one elects to submit to the demands of answers, the questions must be such as to permit tidy (however complicated) answers. If, on the other hand, the material is given free rein to find its way to the central questions, the answers will inevitably be less neat.

I have chosen the second course. Addressing myself to the problems of business and government policy making, I have tried to explore the essential implications of the fact that uncertainty is ubiquitous. It seemed clear at the outset that the search would need to be made in steps that start with analytically well-behaved decision problems, and move progressively toward the full range of situations which policy confronts. Indeed, "decision" evolves finally into an ongoing deliberative-administrative process, having inseparable economic, broadly political, organizational, and even societal dimensions.

The study has been a safari which, like most, alternates between excitement and frustration. Needless to say, one cannot survive or carry through such a process without the help of friends, who may likewise suffer hardship en route. It was hardest on my best friend, Edward C. Mack, for several reasons, including the work of criticizing several versions. Harvey S. Perloff and Lyle C. Fitch made the book possible; it was prepared under the auspices of Resources for the Future and the Administration of Public Administration. Others whose comments have improved the manuscript are Carl S. Shoup, Gerhard Colm, James W. Angell, William Fellner, Alfred J. Kahn, Jacob Marschak, Harold J. Barnett, Yehezkel Dror, Luther H. Gulick, Peter C. Fishburn, and Annmarie Walsh. For this aid I am truly grateful. Mrs. Walsh also undertook a fundamental editing and pace setting for the entire manuscript; the reader as well as the writer will thank her. Thanks are due as well to Betty Geenty for her skilled typing and checking of copy.

RUTH P. MACK

New York
March 1971

Contents

Contents   xi

Planning on Uncertainty

CHAPTER 1

Uncertainty in Administrative Decision

Uncertainty is the complement of knowledge.[1] It is the gap between what is known and what needs to be known to make correct decisions. Dealing sensibly with uncertainty is not a byway on the road to responsible business and governmental decision. It is central to it. The subject is complex, elusive, and omnipresent.

I head across the lower level of the Grand Central Terminal on my way to work on West 44th Street and subconsciously cope with uncertainty. I must cut across streams of other commuters without collision or undue delay. I am helped by remembering the sign used by sailors— the unchanged profile as two ships approach one another is "collision course" (cope by obtaining information). Outdoors, there are three east-west crossings and one north-south crossing. I head west unless the light has turned quite recently, as evidenced by the size of the crowd at the corner (cope by using ready information). How long to wait is a function of the length of the light (supply the probability distribution for all states of the world). If I miss the next light, I have one more northward block to keep me moving (cope by using the correct decision-matrix). This puny scheming is unexceptionable when done, as it usually is, silently and without explicit thought.

In more significant context, we give our children above all else an education because it is the form of capital judged most flexible and resistant to mishap. We try to take major vocational risks when the penalty of loss is relatively light—before family responsibilities are severe. We hedge bets, make decisions in steps, use information feedbacks, all as a matter of course.

In business and in government coping with uncertainty also takes place as a matter of course and as a matter of design. Design has reached a highly sophisticated form in connection with types of business or government decisions that are repeated under much the same conditions

[1] Kenneth Arrow, "Control in Large Corporations." *Management Science,* Vol. 10, No. 3 (April 1964), p. 404.

again and again, and for which goals can be sharply defined. The business problems of inventory and quality control and of production scheduling fall in this group. Analogous well-structured decision problems appear in government. Indeed, some urgent problems in the field of the military during World War I were responsible for speeding "operations research" on its way: methods built on mathematical development of probability theory were used to expedite quality control in munitions manufacture; the optimal design of naval convoys was another famous example.

However, in both business and government the vast majority of decisions are not of this well-structured variety. It may even be that the more important they are—that is, the more they are capable of affecting the total product of the enterprise—the less they tend to present the repetitive probabilistic profile. Between the highly structured and the broadly diffuse decision, range, in a long continuum, all of the administrative problems of organizations.

At the more diffuse end of the continuum, targets may be hard to describe, alternative actions almost infinite in number, results of each very difficult to foresee, chances of a specified occurrence almost impossible to estimate. Should, for example, a company open a posh central office, a plant in Latin America? Should a local government break an illegal transit strike? Should a national government spend an additional one billion dollars on poverty, on urban renewal, on medical and social research? The uncertainty that permeates decisions of these sorts is not bounded by the alternatives considered. Rather, the greatest opportunity for improvement may lie in bringing still other alternatives within the compass of review and in contriving to modify previous decisions as the situation clarifies or changes. In any event, coping with uncertainty inherent in these broad policy problems requires modified and additional devices and strategies to those suitable to games of chance and quality control.

This book endeavors to explore the implications of uncertainty in the context of the whole range of deliberative administrative procedures. Although the separation cannot be sharp, legislative processes are excluded.

Uncertainty deteriorates the results of most purposive procedures relative to what they would be if all relevant information were readily available—that is, were knowledge complete and its complement, uncertainty, zero. The deterioration constitutes a cost that it is essential to reduce. How this can be done is the central subject of our analysis.

But the persistent attention to the cost of uncertainty, it is important to note, should not carry the suggestion that uncertainty itself is a bad thing. Actually, it will be shown that the cost of uncertainty can sometimes be reduced by increasing the amonut of uncertainty.

More generally let me say most emphatically, uncertainty is truly a good thing. Could anyone face a life of certainty? Success preknown would be tasteless; defeat and grief known to lie ahead would erode the pleasures of today; such knowledge might often indeed be insupportable. Not only the future but the present would be completely mapped—no need for experiment, no open end to learning, the siren whistle of adventure silenced, the deep breath before the plunge replaced by the deliberate gaze of total calculation. I think one must find as much satisfaction in the fact that uncertainty "is there" as did Sir Edmund Hillary in the fact of Mount Everest.

COSTS OF UNCERTAINTY

But although uncertainty is as necessary as the air we breath, it is not, like the air, costless. Of what, then, do the costs of uncertainty consist? They are of several sorts. The first is legitimate and necessary; it derives from a preference for sure bets which sets uncertain ones at a discount. The second and third are undesirable and sometimes avoidable; they reflect the deterioration of behavior due to uncertainty.

The Uncertainty Discount

The most obvious impact of uncertainty on a clear and constrained choice is contained in the aphorism, "A bird in the hand is worth two in the bush." Given that what is desired is the possession of a bird, uncertainty discounts the one in the bush to one-half value. We are advised that the utility of a *chance* of catching a bird is half as great as that of the delivered bird.

Take a second example which focuses more naturally on costs. From my office in New York City, I wish to speak with an individual in Washington. Should I dial his number or put in a person-to-person call? Concentrate solely on the chances that the individual with whom I wish to speak will be in or out, and thus ignore all other possible advantages of a person-to-person call such as the sleuthing capability of the telephone operator. The choice then hinges on the uncertainty discount implicit in the telephone rates and my judgment concerning whether, applied to my problem, they are high or low. A station-to-station call to Washington costs $.80 which is .67 of the $1.20 charge for the person-to-person call. In other words, the uncertainty discount for station-to-station is $1.00 - .67$; the chance at having the conversation is worth two-thirds of having it for sure. Thus, if the person were twice as likely to be in as out, time after time, the cost per conversation would be the same either way—$2.40 for three station-to-station calls (which would connect with the person on two of the three occasions) and $2.40 for two person-to-person calls. If I judge that the chances of his being out are greater than two out of three, the person-to-person call is indicated; if less, the station-to-station call should be made.

Interestingly, the odds change if the call is to San Francisco. The telephone company's rates place the uncertainty discount for the station-to-station call at 1.00 − .51—the charges are $1.70 compared with $3.30. Now, the person-to-person call is indicated only if the person is about as likely to be out as in. Unless San Francisco folk are in fact less likely to be where they are expected to be than are folk in the nation's capital, station-to-station calls across the continent are more often indicated than are those part-way down the coast (assuming, still, that attention is confined to the price differentials).[2]

Placing a lower value on the chance of a desirable result than on the result for sure is entirely rational. Indeed, it would be irrational to do anything else, although the extent of the appropriate discount for uncertainty is often most difficult to determine. In the case of the telephone rates, at least the criterion for the appropriate discount is clear; a further judgment has been required as to what in fact are the chances of a person being in.

In many if not most decision problems in business and government,

---

[2] Rates are those of the winter of 1970. Perhaps I should add how overtime affects choice. Overtime rates per minute are the same for both sorts of calls—$.20 from New York to Washington and $.45 to San Francisco. As it works out, the choice between the two ways of placing longer calls rests on the same probability of the person being in or out as it does for the three-minute call. Take, for example, the call to Washington and assume that the chances of the person being in or out are again, in fact 2 to 1. The average occurrences over a large number of calls would be as follows for a *nine-minute* call:

	Station-to-station		Person-to-person	
Person is:	in	out	in	out
Probability	2	1	2	1
Cost to caller	$2.00	$.80	$2.40	0
Average cost of *completed* call:	$2(\$2.00) + \$.80 = \dfrac{\$4.80}{2}$		$2(\$2.40) + 0 = \dfrac{\$4.80}{2}$	
	= $2.40		= $2.40	

For the San Francisco call, indifference between the two methods again is at the point where the individual will be in as often as out for which both sorts of completed calls average (after rounding) about $7.40 for nine minutes.

predictions may be complicated by goals or utility that can be only partially envisioned and by causality that is complex and obscure. Nevertheless, the discount relative to the result-for-sure is part of the proper cost of uncertainty and must be assessed. It is the source of the first type of cost which uncertainty engenders.

Deterioration of Behavior

But this entirely rational discount for uncertainty is often accompanied by two other costs that imply deterioration in decision behavior which ought to be held in check. They result from befuddlement on the one hand and from externalities on the other hand.

Befuddlement, obfuscation, and passivity constitute a second cost of uncertainty because deterioration in the wisdom, vigor, and effectiveness of administrative decisions results. To illustrate:

The disagreement and confusion that can follow paucity of relevant information deteriorates the ability of the decision maker to deal with the problem even as he sees it. He loses his cool. He suppresses the fact of uncertainty or copes with it improperly.

Uncertainty often narrows the list of alternatives considered; the more uncertain ones may be discarded or not considered at all. Innovation may be eschewed even though its net utility (after allowance for the uncertainty discount) could be expected to be greater than that of the tried and true. An effort to avoid uncertainty may cause decisions to be made in the context of too narrow a "system" or framework. In the extreme, the decision to decide may not even be made. For, when serious uncertainty is present, the mind often shys from a problem; it is repelled by it.

Uncertainty may cause the action that is finally chosen to be badly executed. A situation heavily shrouded in uncertainty may produce poorly motivated follow-through, shilly-shallying, and lackadaisical action. Action haunted by uncertainty also may be unconvincing to others and therefore ineffective. Uncertainty is felt unbecoming to the young man on the way up, to a platoon commander, or to a physician. The government administrator or legislator can still less afford to appear uncertain; if the viscosity of the political process can strangle action having clear benefits, how much harder must it be to achieve action when benefits are doubtful even to its sponsors.

To anticipate a finding of this study, there appears to be a tendency for uncertainty to produce a bias toward overconservatism, toward routine ways to solve problems, toward doing nothing. Such a bias limits targets more than even a realistically large discount for uncertainty would require. The benefits experienced by the decision maker are, then, dwarfed by uncertainty.

The third type of uncertainty's cost results from the tendency of uncertainty to exacerbate disadvantageous externalities—the impacts of an act other than those of direct concern to the decision maker. Thus it is easier to ignore the impact of a decision to withdraw water from a river on the ecology of the estuary if no one really knows just what that impact will be. There are also further costs of this type which are less self-evident. They concern how the costs of uncertainty borne by the individual decision makers add up in their impact on society at large. To anticipate, the total impact is more than their simple sum.

Benefits of Uncertainty

But the impact of uncertainty is not always a cost; it can occasionally actually improve an outcome. Administrative action is not simply a matter of deciding what to do. Decisions often result from lengthy processes that involve all sorts of interpersonal wrangles and Machiavellian tactics. Uncertainty can help to bring these processes to the point where some measure of agreement is achieved. Given the ambiguities and cross-pulls of political life, given honest differences in values and factual judgments, I wonder how often people would agree on a course of action if everyone knew precisely what they were agreeing on. The uncertainty inherent in all aspects of decision can provide the leeway for a rearrangement of fact and emphasis which makes coalition possible and a strategy of achieving consensus effective. The uncertain world must fight fire with fire. In this sense, the obfuscation of uncertainty can be an advantage rather than a cost.

MINIMIZING UNCERTAINTY'S COST

I have used the notion of the cost of uncertainty, as generated in these several ways, as a pivot for analyzing "planning on uncertainty." *The problem is how to minimize the cost of uncertainty in terms of the net expected utility of purposive, deliberative conduct.* A few words on the meaning of this sentence:

First, *minimize* is used in the dictionary sense of "reduce" rather than the special sense assigned to it in economic theory. Indeed, as one explores the full implications of uncertain and probabilistic knowledge, particularly when innovative opportunities are present, the notion of a best result must often give way to that of a better result; what is best is an open-ended question.

Second, as the previous section suggested, reducing the *cost* of uncertainty is by no means the same thing as reducing the *amount* of uncertainty. The cost of uncertainty can actually often be reduced by increasing the amount of uncertainty. This occurs if an alternative is chosen that has a smaller chance of achieving a sufficiently larger utility.

Third, there are many acceptable ways of defining *expected utility*—in terms of net profits, benefits minus costs, advantages minus disadvantages, or progress toward an objective. However, the argument here takes the position that utility and disutility must be defined to include whatever elements are actually relevant to policy—both economic values and noneconomic values, values subject to measurement in terms of money (or other quantifiable units) and those subject to no more than a vague hefting, and values which are directly comparable and those which are not.

Fourth, by *deliberative conduct* I mean conduct that attempts to deal thoughtfully and appropriately with the recognition and solution of problems. Deliberative behavior, since it concerns problems, is purposive. This presupposes a value scheme (and an implied definition of utilities) that provides a basis for preference. Deliberative behavior is also necessarily rational in the sense that it collects and uses information in both a logical and imaginative way. But its power to do either is constrained, among other things, by the characteristics of man and of decision situations.

Some situations are tight little islands. Problems routinely present themselves; values are clear and alternative paths toward achieving them well defined; information on which to base choice is rich and precise; decision agents can behave in a highly expert and rational way, singly and in combinations. Examples of this type of situation in business or government are often found in the fields of inventory or quality control and production scheduling. In contrast, other situations may spread amorphously in time and space: Should a businessman build a canning plant in Nigeria, or a central office in Atlanta? Should a municipality undertake an urban renewal project in a given locality? Should the federal government set national support minimums and how? Such problems first need to be discovered, brought into focus, alternatives thought through and fought through; and only then can a choice be made, at least as a start from which further tests, suggested changes, and further "decisions" may proceed. Clearly this is a process in which participants, trying to do the best they can, behave as human beings with whatever admixture of rationality is, under the circumstances, accessible to them.

Minimizing the cost of uncertainty in such drawn-out, time-consuming situations—situations where at best only loosely quasi-optimal solutions are possible, where deliberative conduct must address itself to people-oriented (broadly, political) as well as task-oriented matters, where an input of good ideas can be as productive or more productive than expert calculation of relative advantage of existing alternatives—minimizing uncertainty's cost in this context must require very different procedures from those needed to devise a sampling method for achieving adequate quality control of machine products.

PLAN OF THE STUDY

I have alluded to a subject of vast scope. And it is this whole range of decisions in business and government executive offices which I shall analyze. Decision processes in legislatures are excluded except insofar as they are reflected in administrative decisions.

The discussion, which is entirely nonmathematical, aims to be of interest to people who approach decision problems from various backgrounds—economics and decision theory, political science, planning, management science, and the like.

This intent has grown out of the work itself. The received doctrine at the narrow end of the range of decision problems consists of an elaborate and elegant expertise—statistical decision theory. At the wide end where policy is shaped, there is an extensive and quite unrelated literature on decisions achieved by means of political processes. This has given rise to a tough problem in organizing the study. However, the actual work has progressively emphasized that each of the disciplines has contributed in ways that are largely *complementary* and not, as many arguments suggest, competing. I find the theme of complementarity repeated in how utility is defined, in how decisions are arrived at, and indeed wherever one turns. Clearly a common language must be found lest the Hindoo fable of "The Blind Men and the Elephant" be reenacted evermore.[3]

---

[3] The fable starts thus:

It was six men of Indostan   The *First* approached the Elephant,
  To learning much inclined,   And happening to fall
Who went to see the Elephant   Against his broad and sturdy side,
  (Though all of them were blind),   At once began to bawl:
That each by observation   "God bless me!—but the Elephant
  Might satisfy his mind.   Is very like a wall!"

The second blind man feels the tusk and concludes that the elephant is like a spear. The other four proceed in like vein.

The basic strategy of the study is embodied in its three-part structure.

Part One sketches the elements of "statistical decision theory." It is concerned with decision proper, taking as predetermined the alternative acts to be considered. It is confined to the uncertainty inherent in a decision situation in which a choice is made when goals are clear and expected consequences, as viewed subjectively by the decision maker, are accessible to quantification. It is the world of economic man and of well-structured decision problems.

Part Two continues to assume that alternative acts are predelineated but develops realistic notions of decision makers and decision situations. Among the many differences between economic man and natural man, three are central: his perception is selective, not total; his aspirations are developmental—they are conditioned by the past and by his image of himself; "he" is typically "they"—a decision maker is usually a collective. Actual decision situations cover, as has been said, an exceedingly wide range. Judgments are required concerning the utility expected to be generated by each of the acts under all possible conditions. Implied is the need to understand causality (make reality judgments) and the need to define goals, utilities to be sought (evaluative judgments); these matters are discussed. Incidentally, to picture how utility is defined and measured, we compare how this is done by consumers, businesses, and government. The answers merge more than one might at first expect. It also becomes evident that the utility to be expected from many possible outcomes, described (completely) in physical objective terms, is itself a range—a probabilistic assignment. In other words, knowledge of how much an outcome will be valued is not certain, just as knowledge that the outcome will take place is not certain.

Decision rules or rather, in this wider context, decision procedures are next considered. However, before appropriate procedures can be selected it is necessary to develop a typology for decision situations. I shall return to both subjects in a moment.

Part Three cuts loose from the tie to predelineated alternatives. "Decision" becomes an ongoing deliberative-administrative process. Typically both economists and political scientists distinguish, roughly, five stages of the process—deciding to decide, specifying alternatives, choice, effectuation, and review. The format is applied to the famous decision of the International Business Machines Corporation to introduce the unified 360 computer line.

In the context of the time-consuming, deliberative-administrative process, it becomes apparent that high costs of uncertainty may often be incurred not because the wrong choice is made among the alternatives reviewed but because better problems and alternatives are not considered. A type of alternative frequently slighted under uncertain conditions is one that tends to be "advancive." Behavior that generates advancive alternatives is discontented with routines; it is inventive, seeking, learning; it features innovation, attention to motivation, and to the growing edge of know-how. It is not risk-avoiding; it tends to extend the world of the actual toward further reaches of the possible. Advancive alternatives should be considered when they promise an acceptable return after being discounted for uncertainty.

To envision the problems of dealing with the deliberative process as a whole, a model is presented in the form of a diagram. It features how the process progresses from one stage to the next. This implies two contrapuntal themes carried along simultaneously. One is person-oriented in the sense of aiming to influence people; broadly political behavior falls in this category. The other is more directly task-oriented. Both are deliberative and intendedly rational. The model must also accommodate the many ways in which the intracollective and intercollective flows of information, both automatic and purposive, take place and (among other things) generate expectations, which in turn shape the course of decision. Finally, the subject covered by decision rules must be looked at again in this broadest context.

I close with a checklist of some fifty ways to cope with uncertainty over and above selecting the proper strategy of the deliberative process as a whole.

SOME MAJOR EMPHASES

The panorama of decision situations covered in the three parts of the book contain recurrent themes.

Attributes of the Decision Situation

First, it is clear that deliberative procedures must be matched to the characteristics of the decision situation. Six criteria are proposed as a key to diagnosis. The first two concern the control which the decision collective has over the deliberative process itself: the homogeneity of the decision collective; and its access to rational rather than opportunistic, satisficing behavior. The next two concern the adequacy of the relevant information: knowledge about process; and knowledge about the values sought. Criterion five, the degree of seriability, concerns the relationship between the problem at hand and others; it asks whether the results of the decision must stand more or less on their own or may be viewed as part of a series for which average results, weighted by their probability, should be the chief concern. Criterion six concerns advancive potential—the breadth of alternatives, present and imagined, to which the situation is open. This last criterion is relevant only to the deliberative process as a whole, not to choice among predelineated alternatives.

Each of these attributes represents a continuum. For example, in a specific situation, information bearing on what is likely to happen (attribute 4) can range from a few scraps and guesses to almost complete information, at least about the probability distribution of outcomes (as for a tossed coin). Where a situation stands with respect to each of the five attributes may be thought of as its attribute profile. Problems to which statistical decision theory applies have profiles that bespeak good structure throughout, though there are interesting exceptions. For example, the degree of seriability and the presence of shifty and ambiguous information (characteristics that imply relatively poor structure for attributes 3 and 4) have been recognized by some statistical decision theorists.

Clearly a decision that is well-structured throughout (such as a production scheduling problem) must be carried through differently than one having generally poor structure (such as a decision by a developing nation whether to emphasize education or transportation). The finesse of the answer—the "aspiration level" for decision—must and should differ. I might add that for the deliberative process as a whole, aspiration levels are affected also by constraints which circumscribe the alternatives that can, realistically, be considered: constraints of money, personnel, time, and risk-tolerance.

Three Types of Decision Rules

Another recurrent theme is necessarily that of decision rules or, more broadly, decision procedures. Statistical decision theorists have developed three sorts of rules for determining which act should be preferred: the decision matrix, in which, theoretically, the expected utility of each possible outcome is weighted by its probability; Shackle's focus-outcome approach, which selects two representative outcomes as the basis for comparing acts; and the stepwise method, diagramed by decision trees, which exploits the time dimension and divides up the total decision into a sequence of choices.

Interestingly, the same three basic decision types designed for the world of economic man may be applied to choice among predelineated alternatives by his natural counterpart. However the complete matrix, applying only to very well-structured situations, must typically be drawn in three, not two, dimensions to accommodate probabilistic utility. Focus outcomes—their number, breadth, and position in the array of possible outcomes—must be chosen freely after preliminary attention to the character of the underlying probability distribution (is it flat, peaked, or bimodal?). Stepwise decision, here of increasing importance, is utilized where opportunity permits.

When the field of vision is widened to cover the total deliberative-administrative process, we still do not lose the three decision types. They apply, needless to say, to the many decisions that pepper the course of ongoing deliberations. But somewhat modified they also apply, at least in a loose sort of way, to the deliberative-administrative process as a whole. Very well-structured situations can deal throughout with conceptual notions featuring complete probability distributions. Much more usually, only selected aspects of the total panorama have to provide foci for consideration. However, there appears to be a step prior to the selection of focus outcomes, a very important one: the selection of focus goals (the utilities sought). This follows from the complex bundle of often partly conflicting purposes that most acts are intended to serve. The third decision type, stepwise deliberation broadened to include learning is, of course, the essence of the time-consuming process here considered. Thus the other rules tend to be set in the branches of decision trees. However, there is a very significant difference: the branches are unlikely to be there to start with; they are grown as the tree is climbed.

Dangers and Potentials

Risk avoidance is a note which has been struck in the context of statistical decision. Perhaps not surprisingly it appears with heightened importance in the broader world of affairs. A *conservative bias,* we find, characterizes choice among predelineated acts and tends to place the do-nothing act in higher favor than it deserves. The impact of this bias spreads in the staged deliberative-administrative process. It has a further implication in situations having advancive potential.

When decision situations are poorly structured, the potential improvement, which formal know-how and rules can bring about, pales relative to the capacity to summon up and fortify intelligent, flexible, effective behavior. We glimpse this shift in emphasis in Part Two in the subtle judgments required to determine purpose and evaluate intangibles and noncommensurables. Its role snowballs in Part Three as the person-oriented as well as task-oriented character of deliberative processes stands out. This points to the importance of the capability and training of the people who participate in deliberations and the extent to which organizations are designed to give these capabilities scope and support. It points to the importance of building experiment and learning into the deliberative-administrative process. Economics, politics and management merge here again.

Finally, the implications of advancive potential have moved like the camel's head into our tent. Where, in situations generally fraught with uncertainty, alternatives are open-ended, there is often more to be gained by pushing along the possibility vector than by efficient choice in a more limited system. Advancive behavior and learning can be built into deliberative procedure. Indeed this can often be achieved at very low cost because resources such as imagination, improved motivation, commitment may not be scarce in the sense of having commensurate opportunity costs; if unappreciated and unused, the resources simply do not exist. When unwisely neglected they impoverish the outcome to the particular decision collective.

Moreover, the particular impoverishment resonates via the interactive cumulative processes of social change. I might add, without trying to explain, that these and other processes and interrelationships are troublesome when referred not only to the central economic notion of optimization but also of equilibrium tendencies. In any event, the processes are little understood—and fascinate the imagination.

PART ONE

Choice by "Rational" Man

CHAPTER 2

Assessing Probability and Utility

This chapter deals with well-structured "programmed" decisions—a tiny sector of the broad spectrum of administrative decision situations. It analyzes only the decision itself, not what has preceded it or what is to follow. It looks at the decision only after the acts worth considering have been selected and the events that affect their outcomes have been designated. Further, the chapter adopts the classic economic figment of "rational" man, who is receptive to and capable of manipulating all relevant information, which is rich and ordered by a highly competitive economy. It is confined to problems free of very substantial judgmental and nonquantifiable elements.

Although this type of decision represents a small slice of administrative life, the literature focusing on it is vast and sophisticated. From the long history of thought concerning philosophy of knowledge and statistical inference there floods current work in operations research and decision theory, in which mathematical structures refine and build upon the logical foundations. A very large part of management science or operations research concerns the application of statistical decision theory to business problems, notably those dealing with inventories, production scheduling, and quality control.

This profuse and expert literature constitutes much of the received doctrine and is the base on which further work must build. Here, however, only some of its central notions are described in summary and nonmathematical form, along with a few less main-line ideas that are particularly useful in the analysis of more complex decision situations. The probabilistic decision model helps in a number of ways to guide thinking about a broad range of problems with which administration must cope. First, it applies in its own right to some decisions; second, modified in ways which will appear as we progress, it applies to a further group of decisions; third, it provides a conceptual frame which, in whole or part, helps to structure more complex and judgmental problems.

THE DECISION MATRIX

Assume that an individual has chosen a problem that he wishes to solve, and has reflected about the acts that are worth considering as possible solutions. He has determined the possible consequences of each act under all mutually exclusive events that might occur (of which one must occur). How then should he come to a decision? Three steps must be taken:

1. Decide the probability that each event will obtain.[1]
2. Decide the utility which each act is expected to generate under each possible event—decide, that is, each possible "consequence."
3. Select the act that promises the greatest utility.

Steps 1 and 2 are contained in the construction of a "decision matrix"; step 3 is covered by a "decision rule." Pounds or perhaps tons of pages have debated or enlarged upon what these seemingly straightforward instructions do or should mean. Some things that they mean are reasonably clear and I shall try to concentrate on these and make interpretations and occasional additions where need be.

Actually, these steps must be taken in most decision situations, if

---

[1] I use this rather stuffy word because it is necessary to refer either to an event which may take place or to one which has taken place without the decision maker knowing it. C.f, Leonard J. Savage, *The Foundations of Statistics*, John Wiley & Sons, Inc., New York, 1954, p. 10.

not explicitly then implicitly, if not deliberatively then as the result of whatever currents wash behavior this way or that.

Statistical decision theory, of course, makes the steps crisply explicit. It describes them under the constraint of rational (logical) behavior. In consequence, the analysis is *normative*—it prescribes how decisions should be made. However, given the assumption of the model including that of a perfectly rational decision maker, prescription and description coincide.

If there is only one possible event, that is, only one *state of* the world, and if the utility of any act (given the event) can be definitely specified, then one will simply choose that act having the greatest utility. The decision is made under conditions of certainty. Our concern, however, is only with situations subject to uncertainty.

Under uncertainty, the consequences of an act are a function of outside events. Exhibit 2-1 expresses steps 1 and 2 in such a situation.

EXHIBIT 2-1
Possible Consequences of Acts
(Measured in Units of Utility)

Act	E_h P_h	E_j P_j	E_n P_n
	Event and Probability		
A_1	C_{1h}	C_{1j}	C_{1n}
A_2	C_{2h}	C_{2j}	C_{2n}
A_m	C_{mh}	C_{mj}	C_{mn}

Each of the acts (A) that are worth considering are expected to have different consequences (C), depending on which of the n possible events (E) obtains. Concerning which event will in fact obtain, it is possible to state only the probability (P). Since one must occur $(P_h \ldots P_n$ sums to 1).[2]

Consider an example: Suppose that the citizens of a small village intend to hold their annual church fair. They consider whether to engage a band (act 1) or whether not to (act 2). The out-of-pocket

[2] For a concise statement of this notion, and its further development, see John W. Pratt, Howard Raiffa, and Robert Schlaifer, "The Foundations of Decision Under Uncertainty; An Elementary Exposition," *Journal of the American Statistical Association,* Vol. 59, No. 306 (June 1964), pp. 353–376.

expense without the band will be $500 for the day, and with it, $700. If the weather is good on the appointed day (event 1) they will have cash receipts of $2000 without the band, and $2700 with it. If the weather is bad (event 2) they will have no receipts. These figures are all expected to be accurate. Assume further, and this is a powerful simplification as we shall see, that the net dollar receipts are a perfect measure of utility. These statements are summarized in Exhibit 2-2.

EXHIBIT 2-2   Net Receipts from the Fair

	Event (Weather)	
Act	Rainy	Fine
1. Band	−$700	$2000 (2700 − 700)
2. No band	−$500	$1500 (2000 − 500)

What should the citizens do about the band? Intuitively it is clear that the probability of rain has some bearing on the decision. If it rains they lose $200 more if the band has been hired. If it is fine they make $500 more. Some estimate of the chances of rain must be made.

The results of making such estimates can be seen more clearly if I change the problem so that *average* results are clearly relevant. Say a group of 20 villages have decided to pool their fair funds for a period of ten years. Each will be entitled to draw out each year the average net receipts per fair for the 200-village-fair days. If the chances of rain were thought to be 50/50, then, assuming that unusual runs of good or bad weather cancelled out, the probable results are shown in Exhibit 2-3 as case I. Case II reproduces the calculation for a countryside in which the chances of rain are 25/75.

The last two lines reflect the assumption that in case I, 100 of the village-fair-days would have been rainy and 100 fine; whereas in case II, only 50 would have been rainy. The weights based on the probability of rain (line 1) are applied directly to the expected receipts on each sort of day (lines 2 and 3), to obtain lines 4 and 5. Lines 6 and 7 are, respectively, the algebraic sums of lines 4 and 5. Each expected consequence weighted by the probability attributed to its occurrence and summed algebraically is the *expected value*. This is the preferred way to represent the desirability of each of the acts to be compared. I shall call attention to the particular meaning of the words, expected value, by capitalizing the first letters. The act having the highest Expected Value should be chosen. In both case I and case II the music is clearly expected to be worth its cost.

EXHIBIT 2-3   Net Receipts from Pooled Fairs

Line		Case I		Case II	
		Rain	Fine	Rain	Fine
1	Probability	.50	.50	.25	.75
		Receipts on Each Sort of Day			
2	Act 1: Band	−$700	$2000	−$700	$2000
3	Act 2: No band	−$500	$1500	−$500	$1500
		Receipts Weighted by Likelihood			
4	Act 1: Band	−$350	$1000	−$175	$1500
5	Act 2: No band	−$250	$ 750	−$125	$1125
		Weighted Average Results ("Expected Value")			
6	Act 1: Band	$650		$1325	
7	Act 2: No band	$500		$1000	

The numbers bring out the size of the uncertainty discount: if the citizens knew what the weather would be in time to change the arrangements, fairs would never be held on rainy days and the net earnings would always be $2000. Instead, the uncertainty that weather conditions imply means that earnings average $650 when it is equally likely to rain or shine; the uncertainty discount is $1350. When the likelihood of rain is less (1 in 4 days), uncertainty about the weather takes a less heavy toll—average earnings are $1325 and the uncertainty discount $675.

This naive example illustrates some fundamental notions about decision under uncertainty. It presents a decision matrix in which (1) *alternative actions* have (2) *possible consequences having measurable utility* under (3) *alternative events* or *states of the world* having (4) *specified probabilities of obtaining*. The appropriate (5) *decision rule* is: choose the act having the highest Expected Value—the sum of the probabilistically weighted potential consequences.

Discussion of two of these fundamental notions is left for later chapters—the selection of alternative actions and of alternative states of the world that are relevant to the decision; in this chapter we assume that each is given in a comprehensive and mutually exclusive fashion. The other three are discussed here. I shall start with probabilities and move, in later sections, to utilities and decision rules.

PROBABILITY

The example of the fair presented a situation in which two mutually exclusive possible acts could have different consequences under each of two mutually exclusive events. But suppose that consequences could be affected by whether it rained or was very windy or both, by whether there were competing events in nearby villages on some proportion of the fine days, by whether for a particular village the previous year's fair had been so good that the carry-over stock of old clothes and books for rummage had been entirely depleted. Obviously, events often do have such additive, multiplicative, and contingent relationship to outcomes. Probability theory, among other things, specifies the nature of these relationships in a set of theorems. It thereby helps the decision maker not only deal with but even recognize and structure the many problems to which these more complicated probabilities apply.[3]

Rules of Definition and Manipulation

Rule 1: The Probability of an Event

The probability of an event may be described as the degree of belief that a given event, rather than any alternative event, will obtain.[4] Thus the probability of a prospective event E is measured with respect to a set of events S, of which E is one element (a subset). In the context of an analysis of a particular probability problem, S is assumed to consist of all possible events which might occur. (For this reason, S is in mathematics termed the "universal set," or, more simply, the "universe.") The probability of S occurring is therefore 1.0.

The set of events S relevant to a particular problem is always part of some broader set S'. E may likewise define a subset consisting of

[3] The following books are suggested for further reading. For a very clear, accessible and attractive presentation see Irwin J. Bross, *Design for Decision*, MacMillan Company, New York, 1953. A classic in main-line analysis is Leonard J. Savage, *The Foundations of Statistics*, John Wiley & Sons, Inc., New York, 1954. An excellent general survey and textbook is Robert Schlaifer, *Probability and Statistics for Business Decisions: An Introduction to Managerial Economics Under Uncertainty*, McGraw-Hill Book Company, Inc., New York, 1959.

[4] Other definitions are discussed below, pp. 27–29.

finer elements. Thus in thinking about the probability of an event, we must consciously or unconsciously define the set, that is, the system of events that is chosen as relevant to the decision.

Consider the analysis of the probability of drawing a heart, or of drawing a nonheart, from a conventional 52-card deck. In the context of this particular analysis, the 52 different possible drawings constitute the universal set. There are 13 hearts in a deck, and 39 nonhearts. Thus, the probability of the event of our drawing a heart is 13/52, and that of drawing a nonheart 39/52.

But notice that if we defined the universal set as consisting of the 52 cards plus 10 more cards, none of which were hearts, then the probability of drawing a heart changes from 13/52 to 13/62. The numerical value of the probability of a specified event, then, is affected by how the "universal set" is defined and which alternative events are considered. Thought concerning the probability of events, occurs in other words, within the confines of a conceptual box. Prerequisite to meaningful analysis is the sensible placement of the walls of the box, that is, the sensible definition of the universal set. This fact is self-evident, and yet too easily overlooked in the rough and tumble of actual administration. It is, I might add, a major concern of systems analysis. In Chapters 8 and 12 we find that failure to pick the set properly gives rise to some common errors even at the level of policy decisions.

Rule 2: Addition

The probability of mutually exclusive events is additive. This is intuitively obvious. If the chance of drawing a heart is 13/52 and of drawing a black ace is 2/52 the chance of drawing either a heart *or* a black ace is 15/52. However, if the events are *not mutually exclusive* it is necessary to make an allowance for the overlap. Thus the chances of drawing *either* a heart *or* a red ace *or* both are 13/52 plus 2/52 minus 1/52 = 14/52, since there is 1 out of 52 chances that the card will be *both* a heart and an ace. Take a different example—boys who drop out in 7th grade. The probability that a boy who drops out of school in 7th grade has an IQ of less than 90 may be .10, and that he is large for his age (and therefore feels foolish in school), .40. But these two causes do not account for 50 percent of the dropouts since (assuming IQs and size are independent) .04 boys have both characteristics. The probability that dropouts have both characteristics is .10 + .40 − .04 = .46.

The rule of addition, which concerns *either, or,* and *both* probabilities, is useful to spell out because, where classifications are not mutually exclusive it is easy to lose sight of the *both* probabilities. Note also that the additive probabilities must be part of a sequence which constitutes one set, that is, sums to 1.0.[5]

Rule 3: Multiplication

The probability of both of two or more independent elements of a set occurring is the *product* of their individual probabilities. The probability of drawing both an ace and a heart is $4/52 \times 13/52 = 52/(52 \times 52) = 1/52$. The probability of a 7th grade boy dropout having *both* a low IQ (.40) *and* a large size (.10) is $.40 \times .10 = .04$.[6]

The rule of multiplication, whereby probabilities concerning *both this and that are combined,* is in one sense intuitively obvious. Nevertheless it has important implications in the administrative context. When, for example, the outcome of a contemplated act depends on a number of independent events occurring, and if each of these occurrences are mildly uncertain—say three events may take place and they each have a probability of .7—*then the character of the outcome is seriously* uncertain—$.7 \times .7 \times .7 = .34$ (assuming the events are independent of one another). In other words, although there is a 70 percent chance of each of the events taking place, there is only a 34 percent chance that all three of them will occur.

Conditional Probability

The previous paragraph has discussed the "both *this* and *that* rule." Under conditions of independence in the probability sense, knowing the probability of "this" does not aid in knowing the probability of "that." But often independence is not present, as in sequential decisions that affect one another. Suppose, for example, the drawings of an ace and a heart, mentioned a moment ago, were performed thus: instead of returning the card to the deck after each draw (in which case independence is maintained), the drawn card is put aside. Specifically, assume that the first draw is a heart other than the ace and it is removed after it has been drawn; on the second draw the probability ratios of the next card being either a heart or a red ace are $12/51 + 2/51 - 1/51 = 13/51$. In other words, probabilities for the second draw are conditioned by the results of the first draw.

[5] In the previous example the set to which the figures belong is the number of dropouts. But suppose I change the example (restricted to 7th grade boys) thus: .30 boys with low IQs drop out; .20 boys who are large for their age drop out; .15 boys with low IQs are large for their age. These figures all belong to different sets and cannot be used to describe dropouts without appropriate conversion. This could be achieved if I knew the absolute number of dropouts, of boys with low IQs, and of those who are large for their age.

[6] Again, the figures assume that size distributions and IQs are not correlated.

Conditional probability must be considered in using evidence to estimate the likelihood of events. Conditional events may be linked as an
event chain. Knowledge of likelihoods develops differently if we move
forward or backward along the event chain. A famous paper by Thomas
Bayes[7] lays the foundation for making the most of the hindsight afforded
by utilizing prior probabilities. It does this in two ways. The first concerns how these probabilities are estimated, a subject reserved for the
next section. The second is simply a manipulation of the axioms of
probability theory. An illustration will indicate the character of the
manipulation.

A firm requires applicants to fill a large number of clerical jobs. It
is believed that a good high school student is likely to do reasonably
well on the job. However, a test can be devised that would seek out
exactly the traits required for successful job performance. Should the
test be given, and if so how could the information which it generates
be used most profitably? The information in the following table bears

**EXHIBIT 2-4   Probability (P) of Students Meeting Two Requirements
Indicative of Chances of Job Success**

High School Group Grade (HSG)	High School Grade (1)	Test Score Pass (T_1) (2)	Test Score Fail (T_2) (3)	"Pass" Scores, by HSG Groups Ratio to All Students (Column 1 × Column 2) (4)	Ratio to All "Pass" Students (5)[a]
Good (G_1)	PG_1 .40	$PT_1\|G_1$ .80	$PT_2\|G_1$ .20	PG_1, T_1 .32	.68
Not good (G_2)	PG_2 .60	$PT_1\|G_2$ .25	$PT_2\|G_2$ .75	PG_2, T_1 .15	.32
All	1.0		PT_2 .53	PT_1 .47	1.00

[a] Column 4 is put on a base of 1.0. That is, line 1 and line 2 of column 4 are each
divided by line 3 of column 4 (e.g., .32/.47 = .68).

on the answer to the question. (Needless to say, for a final decision one
would need to add further information on costs of the tests, and avail-

[7] Thomas Bayes, *An Essay toward Solving a Problem in the Doctrine of Chance*,
originally published with Richard Price's Forward and Discussion in *Philosophical
Transactions of the Royal Society*, 1763. The paper was published postumously.

ability of applicants.) Assume that high school students are "good" (G_1) or "not good" (G_2). Test scores are "pass" (T_1) or "fail" (T_2).

Exhibit 2-4 indicates, in column 1, the likelihood of people passing the first set of requirements—adequate high school grades. Columns 2 and 3 indicate how each student passing the first hurdle fares in the second—the test (in symbols, $PT_1|G_1$, that is, the probability of passing the test, *given* the good grade classification). Column 4 concentrates on those having both qualifications (in symbols, PT_1, G_1), that is, the probability of passing the test *and* having a good grade. Column 5 is simply column 4 put on a base of 1.0. (In symbols, it is derived from columns 1, 2, and 4 by the formula, Bayes theorem:

$$P(G_1|T_1) = \frac{P(T_1|G_1)P(G_1)}{P(T_1)}$$

$$.68 = \frac{.80(.40)}{.47}$$

The construction is developed by operations that move from left to right in the table. But most of its usefulness lies in reading it in the opposite direction, that is, in the hindsight it conveys. *Without the test,* the best that we can do is to bank on the information in column 1, probabilities based on high school marks, and select 40 out of every 100 candidates as having a good chance of success. *With the test* and no information about high school marks, 47 out of 100 applicants would be selected (column 4, bottom line). However, *the test scores can be used in conjunction with the academic ratings* to aid in identifying good prospects at a lower cost per employee. Column 5 shows that 68 percent of the prospective employees who pass both requirements come from the 40 percent of all students having adequate high school records. Testing the additional 60 out every 100 students will only add 32 percent to the number identified as good job prospects. Whether it would pay to do this depends on the cost of testing and how many additional employees are needed.

These "posterior probabilities" are useful in two ways. For one thing, they refine the estimate of how many students with a given high school record will do well on the job. For another thing, they make it possible to confine the search for additional information to a very rich pool of prospects—the good student. Needless to say, this is a cold-blooded example of how an individual firm might minimize hiring costs in an ample labor market. The social costs of such procedures are another matter—one which, fortunately, is receiving some attention in the private as well as the public sphere.

In the example, statistical evidence was available on both high school marks and on test scores. Often this is not the case. For example, the enforcement of quality standards very typically involves only vague information about the conditions that produce high risk of defective units. Prior probabilities based on such information, combined, by means of Bayesian methods, with sampling tests for defective parts, can enforce specified quality standards at lower cost than across-the-board sampling. Sequential sampling, which progressively improves estimates of prior probabilities, is a common further extension of Bayesian concepts for the purpose of quality control.

PROBABILITY THAT AN EVENT WILL OBTAIN

We turn now to the group of measures concerning probability and ask what the figures signify and how they are determined.

The Meaning of a Probability Judgment

Consider first what they signify. What do we mean when we claim that we know the probability of an event, when we claim, for example, that a "fair" coin has a 50 percent chance of landing heads up? How do we justify such an assertion?

Three main schools have emerged.[8] The school holding the "necessary view" concentrates on the logical basis of probability. We know that a perfectly constructed coin flipped an increasing number of times by a perfectly randomized apparatus, like an unschooled thumb and forefinger, will converge on a .50 chance of heads. This must be true on the basis of the theory of gravity, the notion of "perfect" mechanical capability, and the mathematics of probability.

The second school, the *objectivist* or *frequentist*, concentrates on the observational and experimental basis of knowledge. Experiments, consisting of actually tossing coins, would provide a series of observations lacing around a 50/50 ratio, and, on a cumulative percentage basis, converging toward a shallower and shallower divergence.

However, both of these schools may charge the other with circular reasoning. The necessary school points with cogency to a flaw in the frequentist's position. For any given tossing experiment, no matter how lengthy, a fair coin could land only on heads. (This is, of course, improbable, but nonetheless logically possible). The frequentist might reply

---

[8] The literature goes back for two centuries and longer. There is a most useful short summary of the history of the "grand controversy" in William Fellner's *Probability and Profit*, Richard D. Irwin, Inc., Homewood, Ill., 1965, pp. 25–34 and p. 39ff. A fuller survey is given by John Maynard Keynes (Lord Keynes) in *A Treatise on Probability*, Macmillan and Co., London, 1921, Chapter 7.

that what he means is that, if a coin is fair, heads will tend to appear approximately 50 percent of the time, given a *sufficient number* of flips. By sufficient number, the frequentist seems to mean a large enough number of flips so that the tendency toward convergence causes something very close to the 50/50 ratio to occur. If this is so, his critic can point out, that the argument is circular and therefore empty, since it asserts that heads will appear approximately 50 percent of the time if you flip the coin long enough for heads to appear approximately 50 percent of the time; moreover, what, precisely, "approximate" means is left in the air.

The frequentist, on the other hand, charges that the necessary view, which translates a probability statement not into predictions of experimental results but into its mathematical implications, likewise runs into circular reasoning. Thus, when the necessary school holds that to say a coin is fair is to say that, for any given number of flips it is *most probable* that heads will appear 50 percent of the time, it is simply defining probability in terms of probability. True, the authority of logic and science may provide a partial escape from circularity (physics and mechanics can explain *why* the coin flipped in a specified way will fall with equal probability on either side and never on the edge) but where observation starts and logic ends is always somewhat vague. The argument intensifies as inquiry extends to how probabilities may be assigned to situations where experiment is limited and causality obtuse.

A third school, the *subjectivist*, or *personalistic* school, has now gained considerable acceptance in the English speaking world and I have used it without a label in earlier pages. It escapes from the problem of circularity, by saying, in the words of one of its most adept exponents, Leonard J. Savage, that "probability measures the confidence that a particular individual has in the truth of a particular proposition, for example, the proposition that it will rain tomorrow." Probability is, in other words, a degree of belief. "These views postulate that the individual concerned is in some ways 'reasonable,' but they do not deny the possibility that two reasonable individuals faced with the same evidence may have different degrees of confidence in the truth of the same proposition."[9] An individual who tries to be rational will base this confidence on the best evidence that is available and that it is worthwhile to try to obtain. The degree of belief that a coin will land heads up, for example, might be based both on the experiment of the frequentist and the logic of the necessary view, along with, perhaps, some testing of the construction of the coin and of the flipping device. The personalistic

[9] Leonard J. Savage, *op. cit.*, p. 3.

view is intuitively appealing for its flexibility and more, as we shall see.

Nevertheless, it is clear that for some events, the person can name probabilities which he believes tend to converge to the stipulated figure. For others, his knowledge may be far too slim, and further test may be impossible. Yet here too, modern probability theory has found a solution in the "rule of ignorance." The essential notion, as introduced by Thomas Bayes and developed by Pierre Simon de Laplace, is that the decision maker should behave as if he were faced by a perfectly converging set of probabilities even if he knows that he is not. The difference in various sorts of probability estimates requires a moment's attention.

Certainty, Risk, and Uncertainty

Whatever system for predicting probabilities is used, it is clear that there are not only quantitative but also qualitative differences in the character of knowledge concerning an impending event. One aspect of the difference is commonly referred to in terms of the distinction between *certainty, risk,* and *uncertainty.*

Certainty is a situation in which only one state of the world is possible—that is, the event Y has a probability of 1.0 and all other events have probabilities of 0. In addition, the assignment of these probabilities is confident. Otherwise *some* other events would actually have a probability of occurring, however minute.

Risk is present when two or more states of the world are possible and the assignment of the probability of each can be made with confidence. The probability, .50, of a fair coin falling heads is an example. The mechanical process that causes the random character of the fall is well understood. Logical inference can be verified by accurate experiments: a long succession of instances of almost identical kinds can be observed. The observations on which information is based are well behaved. The same would be true if the quantitative aspects of the guess were quite different, say the .167 probability that applies to the chances that a six-surface fair die would fall on side 2.

Placing money on chances of this sort, at the odds that the assessed probabilities imply, involves a *risk* of loss in a particular instance; but if bets are repeated a sufficient number of times, the average take will correspond closely to the Expected Value—the prize times the probability of winning, minus the penalty times the probability of losing. The risk in the individual case could be insured at an actuarial rate based on the Expected Value. But needless to say, few events of which the chances need to be assessed belong to collectives as orderly as that of tosses of a coin.

Uncertainty characterizes the more usual probability assignments—cases where information is inadequate and observation disorderly. Moreover, both inadequacy and disorder are a matter of degree. If you permit your mind to wander over decisions encountered in the past month, can they not be arranged on a continuum on which both of the sources of knowledge—inference and observation—deteriorate? Without spelling out the character of the deterioration, it is clear that both can move gradually toward an almost complete absence of knowledge.

When a process is simply not understood at all, inference can lose virtually all of its power to help. Logic, then, cannot help to stipulate the probability of a given outcome. If so, stipulation about likelihood must rely heavily on the evidence provided by experiment. This does not mean necessarily that the outcome is deeply uncertain. In the field of medicine, for example, outcomes can sometimes be quite well predicted from experience although the chemistry or physiology of the reaction is not well understood—the antibiotic qualities of penicillin are a case in point. But experiment loses its power to help when an event seems unique or does not occur in sufficient instances to tell us much about probabilities. This nadir of experiment is described by Frank Knight as "true uncertainty."[10] Deep uncertainty implies that *both* inferential and experimental bases of knowledge are poor.

However, even when the assessments of probabilities are deemed poor, the Bayesian approach implies that the correct assessment, and therefore the correct bet, must nevertheless focus on Expected Value, regardless of how poorly expectations can be formulated. If this is done, the decision belongs within the edifice of probabilistic statistical theory.

There are elaborate mathematical arguments in support of Bayes' theorem but there is also a common sense argument which seems very well understood by insurance companies: *providing the estimates are unbiased,* an actuarial basis of prediction can be achieved by making probability estimates about diverse occurrences as if they are repeated drawings from one collective like coin tosses. If estimates are unbiased, the divergence of actual outcomes from the estimated Expected Value will be wider when information is poor than when it is good, but the Expected Value for a long series of bets should be about the same.

[10] Frank H. Knight, *Risk, Uncertainty and Profit,* Houghton Mifflin Co., Boston and New York, 1921, p. 232. True uncertainty is described thus: "The essential and outstanding fact is that the 'instance' in question is so entirely unique that there are no others or not a sufficient number to make it possible to tabulate enough like it to form the basis of any inference of value about any real probability in the case we are interested in," p. 226.

Ambiguity

If uncertainty goes too far—if belief becomes *shifty and inconsistent*—the logic of probability theory is violated. This difficulty is recognized and then dropped by Leonard J. Savage in his 1954 book. If opinion is *very unsure*, the development of laws of manipulation, in accordance with personalistic statistical decision theory, is fraught with "unsurmountable difficulties." "When our opinions, as reflected in real or envisaged action, are inconsistent, we sacrifice the unsure opinions to the sure ones. The notion of 'sure' and 'unsure' introduced here is vague, and my complaint is precisely that neither the theory of personal probability, as it is developed in this book, nor any other device known to me renders the notion less vague."[11] Accordingly, Savage at that time acted like a decision maker and sacrificed the unsure opinion to the sure one, abjuring vagueness, a position which he has since somewhat modified.

Although main-line probability theory has also largely succumbed to the "unsurmountable difficulties" of unsure opinions by ignoring them, a number of writers have been unwilling to do so. William Fellner has given full-length treatment to the subject in *Probability and Profit*, where he develops what he terms a "semiprobabilistic view," applicable to an "elusive hypothesis," in that it does not carry a decision weight equal to the best estimate of its probability of occurrence. The decision weight is "slanted." "Slanting expresses an allowance for the instability and the controversial character of some types of probability judgments. . . ." Ordinarily the weight or probability that is assigned, is decreased and consequently its power to evoke action is reduced.[12] In the terms of our discussion, there is a higher discount for uncertainty than is warranted by the best estimate of probability that can be made. This best estimate has, presumably, used all of the information, inference, hunch, and anything else available. But, thereafter, the decision maker draws back and reviews his judgment and gives it a low grade. Daniel Ellsberg, in a paper published at the same symposium at which William Fellner's

[11] Leonard J. Savage, *op. cit.,* pp. 57 and 58. In later works, Savage has returned to the problem of "vagueness." See, for example, B. De Finetti and L. J. Savage, "On the Way of Choosing Initial Probabilities," in Bibleotecca Mentron, Serie C, Rome (1962) 1, pp. 81–154.

[12] The quotation is *op. cit.,* p. 5. Fellner defines decision weight as follows: "If a prize is made contingent on the occurrence of an event, then a person acts as if he had been promised unconditionally an amount of utility which equals the algebraic product of the utility of the prize with a specific numerical factor." The factor is the decision weight which is bounded by 1 and 0, *op. cit.,* p. 11. Elsewhere he says more simply that ". . . weights equal the probability which an individual assigns to the event in question," p. 12.

discussion of the subject originally appeared, referred to the impact of "ambiguity." "Any scrap of evidence bearing on relative likelihood should already be represented in those estimates. But having exploited knowledge, guess, rumor, assumption, advice, to arrive at a final judgment that one event is more likely than another or that they are equally likely, one can still stand back from the process and ask: How much, in the end, is all this worth?"[13]

The point at issue is, I believe, an exceedingly interesting one having broad implications. The presence of *ambiguity* or the absence of confidence in a guess is familiar enough. Ordinary language deals with it in the difference in confidence expressed in a series of words such as "calculate," "estimate," "guestimate," "guess," and "hunch." Which of these words a man selects as describing the attribution of probability that an event will take place, and a state of the world obtain, bears witness to that interesting capacity of *Homo sapiens* to be aware of awareness. In judging the assessment of probabilities associated, say, with a hunch, the judge feels that he has done a poor job; he believes that others in command of the same evidence might well disagree with him; he thinks his own opinion subject to change.[14]

Main-line statistical decision theory can recognize at least a part of these evaluative judgments. If confidence is low, the assignment of probabilities for each of the various possible outcomes is likely to be relatively uniform. For example, if a purchasing agent is assessing the likelihood of a price rise, and information about markets is very poor, he might assign almost equal probability to a small fall, no change, a small rise, a moderate rise, or a large rise; if information were abundant, the likelihood of one outcome—say a moderate rise—might gain relative to the other possibilities.[15]

If ambiguity is to be considered in the full sense to which Fellner and Ellsberg refer, its relationship to statistical decision theory can be

---

[13] Daniel Ellsberg, "Risk, Ambiguity and the Savage Axioms," *The Quarterly Journal of Economics,* Vol. LXXV, November 1961, pp. 659–660.

[14] The last two points were made by William Fellner, *op. cit.,* p. 4. I added the first in the firm belief that a man's severest critic is not his wife but his wife's husband.

[15] This may change the expected value expressed in a dollar numeraire, or it may not. The following is an example of a case in which Expected Value (EV) changes:

Expected rate of price rise, percent	−1	0	+1	+2	+3	EV percent rise
Probability of obtaining:						
Low confidence	.2	.2	.2	.2	.2	+1.0
More confidence	.1	.1	.2	.5	.1	+1.4

described in at least two ways. The first supposes that the *utility of a reward,* other things being the same, is *deteriorated* by these uncomfortably shifting expectations. For some people under some circumstances, the awareness that others may disagree with them, that they risk not only the prize but the humiliation of being thought a fool, may, in a sense load any outcome with a veneer of distaste. Dollar for dollar, expected rewards have a lower expected utility. It is true that, for some people, the reaction could be just the reverse. But the notion of "slanting" or "ambiguity" assumes that the first reaction is more usual than the second or than none at all.

A second interpretation, the one which William Fellner favors, is to view ambiguity as *reducing the decision weights* associated with a given estimate of likelihood.[16]

Whether in fact people seem to exhibit distaste for ambiguous bets, other things the same, has been the subject of experiments.[17] An example

[16] Deterioration of the willingness to make the bet at all is really a third interpretation of ambiguity. It implies the possibility that ambiguity can affect also the *amount* of money which the decision maker is willing to risk. It seems reasonable to me that this sort of reaction does tend to be present. Reactions of this sort should be reflected in experiments that permit participants to vary *the stakes that they wish to risk* on bets some of which are more ambiguous than others.

Reactions that affect what people are willing to risk on the basis of evidence of different qualities have elements of similarity to the postponement of decisions as a step in "buying information." Carried a step further, the reaction can be an unwillingness to bet at all. Concerning such reactions in terms of withdrawal, in addition to that of indifference and preference, Jacob Marschak asks, "Is not the avoiding of choice itself a decision which, like other decisions, is made more or less desirable by the prizes and penalties it entails?" (*Decision-Making,* July 1966, Working Paper No. 93, Western Management Science Institute, University of California, Los Angeles, p. 2.1). A "yes" answer to this question may nevertheless point to the fact that it is a separate and preliminary decision which should not be confused with what happens next. Certainly the decision to avoid decision in ambiguous situations, or to lower the stakes, takes on increasing importance as we proceed to more and more diffuse decision situations.

A fourth position admits that people recognize ambiguity but that they can learn that they should not.

Raiffa criticized the Fellner-Ellsberg thesis, and reported on an experiment of his own at which subjects showed some behavior that could be interpreted as "slanting" (in Fellner's terms) or as reflecting "ambiguity" (in Ellsberg's terms). However they "corrected" (in Raiffa's terms) their bets when the probabilistic meaning of their first bets was explained (*Quarterly Journal of Economics,* Vol. LXXV, 1961, No. 4).

[17] William Fellner, *Probability and Profit,* Chapter 9, "Appendix on Betting Experiments with Yale Students," pp. 203–209. Ward Edwards, "Probability-Preferences among Bets with Differing Expected Values," *American Journal of Psychology,* January 1954, pp. 56–57; and "Reliability of Probability-Preferences," *ibid.,* pp. 68–95.

of such experiments was reported on by Ellsberg in his symposium article.

Subjects were asked how they would bet on Red or Black balls which would be drawn out of two urns. They win $100 or lose 0. Urn I has 100 Red or Black balls; there is no further information given. Urn II has 50 Red and 50 Black balls. The following questions were asked:

1. Which would you prefer to bet on, Red I or Black I, or are you indifferent?
2. Which would you prefer to bet on, Red II or Black II?
3. Which would you prefer to bet on, Red I or Red II?
4. Which would you prefer to bet on, Black I or Black II?

For questions one and two, the typical response is indifference. Question three was usually answered in favor of Red II. And question four in favor of Black II. (That is, they preferred to bet either on winning or losing from the urn in which probabilities are clearly given.) This is, of course, an inconsistent choice since choosing Red II suggests that it is more likely to occur than Red I (which has a 50 percent chance of occurring); if this is so, then why prefer Black II? "Responses from confessed violators [of the Savage axioms] indicate that the difference is not to be found in terms of the two factors commonly used to determine a choice situation, the relative desirability of the possible pay-offs and the relative likelihood of the events affecting them, but *in a third dimension in the problem of choice: the nature of one's information* concerning the relative likelihood of events."[18]

To summarize the discussion of probability, even for the well-structured decision problem, the assignment of probabilities to each possible event (the figures required as weights for each column of the decision matrix) is a subjective evaluation based on all the evidence, logic, intuitive judgments, and clairvoyance that the decision maker can summon. The resulting evaluations differ in quality. The differences form, in effect, a continuum stretching from pure risk, where observations are well behaved and well understood, to deep uncertainty, where evidence of any sort is sparse and admittedly poor—uncertainty which may take the form not only of believing any of the possible results equally probable, but even of mistrusting the belief itself. Bayesian interpretation specifies that, however poor the information, the best estimate should be made and used to weight utility that is expected to be derived from each possible outcome. However, at the end of the continuum where uncertainty is deepest, distaste for unstable and shaky judgments tends to be reflected either in a write-down of expected utility or of its probability.

[18] Ellsberg, *op. cit.*, p. 657. Italics mine.

In later sections, response to ambiguity plays a role of increasing importance. Perhaps the most significant aspect of its impact is in its influence on how decision situations change over time. To anticipate, the time-pattern of change in opinion (and of consequent actions) differs if changing expectations are primarily a function of cumulating confidence in a specific probabilistic opinion rather than if they are primarily a function of change in the opinion itself.

MEASUREMENT OF UTILITY

We turn now to an examination of the second set of numbers for which the decision matrix calls—a measure of the utility of the consequences. In most of the examples in the previous sections this second step of the decision process presented no problems. On the one hand the conjunction of an event and an act could be described directly in terms of dollars and, on the other hand, dollars were assumed to have a constant relationship to utility. These assumptions apply to many of the central examples and analysis of statistical decision theory.

Three Levels of Consequences

However, assessing consequences can actually involve three questions: (1) What, in objective operational terms, is likely to happen if this or that is done under each relevant circumstance? (2) How can these operationally described results be converted to quantitative terms? (3) How can those quantities, whatever their unit, be converted to a corresponding measure of utility? The previous examples hopped directly to the third question (by expressing occurrences directly in terms of dollars and assuming that dollars have constant utility). But, the result of an act under specified circumstances may not always be capable of comprehensive description in terms of a single unit—dollars or any other. Moreover, its value or utility, does not necessarily bear a constant relationship to money.

This section confronts these questions explicitly in the effort to take the second decision step, that of assigning utility to the act-event conjunctions—assigning the utility of an act under a given "state of the world"—thereby filling the cells of the decision matrix in order to determine which act is preferred.

To distinguish these three concepts, we will use *consequences* in three different senses. *Primary consequences* or *outcomes* are the straightforward operational results of an event (it rains, the coin lands heads up). *Surrogate consequences* are the quantitative *payoffs*, the values of an *objective function* concomitant to the result ($700 loss to the fair, $1.00 loss of wager). This is the numerical unit entered in the decision matrix to be weighted by probability. Dollars are the most frequent surrogate for value of this type. As long as the value generated by all outcomes is completely reflected by dollars, there is no problem achieving measurement in cardinal numbers, as required by the matrix. In that case, surrogate consequences or payoffs are the complete representatives of value. But in many cases, readily available numerical units do not have a constant relationship to the subjective desirability of an outcome. Thus we must use the third concept—that of *evaluated consequences* or *utilities, values of a utility function.*[19]

Utility is a deeply subjective matter for which the only objective measure is relative—that of preference (*A* is preferred to *B*). The utility of two outcomes, *A* and *B*, may be deemed identical if an individual is indifferent to which one takes place (*A* or *B*). If there are more than two possible outcomes, the preference scale must be transitive in the sense that if *A* is preferred to *B*, and *B* is preferred to *C*, then *A* must be preferred to *C*. This implies an ordinal or ranked measurement (first, second, third, etc). However, the matrix previously described and the decision rule for calculating Expected Value demand use of cardinal numbers. How can this be achieved? This is the difficult problem of the relationship between surrogate consequences (payoffs) and evaluated consequences (utilities).

A first difficulty arises from the fact, previously noted, that the utility attached to each of a number of dollars, and under all circumstances, is not identical. For one thing, the marginal utility per dollar of income typically declines as income rises; if so, rich people may decide some

[19] I am greatly indebted to Peter C. Fishburn for calling my attention to the need for a carefully devised nomenclature and for assistance in formulating it. This is not to say that he would necessarily agree with the end product. The terminology aims not to conflict with the usual meaning of "consequences" in decision theory but to add some submeanings. I do however use "outcomes" in a restricted sense, in that in my lexicon it refers to one of the submeanings whereas it is often used as synonymous with consequences.

Savage says that "A consequence is anything that may happen to a person" (*op. cit.,* p. 13). This can be a very complicated sequence of happenings. In the words of Peter C. Fishburn "The statement of a consequence is, in the ideal, a complete description of the individual's future insofar as it is affected by or concerned with the decision situation at hand" (*Decision and Value Theory,* John Wiley & Sons, Inc., New York, 1964, p. 25). My terminology attempts to make steps explicit which seem implicit in determining which of the expected consequences of alternative acts are preferred. The ways in which descriptive and evaluative procedures at the three levels of consequences differ are enlarged upon as the analysis proceeds.

questions differently than poor ones. For another thing, asymmetrical reactions to gains and losses can imply differences between buyers and sellers in their reactions to uncertainty.[20] Declining marginal utility can also characterize the amounts won in connection with a particular decision; thus for a particular person big winnings may have a smaller per dollar utility than smaller winnings. Losses, on the other hand, often have a more serious impact per dollar when the total loss is large than when it is small. If so, the dollar measure, though still a cardinal number series, is elastic, and stretches more at some spots in its length than at others: the dollar payoffs undergo a nonlinear transformation when converted to a measure of utility. Ambiguity and the degree of riskiness (variance) can itself affect the utility associated with a specific Expected Value; more of this in a moment.

We have been speaking thus far about situations in which primary consequences, outcomes, can be measured in dollars. But for many sorts of outcomes, dollar values are largely absent or deceptive makeshifts. Of course, surrogate measures are not confined to dollars. Output can be measured in physical units. If appropriate uniform physical units exist, they can often be transformed directly into units of utility without a dollar intermediary. The operation is familiar to any child: how many candy bars is a movie worth? It may still be the rule in rural communities to judge whether to give up bushels of wheat to get tons of hay without encumbering the judgment with a transposition to dollar units. Indeed, merit-weighted physical units can provide useful units of payoff for complex government decisions—person-days of outdoor recreation, school-days of education, etc. In any event, if a physical unit is pertinent, many of the previous remarks concerning the transformation of dollars to utility, at least in the context of choice among similar goods, apply to the physical measures as well.

---

[20] This appears to be the assumption underlying the assertion familiar in price theory: "for sellers the risk premium is positive, for buyers it is negative" (Oscar Lange, *Price Flexibility and Employment,* The Principia Press, Inc., Bloomington, Ind., 1944, p. 31). Say a seller and buyer of 100 units both contemplate a unit price which they think most likely to be $1.00 but which might easily be expected to be as low as $.80 or as high as $1.20. The seller, if the price turns out to be $1.20, is less pleased by the prospect of a $20 gain than he is displeased by the possibility of a $20 loss if price turns out to be $80. He is therefore indifferent between a sure receipt of, say, $95 and the risky situation with an Expected Value of $100. His risk premium is positive. The buyer, if the price turns out to be $1.20, is more displeased by the prospect of a $20 loss than he is pleased by the prospect of a $20 gain if prices turn out to be $.80. He is therefore indifferent between a sure payment of say $105 and the risky situation implying an expected payment of $100. His risk premium is negative.

All of these difficulties are heightened when intangible values, such as political success or employee goodwill, constitute all or part of the value of a venture. Intangible values of this sort can presumably be incorporated in a utility judgment if they supplement measurable values or if they are the sole utility that a contemplated act is expected to generate. True, they cannot be handled in a precise fashion, and if alternatives are close, they greatly embarrass choice. However, it seems clear that man has the capacity to make not only qualitative but quantitative judgments based on entirely nonnumerical evidence. We judge very accurately whether an auto is approaching at a speed which would make it dangerous to try to pass; we heft two stones and say which is heavier and roughly in what proportion; we estimate whether one garment is more attractive than another and how much difference in price is thereby justified; we judge the prestige value of a business location and add it to the value of other advantages or disadvantages that the place may have.

The Standard Gamble

Conversion from ordinal to cardinal numbers for measurement of utility is often impractical except in terms of an ingenious device known as the *standard gamble*.[21] The procedure trades on the disutility of uncertainty. Assume that I know there are four alternatives, which I prefer in the order A, B, C, D, and the preference is firm and consistent, that is, transitive. The ordinal sequence can be converted to a cardinal one, though only in relative terms (in the sense that index numbers are relative). My interest in B is, by definition, greater than in D and less than in A. I can find out just *how much* less than A if I ask: What chance of getting A (I get D if I lose) would I just be willing to exchange for the certainty of getting B? Say my answer is, a chance of two out of three. Now, to the same question concerning C, I answer, a chance of one out of two. (It must be less than my answer to B.) Then, assuming that the utility of A is represented by the number 1 and of D by the number 0 (any other two numbers would do, so long as the one for A exceeds the one for D), then that of B is .67 and that of C is .50.

[21] The method was developed by John von Neumann and Oskar Morgenstern in their renowned book, *The Theory of Games and Economic Behavior*, Princeton University Press, Princeton, N.J., 1944. My description is approximate. For a good three-page presentation see David W. Miller and Martin Starr, *Executive Decision and Operations Research*, Prentice-Hall, Inc., Englwood Cliffs ,N.J., 1960, pp. 69–72; R. Duncan Luce and Howard Raiffa give a fuller treatment in Chapter 2 of *Games and Decision: Introduction and Critical Survey*, John Wiley & Sons, Inc., New York, 1957.

The standard gamble is a striking conception—simple and efficient. It assumes that people are willing to exchange a lower (or higher) reward for more (or less) assurance that they will get it along a continuous and consistent preference system. The question that it puts is what chance of getting a particular clearly desirable result would one accept in even exchange for the certainty of a particular less desirable result. It is a useful question to ask under a wide variety of circumstances involving even poorly structured decision problems.

Noncommensurable Values

However, the problem takes on a somewhat altered character when outcomes have values that are complementary or otherwise hard to compare. How, for example, can one compare the utility of:

1. The partial immunity to business recession of a general-purpose machine, with
2. The added efficiency of a special-purpose machine?

Indifference Analysis

To make the comparison, there is a venerable piece of standard equipment in economics having great beauty and power—the indifference curve. It can structure the question, how much efficiency will you exchange for specified amounts of flexibility? Answers can be drawn on a two-dimensional surface as shown in Diagram 2-1. Point B represents

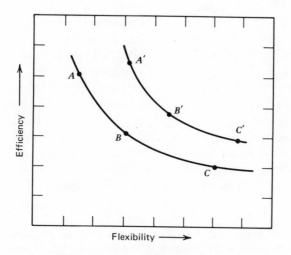

Diagram 2-1   Indifference curves.

a machine having a moderate efficiency and moderate flexibility; it has an Expected Value, which has been determined. If I could greatly increase efficiency, I would give up half the flexibility, point A. If I could greatly increase flexibility, I would give up about a third of the efficiency, point C. A smooth curve through these points, the "indifference curve," locates other alternatives sharing the characteristic of providing the same utility as the machines located by points A, B, and C. There are, of course, different sets of alternatives, typically ones having a higher (or lower) cost for which total utility is greater (or smaller). Point B' indicates an example. Here again, I will trade more efficiency for flexibility and vice versa. But perhaps at this higher level of cost, I am less willing to give up flexibility. If so, my indifference curve is now not only to the right of the previous one but somewhat steeper toward the upper left and flatter toward the lower right corners. At any point, then, on either curves AC or A'C', total utility is a uniform amount, a larger amount in the second case. Converted to expected yield per dollar of cost under, say, different assumptions about business conditions over the useful life of the equipment, the observations would fit into the framework of a choice matrix as C values in Exhibit 2-1.

Risk Aversion

Risk aversion and yield constitute noncomparable values of particular pertinence in connection with planning on uncertainty, since ordinarily higher yields are associated with greater risks, other things being the same. Greater possibility of loss is often the price that must be paid for the possibility of higher gain. Someone who dislikes risk, the risk-avoiding individual, may prefer an alternative having a lower to a higher Expected Value providing the losses (as well as the gains) that he considers at all likely are smaller. The preference system whereby he trades higher yield for lower dispersion of possible outcomes, can be particularized by indifference curves: simply substitute Expected Value of payoff for efficiency on the vertical axis of Diagram 2.1, and dispersion (decreasing to the right) for flexibility on the horizontal axis. An individual will always prefer an outcome on a higher indifference curve than on a lower one. However, there may be no direct way to achieve cardinal measurement of utility. One would have to resort to further devices which might achieve this result at least under sure conditions.[22]

[22] See Harry M. Markowitz, *Portfolio Selection, Efficient Diversification of Investments,* Cowles Foundation for Research in Economics at Yale University, Monograph No. 16, John Wiley & Sons, Inc., New York, 1959. Markowitz achieves the single

Futurity

A prize to be received one year hence is not as valuable as one received today—the recipient is deprived of its use over the coming year. Likewise a future cost is less onerous—the resources can be put to other uses during the interim. This implies that the utility expected to accrue from an act is less, and the costs less, insofar as the consequences occur in the future. This discount for futurity applies to certain as well as uncertain outcomes. Thus uncertain future events carry a double discount.

The amount of the discount of a future monetary cost is theoretically given in terms of the "riskless" interest rate, although in actuality other elements inevitably enter into any market rate. The discount for future benefits is less likely to have a clear monetary measure even in principle. If so, the indifference curve analysis of noncommensurables applies: if you could exchange five Hershey bars today for more next week, how many would you have to surely get next week to give up the five today?

Noncomparables and "Ordinary Argument"

As noncomparable values multiply or increase in relative importance, we move away from the well-structured decision situation. Although we can compare two such criteria, relationships among more are difficult even to conceptualize much less to quantify. Not only the page but the mind runs out of dimensions in which to sling indifference curves.

Noncomparables may also present logical contradictions which mean that appropriate combination is no longer the answer, even in theory. Take an example used by Nicholas Georgescu-Roegen in an early discussion of this point. A textile manufacturer contemplates moving one of his plants to the South. "He probably will have no difficulty in ranking the various regions according to the frequency of success of other firms that have moved their plants there. But how is he going to reconcile

---

dimension necessary to cardinal measurement for portfolios of individuals having the same risk preferences by assuming that yield and risk of all "efficient" portfolios (ones having, roughly, both a higher likely return and a lower uncertainty of return than alternatives) have a systematic inverse association. The utility of yield in dollars then declines (because of risk) with percentage yield; the transformation functions would differ for different individuals. See particularly p. 208.

Other possible ways of achieving cardinal measurement for two noncommensurables would be by using a second indifference analysis to compare the joint utility of the two with a third measurable utility, thereby achieving a standardization procedure a la Shackle. The standard gamble might also provide a conversion device.

this ranking with the logic of economic theory, according to which increased demand leads to increased prices of factors of production? Will he decide to move into the region where there are already the greatest number of successful plants or into that where there is no competition for the local factors of production? To make a choice, the manufacturer must *weigh the opposing hierarchies, as one weighs the pros and cons in ordinary argument.* . . . And since the weighing of arguments seems refractory to any numerical analysis, it is hard to visualize how the entire operation may result in a number being assigned to each expectation involved."[23]

But the story of statistical decision theory is only half over. It remains to indicate how the materials of decision may be used to construct the finished product—rational choice among alternative acts. The step is incorporated in a "decision rule."

[23] "The Nature of Expectation and Uncertainty," in *Expectations Uncertainty and Business Behavior*, Mary Jean Bowman, Ed., Social Science Research Council, New York, 1958, p. 27. Italics mine.

CHAPTER 3

Decision Rules

The third step of the decision process—choosing the best act to undertake—necessarily involves devising ways to assemble all of the possible consequences of an act and to determine, in the light of their several probabilities, which of the alternatives seems most promising.

EXPECTED VALUE

Comprehensive Dollar Metrics

When hard numbers are available, the Expected Value rule applies in a straightforward fashion. The expected consequences of an act under each state of the world are weighted by the probability that the state will obtain. Obviously, one should select the act for which this expected payoff is highest, assuming the measures of payoff are unbiased.

The rule incorporates the *uncertainty discount,* the first source of uncertainty's cost mentioned in Chapter 1. To illustrate, assume that if an act is undertaken, it results in a reward of $3 if event A occurs, $7 if event B and $10 if event C occurs. Desirable as is the $10 reward, it is an uncertain one, since it is contingent on event C for which the probability of occurrence is 2 out of 10 tries. Thus if one tried again and again, the average reward from the act and event C would be $2 (i.e., 0.2 × $10)—the uncertainty discounted value of the $10 reward. But, of course, when event C does not occur, other events do—A, 3 times out of 10, and B, 5 times out of 10. Thus the uncertainty discounted reward from A alone is $.90, (i.e., 0.3 × $3), and from B alone $3.50 (i.e., 0.5 × $7). Since one of the three events must, by definition, always occur, the total reward from a large number of tries approaches $2 + $.90 + $3.50 or $6.40—the Expected Value, or the sum of the uncertainty discounted values for all possibilities.

Variants

When the primary consequences are measured completely by the surrogate, money, and money has a constant relationship to the utility of oft repeated acts, the rule works smoothly. However, our discussion of how likelihood and utility can be ascertained has raised many questions and qualifications concerning the meaning of the numbers that may be assigned.

One large class of problems bearing on the adequacy with which consequences are measured concerns, in effect, the relationship between the three levels of consequences. The relative inadequacy can be of several types.

A variety previously discussed implies a nonlinear surrogate-utility transformation function—the utility per dollar of payoff differs depending on whether the payoff is large or small, positive or negative. This can be dealt with by using an appropriately responsive transformation function and involves merely an adjustment of the Expected Value rather than a variant of it.

Some problems require changing the decision rule to reflect the particulars which cause the nonlinearities in relationships. There are many examples in the literature. There is, for example, the "maximin" rule of pessimism proposed by Abraham Wald. His injunction is to minimize the maximum risk (or maximize the minimum payoff). The decision maker is advised to select the act which, if worst comes to worst, will be better than other alternatives. The rule recognizes special sensitivity to losses. In a particular situation—a two-person game with wise opponents—pessimism maximizes the winnings of both players; both players should assume, since it is so often true, that they will systematically be forced into the worst possible situations.[1] Leonid Hurwicz, reflecting that for some people, in connection with some situations, pessimism and sensitivity to loss are replaced by optimism or interest in games, suggests the use of a "coefficient of optimism" which particularizes the actual position of the decision maker on the pessimistic-optimistic continuum.[2] L. J. Savage has suggested a variant of the pessimistic rule. His pessimistic assumption is that nature will continue to make you feel as sorry as possible that you did what you did. Accordingly, pick the act which will minimize this regret.[3] By focusing on regret, the decision maker seems to be visualized as holding the several possibilities in his mind and worrying more about how much of a chump he may turn out to be than how well off he may turn out to be. Although I recognize this utility scheme, I prefer to attribute it to my enemies than to my friends.

Incomplete Metrics

For some decision problems the difficulty lies in what eludes measurement rather than how it is measured. Intangible values are one source of this difficulty of which noncommensurables are a particularly troublesome variety.

One way to incorporate the recognition of intangibles and noncommensurable elements in a decision rule is simply to superimpose appropriate additional values onto the answers generated by the Expected

[1] This fact has been elegantly demonstrated by John von Neumann and Oskar Morgenstern, *The Theory of Games and Economic Behavior*, Princeton University Press, Princeton, N.J., 1944. If players are assumed to have the attributes of economic man, the pessimistic assumption, the assumption that the players will always produce the worst results for their opponents, gives rise to solutions, "saddle points" at which both players are better off than they would be if they used a different decision rule.

[2] *Optimality Criteria for Decision Making Under Ignorance*, Cowles Commission Discussion Paper, Statistics, No. 370, 1951 (mimeographed); cited in R. D. Luce and Howard Raiffa, Games and Decisions, Wiley, New York, p. 282.

[3] Leonard J. Savage, "The Theory of Statistical Decision," *Journal of American Statistical Association*, Vol. 46, pp. 56–57, 1951. The payoff matrix is converted to a regret matrix in the following way: for each column (for each state of nature) the act is selected having the highest payoff; the payoff under the same state of nature for each of the other acts is subtracted from the one having the maximum payoff; these differences replace the payoff figures in the matrix (the entry is 0 for the act having the highest payoff); for each line (each act) the state of nature producing the largest regret is the one assumed to obtain. The rule is: select the act for which this unfortunate result is the smallest.

Value rule applied to the fixed-unit surrogate. In this way, the decision, in effect, is adjusted for factors not previously included.

In some cases it is possible to take account of intangible and noncommensurable values in terms of the numbers themselves. The devices of the *standard gamble* and *indifference analysis* are examples. They can sometimes apply to the important class of problems in which the utility associated with risk avoidance and dispersion of outcomes should be taken into account.

Ambiguous evaluations call for another type of adjustment. We noted earlier that shaky evaluations may be viewed as reducing the utility attributed to an outcome expected with a given probability or as reducing the probability with which a given outcome is expected. If the former interpretation is espoused, the decision rule would call for adjustment of the relationship between the numbers arrived at for the payoff and the utility attributed to it.[4] If the latter is more appealing, then the adjustment is introduced at the point of estimating event likelihood and there is no need to tamper with the payoff.[5]

SERIABILITY

There is one further respect in which the substance of even well-structured decisions may fail to fit comfortably in the format of decision theory. The expected value rule and its variants optimize expected average results. But at times, average results are sometimes of little or no interest to a decision maker.

[4] Ellsberg, for example, elaborates the notion in terms of a preference scheme since he believes ". . . that trades are possible between security level and estimated expectation. . . ." But he believes that trades take place along a function that is not linear: "the less confident he (the decision maker) is, the more he will sacrifice in terms of estimated expected pay-off to achieve a given increase in 'security level'; the more confident, the greater increase in 'security level' he would demand to compensate for a given drop in estimated expectation." Also, Ellsberg thinks that the minimum expected payoffs are more sensitive to a confidence rating than are the other possibilities. These notions are incorporated in an index on the basis of which people decide how to act. Implied is a tendency "to act *'as though'* the worst were somewhat more likely than his best estimates of likelihood would indicate." Daniel Ellsberg, "Risk, Ambiguity, and the Savage Axioms," *Quarterly Journal of Economics,* Vol. LXXV, November 1961, pp. 664 and 667.

[5] William Fellner visualizes the effect of "elusive hypotheses" as causing decision makers to "slant" their true probability judgments downward. That is, to place them at a discount relative to the more reliable judgments; these discounted probabilities are then used as decision weights in a Bayesian formulation of the Expected Value matrix. *Probability and Profit,* Richard D. Irwin, Inc., Homewood, Ill., 1965, pp. 25–34 and p. 39ff. Further details of the decision rule are given on p. 57.

The situation is such that each possible outcome must be individually tolerable. It cannot be viewed simply as a member of a probabilistic series for which the average result for the whole series is all that matters. In other words, the particular decision, or some one of its particular possible outcomes, is not in this sense "seriable." It maintains some "one of a kind" attributes. It is not a member of a series subject to insurance on an actuarial basis. We shall call such situations *nonseriable* or *having low seriability*. For decisions characterized by low seriability, the evaluated consequences which are of interest are those associated with the cumulated possible results of each sequence of act-event conjunctions which might take place.

In its most extreme form the sequence is a set of one. If I consider swimming a broad river alone at night, I will either get to the other side or drown; an average result is hard to visualize this side of the great divide.

A new business may be judged to yield an annual income having an expected value of $10,000; but it could lose $25,000 in one year. If the loss would mean bankruptcy to the proprietor, and the chance of it occurring was thought to be one in five, the venture might seem ill-advised. Even if the proprietor could withstand a loss of $50,000 there would still be a chance of 4 in 100 (0.2 times 0.2) that the first two years (or any other two years assuming the figures do not alter) would wipe him out.

These examples concern situations which are dichotomous: win or lose. But nonseriability can evoke concern for each of the whole array of possible outcomes. To illustrate, consider once again the village fair. Suppose that it were feasible to continue the fair for as many as five days. Suppose that the weather on sequential days is uncorrelated (that is, as each day breaks, the chance of rain is always 50-50); also make the thoroughly unrealistic assumption that earnings per day will not be deteriorated by increasing the number of days. Exhibit 3-1 shows in successive lines each possible result for total receipts (for all days) of fairs running one, two, three, and five days, and the probability that each of the possibilities will eventuate.

The first column duplicates the earlier example. The others are derived as explained in note *b*. The point that I want to bring out concerns the total amounts actually at risk under each situation. Look at column 2. If the village bank account was limited to $700 it might be unwise to take a 25 percent chance of $1000 loss, regardless of what one stood to gain. The same might apply to the 3-day fair because even the 12 percent chance to a $1500 loss might not be acceptable.

The average results are irrelevant as a basis of decision because there

EXHIBIT 3-1   Possible Payoffs for Fairs of Specified Duration (.50-.50 Chance of Rain, Net Take on Fine Day $1500, Net Loss on Rainy Day −$500)

Duration of Fair, Days	1		2		3		5	
	P^a	$\$^a$	P	$	P	$	P	$
							.03	−2500
					.12	−1500	.16	− 500
			.25	−1000				
Array of out-	.50	− 500			.38	500	.31	1500
comes, lowest			.50	1000				
to highest^b	.50	1500			.38	2000	.31	3500
			.25	3000				
					.12	4000	.16	5500
							.03	7500
Expected Value								
Total		500		1000		1500		2500
Per day		500		500		500		500

^{a} Possible payoffs ($) and probability ($P$) of each.
^{b} The net dollar take, as given, covers all of the possible actual occurrences, given the duration of the fair and the stipulations as stated in the subtitle. The likelihood of each occurrence is derived by the rule of multiplication from the assumption of a .50-.50 chance of rain. E.g., for a 3-day fair, the chance of all rainy days is .50 × .50 × .50 = .125 or, rounded to 2 places, .12 (numbers are rounded up for odd and down for even numbers).

is, in spite of the favorable Expected Value, a greater chance than one can afford to ignore of entirely unacceptable consequences.

This sort of constraint is likely to intensify when utility-payoff functions are nonlinear. Exhibit 3-2 interprets the previous example in terms of evaluated consequences based on low utility per dollar as reward increases and high disutility per dollar as loss increases (see the ratios in the $U/\$$ columns). The increasing sensitivity to increasing loss is due to the worries about injuring credit, overdrawing bank accounts, and generally appearing foolhardy; the decreasing utility of increasing receipts is due to established patterns of annual village expenses, which make earnings over this amount less urgent. In other words, plotting utilities vertically and dollars horizontally, the function approaches a vertical line in the left lower sector (as loss increases) and a horizontal line toward the right upper sector as earnings increase. Note that Ex-

EXHIBIT 3-2 Possible Outcomes for Fairs of Specified Duration, Utility Values

Duration of Fair, Days	1			2			3			5		
	U/$ᵃ	Pᵇ	Uᶜ	U/$	P	U	U/$	P	U	U/$	P	U
Array of outcomes, lowest to highest	1.00	.50	− 500	2.00	.25	−2000	2.67	.12	−4000	4.00	.03	−10000
	1.00	.50	1500	1.00	.50	1000	1.00	.38	500	1.00	.16	− 500
				.83	.25	2500	1.00	.38	2000	1.00	.31	1500
							.75	.12	3000	.80	.31	2800
										.70	.16	3850
										.50	.03	3750
Expected Value			500			625			830			1680
Total per day			500			312			277			336

ᵃ Utility-dollar transformation ratios (U/$). Dollar-utility transformations coefficients are assigned on the basis of reasoning given in the textual discussion.
ᵇ Probability of outcome (P). As in Exhibit 3-1.
ᶜ Utility value (U). Derived from Exhibit 3-1 by multiplying the dollar outcome by the utility-dollar transformation coefficients, column U/$ in this table.

49

pected Value per day, as well as the total array, now bear on which duration is more desirable. The 2- and 3-day fairs are banned on both counts. The 5-day fair looks good only if we assume that the villagers do not much mind spending time on fairs (and that adding days does not decrease the daily take).

In the decision situation characterized by relatively low seriability, then, expected values may be of little or even no interest. Repetitions are typically not sufficiently numerous to give rein to the tendency for actual outcomes to converge on Expected Value. Consequently, actual outcomes may diverge so widely from average outcomes that the average result is a poor basis of choice. The decision maker needs to consider *all the possible consequences which might obtain with a likelihood that he cannot afford to ignore.* All of these consequences must appear tolerable and some, of course, clearly desirable.

Moreover, this tolerance of the range of actual evaluated consequences needs further subdivision. Not merely the worst of the cumulative end results must appear tolerable but likewise each possible *time path to it* (the years of severe loss in a new business, the loss of $1500 the third day of a five-day fair).

These characteristics of the nonseriable decision situation tend to be intensified by nonlinear surrogate-utility transformation functions, but they are not confined to these situations, nor is the difficulty a function of nonrational value systems, sparse information, or other derilections from the stereotype of economic man and rational decision. The problem arises from the character of the decision situation itself—its element of uniqueness, in contrast to membership in a group in which acts will be repeated again and again. Adding a measure of dispersion to that of expected value is a familiar way of addressing the problem, though it by no means solves it.

Nonseriability is, however, sometimes subject to correction. The method is *insurance.* It has the capacity of making nonseriable decision problems seriable if three conditions can be met: (1) all estimates—those of probabilities and of consequences—are *unbiased* (so that expected values for each eventuality are unbiased); (2) the number of eventualities covered are large enough for convergence toward Expected Value to be substantial; (3) resources are adequate over relevant time periods to cover such runs of bad luck as may take place. Insurance meeting these requirements is not confined to the usual commercial sorts. Each man can be his own Lloyd's of London. Thus an art collector may not guess right each time, but if he sells his mistaken purchases, his success will be a function of his ability, not primarily of his luck. Large businesses and upper-level governments can deal on a seriable basis with decision situations that would be nonseriable for a small enterprise.

MODELS FOCUSING ON SELECTED OUTCOMES

Nonseriable problems require attention to individual outcomes. This complicates the decision rule. If relevant states of the world are complex (not simply loss or profit, rain or not rain), and if acts are various and subject to modulation, decision matrices take on additional dimensions. Problems of these kinds usually require some sort of powerful simplification before the mind can grapple with them.

Shackle's Model

Perhaps the best known scheme for such simplification is that of G. L. S. Shackle. He believes that ". . . the individual reduces any uncertainty-situation to the simplicity of an ordinary bet, in which only two possible outcomes are considered, one of which is a definite amount of gain and the other a definite amount of loss."[6] The decision maker selects these two outcomes on the basis of their capacity to command his attention, their "interestingness." He contemplates the dollar outcome that he expects and the uncertainty he associates with that outcome.[7] The less the uncertainty, the greater the interestingness of the outcome. People will differ with respect to the particulars of their ability to be attracted by the exchange of larger gains for less uncertainty. However, any individual, contemplating a particular act in a given decision situa-

[6] *Expectation in Economics*, 2nd ed., The University Press, Cambridge, 1952, p. 18. My description of Shackle's theory takes liberties with his construction in order to show, in brief compass, its relation to the more usual decision theory. This relationship is also the subject of a paper by Ward Edwards, "Note on Potential Surprise and Nonadditive Subjective Probabilities," in *Expectation, Uncertainty, and Business Behavior*, Mary Jean Bowman, Ed., Social Science Research Council, New York, 1958.

[7] Other useful expositions of Shackle's theories are: G. L. S. Shackle, "Expectation and Liquidity," in *Expectations, Uncertainty, and Business Behavior*, M. J. Bowman, Ed.; and G. Patrick Meredith, "Methodological Considerations in the Study of Human Anticipation," in *Uncertainty and Business Decisions*, a symposium edited by C. F. Carter, G. P. Meredith, and G. L. S. Shackle, University Press, Liverpool, 1957. The same source has as frontis-piece a photograph of a three-dimensional model of the Shackle decision construction.

Shackle uses a notion, "Potential Surprise," which is close to one minus subjective probability, though not identical to it. But for the purpose of this discussion, I have, with apologies to Shackle, turned his notions upside down in order that the reader may stay right side up. Though some subtleties are lost, the net communication is, I expect, optimized.

tion, will arrive at the two judgments on which his final evaluation will depend: they will be the particular combinations of reward and likelihood, and the particular combinations of penalty and likelihood toward which his mind gravitates.

In order to decide between alternative actions, four figures—two dollar values and two probability estimates—need to be collapsed into a single figure for each alternative. This is done in two steps. First the estimates of gain and loss are, in effect, both discounted for uncertainty.[8] Second, these two values—the foci of interest—are, in effect, adjusted for asymmetrical utility before the net value of the act is ascertained.[9]

Shackle's model, and its associated decision rule, features the notion that people do not visualize all possible outcomes of any one act and attach likelihoods to each which sum to 1.0. Instead they do something simpler—pick two possible outcomes, a good and a bad one. The simplification makes it possible to allow considerable flexibility and richness in the subjective evaluations that are made with respect to the two chosen values. However, these evaluations have some serious rigidities; they are made entirely in dollar terms; they insist that just two possibilities are considered and that the preference surface is continuous.[10]

It is easy to picture a decision model in which these rigidities are removed. However, by removing the rigidities one also removes the optimizing properties which Shackle attributes to his model.

[8] These values Shackle calls standardized focus gain and focus loss. They are close cousins to two Expected Values e.g., "the focus gain is the point with the highest expected value obtainable" (Edwards, *op. cit.*, p. 46). Shackle's actual construction involves replacing the two primary focus outcomes by "equivalents carrying nil potential surprise." This is accomplished by the use of what is virtually an indifference curve structure to project a primary focus outcome to a result, involving nil potential surprise, which would be deemed equivalent; that is, to the certainty equivalent of the gamble (Shackle, *op. cit.*, 1952, pp. 24 and 25).

[9] A gambler's "indifference map" traces the structure by which the individual will trade focus gain for focus loss. Each indifference curve will be a set of points located by a focus gain (vertical axis increasing values upward) and a focus loss (horizontal axis increasing losses to the right), "all the members of which are mutually equal in attractiveness to the given person in his given circumstances" (Shackle, 1952, p. 29). The venture is preferred which lies on a curve to the left of that of the challenger (*ibid.* p. 30).

[10] A number of cogent criticisms have been made of the Shackle model and they make interesting reading. Three recommended examples are: G. P. Meredith, "Methodological Considerations in the Study of Human Anticipation," in *Uncertainty and Business Decisions, op. cit.*; C. F. Carter, "A Revised Theory of Expectations," in *Uncertainty and Business Decisions, op. cit.*; and Ward Edwards, "Note on Potential Surprise and Nonadditive Subjective Probabilities," *op. cit.* The continuous preference surface has specifically been questioned by Meredith, *op. cit.*, pp. 42–43, and Edwards, *op. cit.*, p. 46.

Accordingly I shall postpone the discussion of these more relaxed selective-focus models until Part Two, where more realistic notions about decision makers and decision situations are introduced.

Decision Trees

Thus far we have thought only about situations for which the acts deemed worth considering are all single alternatives in the sense that, at a given point of time, one chooses one or another (including the alternative of doing nothing). But sometimes an alternative consists of a *series of acts to be undertaken in sequence.* At each of the points in time at which secondary and tertiary decisions are possible, the decision maker may choose between two or more alternatives. This situation comes under the constraints of this chapter if the alternatives to be considered in the future are *presently recognized as possibilities.* Needless to say, they often are not.

Just *when* all or parts of a decision should be made must usually itself be decided. Postponement is possible when the period relevant to the decision, the entire period over which consequences accrue, is longer than the periods when new decisions concerning the same problem can be made or previous ones revised. Serial decision or outright postponement is desirable when it may be expected to enhance the final consequences. For the moment we consider only serial decision among presently delineated alternatives.

Take the example of a manufacturer who produces only one product on one type of machine, of which he has five. His plant is running close to capacity and he considers purchasing an additional machine. The alternative, overtime work, is economical for small spasmodic additional sales but uneconomical for a large persistent increase. Investment criteria require a cash flow that will cause the machine to "pay for itself" in two years and we shall assume, accordingly, that the decision horizon is at least two years.

The decision tree has three branches if we limit decision points to one a year. It may be represented as shown in Diagram 3-1 (the figures, the cumulated payoffs, are developed in Exhibit 3-3).

The initial choice must be made on the basis of expectations concerning the whole subsequent sequence of events and the payoffs that they are expected to yield over the two-year period (later payoffs are for our purposes just gravy).

Assume that the payoffs (in terms of net cash flow) depend primarily on sales, which may be either high (H) or low (L) (although the actual levels in any case in the second year are assumed to reflect an upward trend). Three matrixes are shown in Exhibit 3-3 in the first

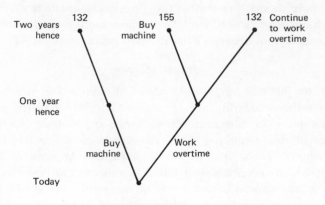

Diagram 3-1

EXHIBIT 3-3 Matrices for Decision Tree

		Year 1		
Sales:		High	Low	Expected
Probability:		(.4)	(.6)	Value (EV)
Acts				
1	(Buy machine)	100	20	52
2	(Use overtime)	70	60	64

		Year 2		
Sales:		High	Low	EV
Probability:		(.5)	(.5)	
Acts				
1.1	(Continue use of machine)	120	40	80
2.2	(Now buy machine)	120	40	80
2.3	(Continue use of overtime)	70	65	68

		Years 1 and 2				
Sales:		H_1H_2	H_1L_2	L_1H_2	L_1L_2	EV
Probability:		(.2)	(.2)	(.3)	(.3)	
Acts						
Year 1	Year 2					
1	1.1	220	140	140	60	132
2	2.2	190	110	180	100	155
3	2.3	140	135	130	125	132

year, for the second year, and for the two years together. The acts
in the first year are shown in the stub of the first matrix. The second
matrix shows acts in the second year, given each act in the first year.

The third matrix—payoffs for the two years together—must consoli-
date the four possibilities for low or high sales each year and their
probabilities (derived by the rule of multiplication) into a probability
weighted outcome for each of the three possible two-year acts. Act
2-2.2—overtime the first year and buying the machine the second year—
is clearly best. The conclusion assumes that the requirements for seriability have been met, although consideration is confined to only two outcomes each year, rather than to the whole range of possibilities.

But if seriability were low in the sense that the manufacturer was
in a position to be severely hurt by a yield as low as 100, act 2-2.2
would be questionable; there is a 3 out of 10 chance of the L_1L_2 case,
and another 2 out of 10 chance of the H_1L_2 case with a yield of only
a little higher—110. The overtime-throughout choice, 2-2.3, would give
him a substantially higher return in these eventualities. On the other
hand, the early machine purchase would be far more attractive if the
jackpot were high (H_1H_2) and sales were high both years. How does
he balance these several situations against one another?

The decision tree is an appealing conception. It seems to accommodate
the harsh outlines of the decision matrix to something closer to every-
man's experience. This humanization, acquired by admitting timing and
sequence into the decision's structure, grows in importance as, in Part
Three, we view the decision process before the acts to be undertaken
have been nominated.

Certainly one advantage of postponing a decision is to gain information capable of improving the judgment about what to consider doing.
Coping with uncertainty by "buying information" or "buying time" is
intimately involved with climbing around in decision trees.

So, for that matter, is all of life. Perhaps it is just as well that the
young take the steps that determine the main trunk-branchings without
full awareness of their import. Clearly, one of the blessings of advancing
years is the sense of scrambling among the fine branches with the abandon of a chipmunk.

SUMMARY OF PART ONE

"Choice by rational man" is the subject addressed by statistical decision
theory. It concerns choice among predelineated alternatives. Its central
application is in decision situations in which information is reasonably

rich and manageable so that opinion has a firm base. The purpose of my exposition is to tell just enough about this expert and voluminous work to reveal its applicability to the whole range of decision problems faced by businesses and government administrators.

To choose among alternative acts the consequences of which are uncertain, it is necessary to review the states of the world that might influence outcomes, the probability that each state will obtain, the consequences in terms of expected utility of choosing the act under each possible state of the world. Finally, these evaluations of probabilities and of expected utilities need to be consolidated to yield a basis for saying: this is the act I prefer.

Starting with the estimate of probabilities, we reviewed first some central theorems describing additive, multiplicative, and directional relationships of probability. They provided glimpses of how uncertainty permeates actuality.

We turned next to the meaning of the probability judgments for which the matrix calls—estimates of the probability that specified events will occur (specified states of the world will obtain). The most usual practice is to rely on subjective judgments as to what these are—judgments which make use of such logical or experimental evidence as is available, but are not confined to the evidence since they are, at core, simply degrees of belief. This distinction between situations involving risk and those involving uncertainty, or even ambiguity concerning the degree of uncertainty, is applicable to all sorts of decision problems.

The notion of ambiguity, an idea that recognizes man's capacity to evaluate his evaluations, has been emphasized. For, although a few economists have asserted its applicability to mathematical decision theory, its applicability to less well-structured decision situations is clearly pervasive. For one thing, we shall see that it contributes to a "conservative bias" which seems to characterize many business and government decisions.

The matrix calls next for an estimate of the utility expected to result from act-event conjunctures. We suggest that it will be useful (particularly in later parts of the book) to distinguish between three levels at which act-event conjunctions can be described: primary consequences or outcomes described in objective physical terms; surrogate consequences or payoffs, which apply the best objective standard of uniform measurement that can be devised; and evaluated consequences, which apply a utility function.

Intangible values are present in some degree in most decision problems, even well-structured ones; and intangibles are less of a hazard than noncommensurables which introduce alternative criteria of value and therefore cannot be directly added to one another. However, in-difference analysis provides a way of formulating exchange relationships or trade-off surfaces among noncommensurables.

Finally, we turn to how the probability-discounted expected utility of an act under all relevant states of the world may be evaluated in a way which makes it possible to choose which of the alternative acts are preferable.

The standard answer is: choose the act for which the Expected Value, the sum of the evaluated consequences weighted by their probability of occurrence, is highest.

The Expected Value decision rule can be adjusted for various sorts of nonlinearities in the relationship between surrogate and evaluated consequences, that is for difference between the numerical unit in which expected outcomes are measured and the utility associated with each unit at the various levels of payoffs. Here again, we meet, in relatively contained form, difficulties that ramify in the majority of real life situations.

However, some decision situations are not well served by the Expected Value rule. Nonseriable decision situations are an important class of problems for which Expected Value is at best only part of the answer. The acts are not repeated often enough for diversity of individual outcomes to average out. This means that the whole range of possible outcomes may need to be kept in mind.

G. L. S. Shackle's decision model concentrates on two outcomes—a good one and a bad one. It thereby can deal with nonseriable decisions but ones for which it is impractical or impossible to consider more than a few of the possible outcomes. Additional possibilities (as well as difficulties) are introduced in decision situations when they can be made stepwise, that is, when time is admitted as one of the dimensions of decision even in the restricted fashion that the notion of well-struc-tured decision admits.

The chapter provides a varied menu of decision rules and procedures among which intelligent choice can be made, depending on the problems and the circumstance. This variety is, I believe, essential. A thoughtful person varies his evaluative procedures with the characteristics of the problem that he faces. When appropriate, the rigor of the formal, tightly quantified matrix and the Expected Value decision rule is the ideal selection. But when not appropriate it is necessary to trade rigor for relevance.

Indeed, one of the purposes that Part One should serve is to fix well in mind the rigor that will be lost as, in the remainder of this book, we pursue relevance. Relevance at any price is written on our banner.

But it is well to know the price, and to keep it as small as possible. It should become evident as we proceed that the price can be kept down in several ways: by using statistical decision theory proper in the situations that conform to its tenets; by applying it as a first step to parts of larger problems; and by using the basic framework for deliberation that it has constructed, modified in ways appropriate to the materials loaded upon it.

PART TWO

Choice by
Natural Man

CHAPTER 4

Decision Agents and Reality Judgments

The workday world is an extraordinarily sloppy counterpart of the world pictured in the previous chapters, in which economic man makes optimal decisions on well-structured decision problems. It is this world of experience to which the discussion now turns. We retain the assumption that all alternative acts worth considering are preselected and known in each decision situation. But we consider the natural decision agent and the problems that he faces as he tries to do the best he can.

THE DECISION AGENT

Decision rests on a number of subjective judgments by men and women of whom the salient characteristics need to be sketched. Judgments are often also made by groups of men who must bring their opinions and desires into some accord in order to reach collective decision.

Natural Man

Herbert Simon has portrayed the contrast between "rational" man and natural man. Man's behavior in organizations is "intendedly rational." He has only limited knowledge and computational capacity relative to what is objectively required. Consequently, in order to deal with most real situations, man must construct a simplified model, and the question is, what is the nature of the model. For one thing ". . . its construction will certainly be related to his psychological properties as a perceiving, thinking, and learning animal."[1] Consideration of these properties leads Simon to reject the notion that man is capable of formulating joint probability distributions or complete and consistent preference ordering of all possible alternatives of action. Instead, he must use some sort of highly simplified payoff function which he considers acceptable or satisfactory.[2] He does not maximize; he "satisfices."

Concerning what is felt to be "satisfactory," Simon has two very important things to say. He points first to the fact that men do not perceive a total situation, but only that portion of the total which is meaningful and, in context, significant to them. In other words, *perception is selective*. Second, he asserts that what is satisfactory at any particular moment is influenced not only by things presently going on but also by achievements or defeats of the past;[3] that is, *aspiration levels are conditioned*.

Maximization, then, is not simply difficult and approximate; *it is intrinsically impossible:* first, because the materials of decision are not approximations of some external objective reality, but inherently subjective (since they are selected and perceived through the screen of the individual's psychological field); second, because goals move away like the carrot tied to the stick at the donkey's neck. In consequence, both current perceptions and ambitions and how they change are subject to forces internal to the decision maker.

The picture of man as a perceiving, thinking, and learning animal is based on work in psychology which seems generally undisputed. It views thinking and learning as part of a broader set of characteristics. Man is possessed of an unconscious as well as a conscious level of being, and the former, judged against "rational" standards, is highly erratic in its influence on behavior; so conceived, thinking and feeling are inexplicably intertwined. Man's perceptions are almost never total, but are selected by what he is ready to perceive and finds functionally significant. His storehouse of knowledge is highly structured on the basis of what he finds meaningful, and this is affected by his moods, needs, wishes, and experiences; this structure is influenced, among other things, by the "roles" in terms of which he conceives his relationships to the outside world. His drives and ambitions are inevitably affected by both

[1] H. Simon, "Rationality and Administrative Decision Making," in *Models of Man*, John Wiley & Sons, Inc., New York, 1957, p. 199.

[2] H. Simon, "A Behavioral Model of Rational Choice," in *Models of Man, op. cit.*, p. 246.

[3] *Ibid.*, p. 253.

internal and external events. He is, finally, conscious and unconscious, thinking and feeling, dreaming and coping, remembering and forgetting—a point in history: his present is simply the growing edge of his past.[4]

This description of man's psychology has implications about his sociology: the environment and its values are part of the content of the individual's psychological "field." But the outer world does not simply intrude on the inner world. It is part of it. Man is a social animal. His kind are part of himself. He has the power of empathy. If so, he differs again from *Homo economicus* since he has necessarily pluralistic values. Jones the family man and the organization man is also a societal man who accepts some and rejects other societal problems as his own. The pluralistic view of the political process relies heavily on this characteristic of the human animal. Three further attributes should be mentioned. They are easily observed though perhaps little understood.

First, there is the power to dream, to imagine, to create, to dare. As Kenneth Boulding has said "Without the heroic, man has no meaning; without the economic he has no sense."[5]

Second, there is the power of judgment. "Judgment it seems, is an ultimate category, which can only be approved or condemned by a further exercise of the same ability."[6] Intuition seems to contribute to judgment; this subrational or perhaps superrational process performs some of the feats of multivariate analysis that *Homo economicus* would

---

[4] Good discussions at a textbook level are to be found in David Krech and Richard S. Crutchfield, *Theory and Problems of Social Psychology*, McGraw-Hill Book Co., Inc., New York, 1948, and C. L. Hull, *Principles of Behavior, An Introduction to Behavioral Theory*, Appleton-Century-Crofts, New York, 1943. See also: Donald W. Taylor, "Thinking," in *Psychological Theory; Contemporary Readings*, M. H. Marx, Ed., 2nd ed., Macmillan, New York, 1963; "Decision Making and Problem Solving," in *Handbook of Organizations*, J. G. March, Ed., Rand McNally, Chicago, 1965; Ulric Neisser, *Cognitive Psychology*, Appleton-Century-Crofts, New York, 1966. For a few articles, selected almost at random, dealing with more particular aspects of some of these problems see I. L. Child and J. W. M. Whiting, "Determinants of Level of Aspiration: Evidence from Everyday Life," *Journal of Abnormal Psychology*, 1949, Vol. 44, pp. 303–314; Kurt Lewin, T. Dembo, L. Festinger, and Pauline S. Sears, "Level of Aspiration," in *Personality and the Behavior Disorders*, J. McV. Hunt, Ed., Ronald Press, New York, 1944, pp. 333–378; and R. D. Luce, "The Theory of Selective Information and Some of its Behavioral Applications," in *Developments in Mathematical Psychology*, R. D. Luce, Ed., The Free Press, Glencoe, Ill., 1960.

[5] Kenneth E. Boulding, *The Skills of the Economist*, Howard Allen, Inc., Cleveland, 1958, p. 183.

[6] Sir Geoffrey Vickers, *The Art of Judgment, A Study of Policy Making*, Chapman and Hall, London, 1965, p. 13.

do on his abacus. In any event, one cannot deal constructively with the problems raised by uncertainty without remembering that some men, under some circumstances, are virtuosos in the art of judgment.

Third, most reasonably healthy people have a preference for doing things well rather than poorly. Whether the "instinct of workmanship" is an instinct or a projection of a father image, it tends to produce pleasure in good performance. For people whose conscious or unconscious levels of behavior are geared to socially benign objectives, this implies deliberative effort to solve problems with a rational regard for how to do the job well. "Well" in this context is defined by norms largely external to the individual.

These norms mute idiosyncratic behavior; they tend to stabilize and rationalize individual behavior since they chain in to the collective wisdom. Influences of an analogous sort are, of course, present in all the evaluative proceedings of individuals because man's inner life is deeply patterned by the basic values, and even fashions, of the society of which he is a member.

Another stabilizing influence derives from the organizations in which most decisions are made and in terms of which roles are assigned or played. Institutions have as one of their primary purposes, the substitution of institutional goals for personal ones. Personal goals "depend on the organizational environment in which the individual's decision takes place. The task of administration is so to design this environment that the individual will approach as close as practicable to rationality (judged in terms of the organization's goals) in this decision."[7]

There is another process that tends to subdue the erratic influences on behavior. Most consequences of general importance represent the cumulation of many decisions by many decision makers. This aggregation affords an opportunity for the idiosyncratic aspects of individual behavior to cancel out except insofar as individuals are subject to shared biases. Insofar as personalistic aspects do cancel out, individual decisions are subject to wider variance than would be true of those of economic man, but their average values would not necessarily be widely different.

However, much of the personalistic aspect of behavior will not cancel out in the behavior of a group. Individual behavior is strongly influenced by that of other individuals and by the environment in which decisions are made. This imparts, I expect, a strong *developmental aspect to decision*. Development may have temporal and spatial patterns, for it is born

---

[7] Simon, *Administrative Behavior, A Study of Decision-Making Processes in Administrative Organizations*, 2nd ed. (1947) 1961, The Macmillan Co., New York, pp. 240–241.

on the tradewinds of men's thoughts and nurtured by a common soil. This theme is reintroduced in Chapter 10.

The Collective Decision Maker

Leonard Savage points out ". . . organizations sometimes behave like individual people, so that a theory originally intended to apply to people may also apply to (or may even apply better to) such units as families, corporations, or nations."[8] But to describe realistically a typical decision maker in government or indeed in business, Savage's statement could also be reversed; it is not so much that a corporation or nation behaves like a person as that a person behaves like a corporation or nation.

For one thing, the individual is himself a group of individuals. He is an *intrapersonal* collective. Thus a government executive, Tom Jones, may in effect behave like a five-man board of directors consisting of: (1) the craftsman who wants to do a "good job," (2) the politician who has an eye on what people back home will think, (3) the organization man who identifies himself with the needs of his bureau, (4) the societal man who wants to be admired for his virtue and wealth, (5) the family man who wants time to play with his childeren. Although over time the interests of these Joneses may tend to merge, at any particular moment they may be sharply opposed. A decision presupposes some reconciliation of that opposition. Thus, even the "person" often functions as a "collective"—an intraperson collective—in administrative situations.

But frequently the interests that need to be reconciled reach outside of the individual decision maker so that collectivity takes on *interpersonal* characteristics. It can do so in different ways and to different extents. One such way features how others will react to one's own decision. The anticipated reactions can be mere wisps in the total evaluation—the reaction of a neighbor to my new television set, the discipline that placing an order with one supplier imposes on his competitors.

At other times anticipated reactions may be central to the decision; ultimately the individual decision maker may view himself as a surrogate of the reacting group. But this pure case is rare even in the standard format of the elected legislator. Ordinarily there is a substantial processing operation whereby the surrogate must learn of, interpret, and perhaps select among the wishes of his constituency; moreover, these

---

[8] Savage, *The Foundation of Statistics* John Wiley & Sons, New York, 1954, p. 8.

semiprocessed wishes may be only one of the raw materials that he may deem relevant to the decision problem. The surrogate is common in businessmen and indeed in the home. The "housewife" trying to arrange the week's menu for a family of five, each with competitive foibles, is a political scientist in fact if not in theory.

Another way in which interpersonal collectivity manifests itself is more direct. In politics and business the decision agent is often actually a group of people rather than a person representing a group. Collective business decisions have been the subject of a good deal of investigation.[9] The theory and practice of the pluralistic process has been elaborately studied in political science; there is agreement at least on the fact of its importance.[10]

These several sorts of collectivity obviously influence the decision process. For example, as Cyert and March emphasize, the conflicts of goals among members of any decision collective are not capable of stable or complete resolution. "Quasi-resolution of conflict" is the usual state within an organization.[11] It tends to increase the uncertainty with which outcomes can be predicted. Of course, this depends upon the patterns of conflict resolution in a particular organization—a habitual pattern of leadership, for example, reduces the difference between collective and one-man decision.

[9] See, for example: Richard M. Cyert and James G. March, *A Behavioral Theory of the Firm*, Prentice-Hall, Inc., Englewood Cliffs, N.J., 1963; Cyert and March, "Behavioral Theory of Organizational Objectives." in *Modern Organization Theory*, A Symposium on the Foundation for the Research on Human Behavior, Mason Haire, Ed., Harper & Bros. New York, 1959; Neil Chamberlain, *A General Theory of Economic Process*, Harper & Bros., New York, 1955; Thomas Schelling, *The Strategy of Conflict*, Oxford University Press, New York, 1963; Kenneth Boulding, *Conflict and Defense*, Harper & Bros., New York, 1962; and many articles in the *Journal of Conflict Resolution*.

[10] There is general agreement in modern political science with respect to the pluralistic nature of political process. David Truman's *The Governmental Process*, Knopf, New York, 1951, was a pivotal work. But parallel notions, each making their own particular contributions, have been written in many areas. Richard Neustadt applied it to the chief executive in *Presidential Power*, Wiley [1960], New York; Wallace Sayre and Herbert Kaufman in *Governing New York City*, Norton [1965], New York, and Robert A. Dahl in *Who Governs*, Yale University Press, New York, 1961, investigated its manifestations in local government.

The general fields of legislation and administration have been extensively explored; see, for example, Aaron Wildavsky, *The Politics of the Budgetary Process*, Little, Brown [1964], Boston; and J. Leiper Freeman, *The Political Process*, Random House, New York, 1965.

[11] Richard M. Cyert and James G. March, *op. cit.* The quasi-resolution tends to be achieved by agreement on major goals in contrast to subgoals, formation of coalitions, bargaining, threats, and other techniques.

A central effect of an interpersonal decision agent is a tendency to draw out the decision process. It takes time to formulate and achieve agreement concerning group action. This implies that strategies whereby the process is governed are part of the fabric of the decision itself.

Collectivity, along with selective perception and conditioned aspirations, also influences the attribution of utility to outcomes. Pluralism typically implies noncomparable utilities; values are differently weighted by various members of a collective. The company's treasurer prefers the policy that provides ample sources of funds, the production manager values the newest machines. The director of a government bureau builds empires in terms of a large staff and large budget; his mayor wants to exhibit the halo of efficiency. Noncomparable values, since they are difficult to relate to one another, tend to complicate the attribution of utility to an outcome, and thereby to blur the meaning of preference.

JUDGING THE PROBABILITY OF AN OUTCOME

In order to choose a preferred act, men, having the subjective characteristics which have been described, must form expectations about objective phenomena. They must determine the likelihood that specified events will obtain which will result in specified outcomes if particular acts are undertaken.

They must, in other words, make judgments about causality. In the previous chapter, it was possible to bypass causal questions partly because only trivial examples of causal linkages were used. It is not very difficult to describe (for practical purposes) the essential forces that determine and fail to determine on which side a fair coin will fall. It is much more difficult to describe how a new machine will affect profits or how an urban renewal project will affect a city. Yet the forces that determine results do need to be understood before it is possible to stipulate the several states of the world whose probability of occurrence must be estimated.

Four Causal Categories

The relevant labyrinths of causality are endless and particular to each situation. There are many ways of grouping them. Yet when problems are broken down into manageable pieces, are not the following four categories of causal factors commonly present?

1. *The basic internal dynamic.* An explosion in the cylinder of an engine creates a force that may be transmitted, by valves, piston rods,

and gears, to the wheel; the transformation has a physics and a chemistry that can be spelled out. Unfortunately, in the economic and social fields, transformations are more nearly smelled out than spelled out; nevertheless dynamics are present. Urban renewal slows deteriorating processes by creating new offices and living quarters which encourage, in such and such a fashion, these and those sorts of business and individuals to locate there; this sets in motion a cumulative process of neighborhood or city development of sorts that must be broadly described, given the character of specified external influences.

2. *The external influences* which bear on the final performance, and their possible conditions. This implies knowledge of the variables in a complete response system, and knowledge also of the qualitative or quantitative characters that they are likely to assume. How is the engine affected by quality of fuel, air temperature and altitude, and what will each be? How will the usefulness of an urban renewal project be influenced by trends in employment in the locality, by the personality and commitment of key people, by the adequacy of the school system, by birth rates of various segments of the population, and by opportunities for migration? What will all these things be like at relevant periods of the future?

3. *The human factors and strategies* which encircle the decision. Outcomes are influenced by people's reactions, and these need to be judged. Human behavior is both part of the internal dynamic of decision and of the external influences that play upon it. However the human elements can not, or need not, be taken as given like the items in paragraphs 1 and 2. They are subject to manipulation in terms of strategies in which moves are initiated to produce a desired result and the moves of others are opposed by countervailing maneuvers. Will the tenants in the urban renewal area fight the new project, and if so, how can their opposition be softened or countered?

4. *Chance.* Even in theory, causality can seldom be entirely determinate for a particular result. Often, of course, the outcome which is of interest concerns not a particular episode (will the next flip come up heads?) but a group of episodes (the result of 100 flips). The chance element is subdued in outcomes subject to extensive averaging. The impact of chance is vastly augmented in practice as opposed to theory, since in practice truly unknowable random elements are likely to be compounded with a great deal of residual *ignorance* about processes that are theoretically subject to understanding.

Note incidentally that uncertainty is by no means the product of futurity alone. Much discussion seems to proceed as if it were. But in

each of the four categories just mentioned there is a double question—
how does it work, and only then, *in what direction, and how powerfully,
will the things that affect how it works be pushing at such and such
a future date?* The first question is particularly important in connection
with the internal dynamic.

Causation and the Definition of an Outcome

There is, then, a complex variety of things that need to be understood
before the relevant "states of the world" can be selected, their impact
on the problem at hand depicted, and their probability judged. Often
the only way to make the problem manageable is to reduce its scope
by reducing the *comprehensiveness of the point of view* from which
the decision is made. This narrowing of focus and framework implies
"suboptimizing." In terms of my four categories, this can mean cutting
a piece out of a larger problem so that more of it is considered in
terms of external influences and less in terms of internal dynamic.

Suboptimizing can also require subduing complexities introduced by
time. The complexities may result from external inanimate influences.
However the human factors (category 3) tend to be especially adept
at stringing out decision processes. If what will happen is a function
of what some gentlemen may do, and what you then do, and what
he then does, and so on, a time consuming "game" is under way. When,
indeed, is the "decision" made? To cope with an unmanageable time
duration, one decision problem can sometimes be chopped into several
sequential ones. This can on the one hand reduce the complexity of the
causal factors which need to be comprehended, particularly categories
2 and 3. On the other hand it can phase-in information, thereby improving the capacity to predict outcomes.

The point is simply that the complexity of the causality with which
the decision collective must cope is in some measure subject to the
control of the decision maker.

In any event, having pictured in objective external terms what is
likely to occur and how likely it is to occur, one must judge how much
one would like it if it did. This judgment instead of looking outward
looks inward, the direction in which our examinations now turn.

CHAPTER 5

Value Judgments

Value judgments imply an appreciative system, a basis for attributing utility to outcomes. What is desirable must be defined in a fashion that makes it possible to say that this outcome is preferable to that outcome.

The previous chapter developed some of the problems of describing outcomes in physical objective terms and of judging their probabilities. This chapter will explore the problem of assessing utility, of developing a value scheme which interprets outcomes in terms of their expected contribution to the achievement of goals, desires, advantage. Typically a step intervenes—the effort to measure output in terms of some objective function, a surrogate for the utility in which the consequences relevant to choice must be framed. This intermediate step will be postponed until the next chapter.

BASES FOR ATTRIBUTING UTILITY

Required is a ruler calibrated in such a fashion that when laid against the outcomes of several acts it will always indicate consistently which one is preferable. How difficult it is to fulfill this requirement can be appreciated by a swift review of the ways in which utility is defined and assigned in connection with consumer, business, and governmental decisions.

Utility in the Private Sector

For the consumer, utility is defined by an internal comprehensive reference—the subjective feeling of desirability that the contemplation of an event evokes. Since the criterion of utility is internal, it may be applied with or without deliberation. Since it is internal, it operates with respect to choice between all sorts of different kinds of goods that an individual may desire, as well as with respect to the diminishing utility of more and more of the same kind of goods.

By and large, the utility of an item is measured by what one is willing to pay for it; this is, in effect, the other things that one is willing to give up in order to have it (its opportunity costs). Particulars can introduce complexities, but the essential is simple: the reference is to a subjective value scheme which equalizes satisfaction at the margin of choice by virtue of pricing mechanisms.

In business organizations utility is customarily defined in terms of expected dollar profits. Yet in addition to ambiguities about how profits are to be read from books of account, it is often difficult to convert a profit standard of utility into a stiff measuring stick. Take the familiar problem of the replacement of a bank of machines. Expected profits can be partially measured in at least fuzzy dollars under specified states of the world (these are hard to predict, including estimates of technological change, wage rates, and levels of output). However, the relationship of other values to profits can only be judged loosely: the effect of the installation on institutional morale, on customer satisfaction, and on flexibility to cope with contingencies.

For still other business decisions, intangible and noncomparable elements may be overriding. Examples are a decision to build an imposing central office, to move a plant from city to suburb, or to enter a new and risky market. For such matters, whatever calculations are made are bound to be secondary to a judgment that is basically an act of faith, a bet on the power of the organization to turn the unknown future to its account. These several examples start with the assumption that utility is measured by profits and then stresses that profits themselves are hard to measure.

But there appears to be a growing recognition of the fact that the optimization of profits is by no means the single utility towards which businessmen strive. Others include a level of sales that maintains the company's "industry position," an adequate rate of growth, an enticing future for promising employees, a high order of financial capability including the power to borrow or float securities at attractive prices, the maintenance of an appropriate company image, prestige and other ego satisfactions for company officials, the general ability to survive, and so on.[1]

These objectives converge on a vague notion of long-term survival and prosperity for the organization. Pursuit of such objectives involves resolution of interpersonal conflicts within the organization as well as comparison of noncommensurable values. The idea seems to underlie theories of business economics which feature the balance sheet and the growth of assets rather than simply the level of profits.[2]

Utility in Government

In government, value, utility for society, must be explicitly designated, and many systems of doing so have been proposed. I shall sketch some of the well-known ones. For the most part they define utility as one part of a broader analysis. However my discussion is limited to the aspects of the theories concerned with defining and measuring utility.

The oldest criterion kicks the question upstairs: pronouncements of a Diety embodied in religious and ethical systems have traditionally had a great deal to say about social welfare on earth and how to optimize it. But ethics appear without a label in many approaches to defining utility.

[1] Neil W. Chamberlain in *A General Theory of Economic Process*, Harper & Bros., New York, 1955, refers to discussion of the profit motive as "whipping a dead horse." His Chapter 2 is entitled "Economic Aspirations" and discusses some of the basic things that corporate participants and, in consequence, corporations, are after. R. M. Cyert and J. G. March in *A Behavioral Theory of the Firm*, Prentice-Hall, Inc., Englewood Cliffs, N.J., 1963, discuss, in Chapter 2, "Antecedents of the Behavioral Theory of the Firm." The chapter contains an interesting review of substitutes for profit maximization. Most textbooks in managerial economics introduce motives other than profit maximization, though they often use profits as a proxy for the others. Two particularly interesting discussions of the subject are in A. Papandreou, "Some Basic Problems in the Theory of the Firm," in *A Survey of Contemporary Economics*, Vol. 2, B. F. Haley, Ed., Richard D. Irwin, Homewood, Ill., 1952, pp. 183–219; and W. J. Baumol, *Business Behavior, Value and Growth*, Macmillan Co., New York, 1959, pp. 45–53. Other interesting points of view are presented by Peter Drucker, *The Practice of Management* Harper, New York, 1954 (see particularly p. 63), and A. Alchian and R. Kessel, "Competition, Monopoly and the Pursuit of Money," in *Aspects of Labor Economics*, H. G. Lewis, Ed., Universities-National Bureau Committee for Economic Research, Princeton, 1962.

[2] See, for example, Kenneth E. Boulding, *A Reconstruction of Economics*, John Wiley & Sons, Inc., 1950, and Neil W. Chamberlain, *op. cit.*

Social welfare functions. The concept of a social welfare function starts with the notion that individuals optimize their economic welfare (only economic welfare is covered) and addresses itself to how one may add or subtract to the sum of individual welfare. A very popular answer starts with that of Vilfredo Pareto and describes a social optimum "frontier." Movement along that frontier must leave no one worse off and at least one person better off. Needless to say, this is hard to do. It implies at best that, although some individuals may be momentarily worse off as a result of, say, paying for benefits to other individuals (distribution effect), the total level of product rises enough to restore the income to its previous level (income effect). Later work has softened the tests by introducing a "compensation principle"—the gainer must be able to compensate the loser and the loser must not be able to compensate the gainers.

These venerable propositions have been subject to attack and counterattack. Damaging objections remain: the distribution of income must be taken as a given; the difficulties of interpersonal comparability of welfare, and of external and interaction effects among individuals, cannot be encompassed.[3] The basic pluralism of the evaluative process is overlooked. Dynamic and noneconomic aspects of welfare lie largely outside of the approaches. Nevertheless the analysis provides valuable perspectives for broad policy with respect to classes of government spending and revenue aspects of public policy. It also sets in sharp relief distinctions between income and distribution effects; direct and external effects; time patterns of impacts on welfare.

Voting. Voting mechanisms throw the responsibility for designating social utility squarely in the lap of the electorate; every man is thought of as voting for what he deems to be his own personal good, a subject on which he is presumed to be an expert. The basic theory proposes that social good is the sum of individual goods as assessed by the individuals themselves. But voting mechanisms are believed to break down in connection with "merit" wants (e.g., free education), which by their

[3] *The Economics of Welfare,* by A. C. Pigou (1920), is the parent volume. For various aspects of the compensation principle see N. Kaldor, "Welfare Propositions of Economics and Interpersonal Comparisons of Utility," *Economic Journal,* 1939, pp. 549–552, and J. R. Hicks, "The Valuation of the Social Income," *Economica,* 1940, pp. 105–124, and T. DeScitovszky, "A Note on Welfare Propositions in Economics," *Review of Economic Studies,* 1941, pp. 77–88. The problems raised by assumptions about income distribution are discussed by I. M. D. Little, *A Critique of Welfare Economics,* Clarendon Press, London, 1950. Good reviews of the subject are: Kenneth Boulding, "Welfare Economics," in *A Survey of Contemporary Economics,* Vol. 2, B. F. Haley, Ed., Richard D. Irwin, Homewood, Ill., 1952, and Jerome Rothenberg, *The Measurement of Social Welfare,* Prentice-Hall, Englewood Cliffs, N.J., 1961.

very nature must be provided at public expense because of the merit attributed to them by society.[4] However, it has been argued that if the voter is regarded as maximizing his own utility in a framework that recognizes decision making rules of the group, a broader though deeply uncertain capacity to define the public interest may result.[5]

But here, as for social welfare functions, the apparatus seems most capable of addressing primarily policy in the large. How do the wishes of the voter penetrate to the specifics of policy in the small?[6] Is the voter merely the Delphic oracle herself whose befumed mutterings are unintelligible until "interpreted" by the high priests—the legislator or administrator? If so, it is the decision maker's interpretation and evaluation of voters' injunctions (along with other matters, such as the interests of particular powerful groups, that the decision maker believes he should bear in mind) that probably define and assuredly measure merit at the level of most actual decisions. Moreover, the administrator's ears may be less sharply attuned to voices he has heard than to those he *expects* to hear. Votes, then, are less a measure than a datum of choice.

Partisan mutual adjustment. "Partisan mutual adjustment," a phrase coined by Charles Lindblom, specializes in getting from the small to the large. In describing it, Lindblom asserts the inherent usefulness of a pluralistic process, which, taking a wide variety of forms in a wide variety of places, and embodying all interests of any importance, tussles its way via partisan advocacy and adjustments, toward actions which are whittled down to manageable proportions.[7] Thus, in situations where

[4] See Richard A. Musgrave, *The Theory of Public Finance,* McGraw-Hill Book Co., New York, 1959, pp. 13–15. Arthur Maass proposes that votes can be cast for the public (rather than personal interest *Design of Water Resource Systems,* Harvard University Press, 1962, Ch. 15.

[5] James Buchanan and Gordon Tullock, *The Calculus of Consent,* The University of Michigan Press, Ann Arbor, 1962. The authors develop the notion that the individual participant in collective decision attempts to maximize his own utility under the assumption that utility functions differ and people choose, of course, more rather than less utility. However, final collective actions insert decision-making rules between the chooser-voter and the action. This means that individuals must guess at the final outcome at the time that he chooses and this adds great uncertainty to his behavior. All this can be viewed as a strategy of game playing in which the political process constitutes a positive-sum game. The authors ask how the rules of government can be changed in a fashion which will increase this positive sum.

[6] There is a large literature dealing with this subject, two fine examples of which are Anthony Downs, *Economic Theory of Democracy,* Harper & Row, New York, 1957, and Wallace S. Sayre and Herbert Kaufman, *Governing New York City: Politics in the Metropolis,* Norton, New York, 1965.

[7] Lindblom's voluminous writings on this subject translate the findings of pluralistic political analysis into the languages of economic and administrative decision making. See particularly his *The Intelligence of Democracy,* The Free Press, New York,

the conditions and information necessary to well-calculated assignment of value are inaccessible, incremental pluralistic policy formation can stumble in a direction which tends at least to correct recognized evils and move toward recognized good, thereby defining both.

Partisan mutual adjustment (basically, complex bargaining) has several implications for definition and measurement of utility. First, it tends to reverse the structure of thinking: the value system in part derives from, and in any event is defined by, advocacy and its effectiveness, rather than vice versa; alternatives are, in effect, valuable because they are chosen by the political process, rather than necessarily chosen because they are valuable.[8] Second, the emphasis on decision in the small (the disjointed incremental decision) means that values may be read from past experience. Finally, it stretches the evaluative process, along with the central decision process, both spatially and temporally.

Heuristic Process. Heuristic judgment about utility is specific to the problem at hand. It consists of two strands: the web whereby individuals or groups decide what to advocate, the woof whereby consensus necessary to progress toward decision is achieved. The heuristic process in the specific case shuttles back and forth over the two strands to complete the decision process. For each individual or group the first strand can take almost any shape. At worst it may be based on no more than the rationalized self-interest of a despot. At best, a man's judgment encompasses his personal values, imagination, habits of thought and analytical capabilities, his sense of history and of problems and what he perceives, knows, and can find out about the specific situation, and his evaluation of the adequacy of this knowledge. The second strand, and the process whereby the fabric is woven, is also infinitely varied.[9]

1965; also David Braybrooke and Charles Lindblom, *A Strategy of Decision, Policy Evaluation as a Social Process,* Collier-Macmillan Ltd., London, 1963.

[8] The notion that a *process* of social change has welfare connotations, which appears central to Lindblom's ideas, has been advanced by Jerome Rothenberg who arrived at the thought via an economist's effort to study social welfare functions: "We are labeling an empirical congeries of individual behavior as a process of social choice, and defining social welfare as that which is ordered by this process of social choice" (The Measurement of Social Welfare, *op. cit.*, p. 324). "A large if not major portion of all social valuation occurs only within the context of institutionalized decision-making processes" (*ibid.*, p. 318).

[9] How the fabric of behavior is woven has been analyzed in the literature on political pluralism and holistic decision processes. William Gore has spelled out the stages that are typical in *Administrative Decision-Making: A Heuristic Model,* John Wiley & Sons, Inc., New York, 1964, and other writings. But aspects of the process are explicit as well as implicit in most of the literature previously cited in this chapter and in footnote 10 in Chapter 4. My description probably overemphasizes, relative to Gore and other political scientists, the rational, deliberative aspects of the process. These matters are examined more carefully in Chapter 11.

Benefit-Cost or Advantage-Disadvantage Analysis. Benefit-cost analysis starts with a definition of goals on the basis of which benefits must be defined. Definitions must be specific to the problem. For the most part, the analysis has a strong economic orientation and is limited to types of benefits and costs to which economic analysis is appropriate. For example, Jerome Rothenberg outlines the purposes of urban redevelopment (one aspect of urban renewal) as including: (1) elimination of the blight of slums, (2) mitigation of poverty, (3) providing decent housing for all, (4) revival of downtown areas, (5) attraction of middle income families, (6) attraction of clean industry, and (7) enhancement of budget balance.[10] The author notes that only the first and, to a more limited extent, the fourth and fifth "provide benefits of the sort that an economic benefit-cost evaluation can consider."

However, in the context of defining utility, it is *all advantages and disadvantages* that need to be set forth—those subject to economic analysis and those having large noneconomic elements. The latter, since they primarily involve public goals and public subsidies, imply that "valuations must be given by decision makers themselves . . .".[11] If the economic group is small relative to the others, as is so often the case, the exercise of developing numbers may, via a semblance of precision, do more harm than good.

Benefit-cost analysis, broadened to cover all significant advantages and disadvantages, is simply another name for comprehensive rational analysis. It can be structured to capitalize on the methodological contributions of economics without chaining it to the conventional subject matter of economics.

INTERRELATED UTILITIES

The previous examples should serve to indicate the diversity in basic systems of evaluation. There are wide differences in how utility can be assigned for consumers, private business, and governments. There are wide differences among theories applicable to two of the sectors.

Complementarity in Value Systems

For the government sector the sample of theories that have been reviewed are widely diverse. Political scientists feature the interpersonal aspect of the process. They consider how values arise, are espoused,

---

[10] Jerome Rothenberg, "Urban Renewal Programs," in *Measuring Benefits of Government Investments,* Robert Dorfman, Ed., Studies of Government Finance, Brookings Institution, Washington, D.C., 1965, p. 297.

[11] *Ibid.,* p. 297.

and advocated. Voting, partisan mutual adjustment, disjointed incrementalism, and heuristic decision processes are names for what goes on. In one sense, the theories imply that those things that are espoused and that prevail under all of the pushes and pulls of the political processes are, virtually by definition, valuable for the society at the time. Economists typically look for sharper answers in terms of welfare functions, aspects of voting mechanisms, or cost-benefit analysis restricted to economic factors and dollar calculations. These are basically orderly techniques for aggregating choice or analyzing the elements of a decision.

Yet the several systems for defining and measuring utility in government seem essentially complementary, rather than competing concepts as the literature seems to suggest. It is clear that the individual must decide what to espouse; and to make the choice well he should use all the analytic tools at his disposal—social welfare concepts, expressed preferences of voters, benefit-cost analysis (extended to cover *all* important advantages and disadvantages). It is equally clear that the process of advocacy, bargaining, and the like adds an additional dimension of goal definition. In particular, the intangible and especially the noncommensurable elements tend to be represented by different individuals; and their differential power to persuade (itself partly a function of public readiness and the justice of their position) shapes the trade-off surfaces which define utility. Furthermore, the relationships between the utility systems of private individuals, businesses, and the public are interdependent and otherwise interrelated.

The framework in terms of which to combine societal and personal values, political process, and economic rationality has not yet been built. That problems call for such a framework is abundantly evident. An example, in a field in which analysis is relatively highly developed, water supply, may help to visualize the elements which need to be encompassed.

The supply of potable water serves or jeopardizes both private and societal interests, comprehensively defined. Likewise its production must often engage both private and government enterprise. Elements relevant to the utility system are:

1. Individuals derive utility from water—marginal amounts that vary from the utility of life itself to virtually nothing. The insurance of standby capacity to meet new needs or years of low precipitation is likewise useful.

2. For business firms, water serves the profits objective as an input to production or, for water utility companies, as a source of revenue.

3. The use of water by individuals and businesses often involves externalties, negative utilities to others, due to pollution, preemption of water, etc.

But water supply involves the dedication of some part of a basic national asset—the total water-resource potential. Thus it affects the national balance sheet of actual or potential productive assets on into the future. This impact is a type of externality a large part of which lies outside of the price system and tends to involve broad societal values (present and future). Therefore:

4. Dedicating some part of the water-resource capital to water supply implies the opportunity cost of other uses of the resource for providing recreation, fish, ecological balance, power, etc. A primary government involvement will be to balance the utility of the addition to potable water supply against the cost in terms of other uses of basic water resource foregone. This is a national asset-related opportunity cost in contrast to the current expenditure-related opportunity cost of alternative allocation of current expenditure. In other words, the elements in paragraphs 3 and 4 involve a value system for society at large, present and future—a concern of governments.

Thus the relevant value systems for designating the expected utility of additions to water supply include those of consumers, business, and the public. The latter can usefully be defined by the apparatus featured in welfare analysis, political approaches such as those described above, and benefit-cost analysis (broadened to include the partly intangible and noncommensurable insurance functions of water supply and opportunity costs). The need for this compound framework of evaluation is perhaps sufficiently self-evident to require no further discussion.

Less obvious may be the thought that in practice the relationship among these several systems is interlocking rather than simply additive. Unless the consumer preference system is engaged (in the sense that a person's needs for more water are automatically compared at an appropriate price with his need for all other things), business and government utility-calculating apparatus is impaired. Analogous remarks apply to relationships among each of the other evaluative frameworks. The point can be illustrated by glancing at a few of the distortions commonly found.

With respect to consumer choices, the price of water is often so low, and its impact on budgets so obscured by lack of knowledge about how much water is used and for what purpose at what time, that individuals use it more like a free than like a scarce good.

For industrial water users analogous malfunctioning of preference systems result from prices that do not reflect costs, particularly the costs of standby capacity, and price structures that encourage wasteful use. The failure to attach a price for water pollution further disconnects private value systems from public ones—a difficulty which laws or regulations typically fail to correct.

These misalignments of private choice mechanisms confuse the public evaluative apparatus. For example, applying political criteria in any of the forms mentioned earlier in the chapter will run into difficulty in evaluating the interests of source areas versus service areas. Obviously, the justice, as well as the increasingly assertive politics, of weighing the value of fish and recreation in the source area—a potential opportunity costs for surface water supplied to the service area—against the value of the potable water is confused and distorted by the maldefinition of consumer and industrial "demand" or "need" for the water. Social welfare analysis or cost-benefit analysis is analogously embarrassed. The difficulty is magnified when present use becomes the bridgehead of estimates of future needs for water-resource planning.[12]

We have been speaking of systems of assessing utility, but a variant of the central problem has introduced itself. What is useful and desirable depends on what is possible. For example, welfare functions and cost-benefit analyses cannot gauge the value of excess capacity of surface water supply as insurance against drought without canvassing the growing edge of the technology for providing water on an intermittent basis; the political tug-of-war between source area and service area is sensitive to new ways to facilitate reuse of water, the optimal use of groundwater, or desalination. Whether consumer preferences can repond to the varying costs and benefits derived from water used in varying amounts or at different times depends on the kinds of meters that are available at an economic price.

Finally, the technology of the possible is not confined to machinery. It includes governmental administrative capability. Laws and regulations can supplement private prices and price structures in inducing water users to serve their own purposes in consonance with wider public purposes. Organizational capacity to plan, to cope with uncertainty, to administer effectively, and to learn is a further dimension of the possible. On all these tools of achieving effective production and use of water does the compound system of assigning its value rest.

[12] This section makes use of insights developed in the course of a study prepared by the Institute of Public Administration for the Department of the Army North Atlantic Division, Corps of Engineers, as a part of the Northeastern United States Water Supply Study, Contract No. DACW 52-69-C-0002.

Apparently evaluative judgments are not independent of reality judgments, as the development of this chapter has thus far suggested.

The Goals-Means Pyramid

In fact, a value system is an elaborate pyramid of goals having the broadest, and largely common, objectives of society at its apex and widening towards its base into ever more specific and programmatic goals. The more specific goals constitute the means for promoting the next higher level of goals. For example, the broad purposes of security and progress are served by means of high standards of living, broadly shared. Viewed as a goal, the latter is served by several means, one of which is the free provision of services that guarantee minimum living standards; this, viewed in turn as a goal, is served by statutory support programs, a goal in turn served by programs for aid to families having dependent children (AFDC), and so on. For a lower-level goal to be thought of as a means for furthering a higher-level goal, a reality judgment is required: the judgment that the means (embedded in a concrete program) will work in a fashion that will in fact contribute to the desired end. What goals are possible or even thinkable depends on the means available. Security and progress were left largely to laissez-faire competition until techniques were invented whereby public policies could influence the level of employment. With increasing capability, have come, and will come, ever more exacting goals.

At each level of the goals pyramid, means compete with other ways to serve the same goals (a negative income tax competes with an AFDC program). At any one level, means (or goals depending on how they are viewed) may complement or compete with one another. Thus a guaranteed minimum living level is complemented, in serving the higher goals of security and progress, by an effective work-training program. But if support levels are too high, the two means (or goals) may start to compete with one another—people may be less willing to bother to train for a job. Just how the several parallel means (or goals) should be combined (the trade-off surfaces between them) involves, again, a judgment about how things will work out—a judgment about reality, not values.

Note that reality judgments enter strongly when an act serves several purposes. For then the multiple utilities require a weighting system before they can be combined into an overall standard of evaluation. Look back at the benefits that Rothenberg attributes to urban renewal and consider the manifold judgments about how the program would actually work out which are required to combine the relative desirability—the trade-offs or exchange rates among the several benefits—into a final basis of evaluation.

The examples that I have used to sketch the goals pyramid have been drawn from the field of government. However, the same propositions apply to business decisions—decisions ranging from very well-structured ones such as inventory control problems to broad policy questions such as those concerning new lines of business expansion. I shall not stop to illustrate. However, were the reader tempted to do so, he would find that the height of the pyramid is likely to increase as the values served are viewed as complex and culminating in corporate prosperity and growth, rather than in narrowly defined dollar profits.

PROBABILISTIC UTILITY

The material that has been examined leads headlong toward an hypothesis: decision agents are usually unsure about which outcomes will materialize; they are also unsure about how they will like them if they do. In other words, the attribution of utility to an outcome even if it is minutely described in objective terms must tend to be probabilistic not single valued.

The Argument

The logical basis of the hypothesis roots back to the characteristics of natural man as a decision maker, discussed in the previous chapter: his selective perception must certainly mean a still more selective appreciative system; his developmental aspirations, in the context of collective decision, must be particularly sensitive to the dynamics of conflict and of progressive conflict resolution. The logical argument continues in the materials of this chapter—the multiple theories or philosophies of value assignment, the difficulty of achieving a unified system, and the interrelated structure among ends of many kinds and between ends and means. The last point alone seems to imply that since expectations about the effectiveness of means are probabilistic and the evaluations of the ends depend on how they can be effectuated, the degree of desirability of an end must likewise be a probabilistic expectation.

Finally, decisions are made today on the basis of utility that is expected to be generated at the time when the evaluated consequence obtains. The subjective estimate of future utility must be based, first, on today's introspection (and other evidence) concerning the utility that a given future outcome has today and, second, on how the utility of the same outcome may change between today and the date when the utility is expected to accrue. The utility is, of course, a net utility, so that both future costs and benefits need to be evaluated. I need not expand on the manifold ways in which time—a day, a year, a decade—can change value assessments even in the case of simple, let alone complex, events.

The argument leads to the judgment that not only event probability but utility assignment is likely to be probabilistic in a very large number of real-life decision problems. The statement applies not only to problems subject to highly judgmental evaluations made by natural collectives laboring under the handicap of skimpy information, but also to relatively well-structured problems made by well-informed decisions agents. Is there evidence in support of this hypothesis?

Evidence

While economists and statisticians have been developing the theory of choice based on a single-valued utility assignment, psychologists have been testing the predictions. The predictions have not come out at all well. "The many experiments undertaken by psychologists in carefully designed repetitive choice situations have indicated that most of the theories tested are not notoriously good predictors of choice behavior for many of the individuals tested." "Dissatisfaction with earlier theories (pre-1957) has led to a new body of theory popularly called 'Stochastic utility theory' in which the assumptions are stated in terms of probabilities of choice rather than preferences."[13]

The tests discriminate as far as possible between uncertainty with respect to outcomes and uncertainty with respect to utilities, and refer primarily to the latter. "Random utility models," which are attributed primarily to Jacob Marschak and his collaborators, present "theories that deal exclusively with outcomes that are probability distributions over a set of 'elementary' outcomes." ". . . the subject's response to the same choice situation is governed by a probability mechanism, and so in general he exhibits inconsistencies."[14]

[13] Peter C. Fishburn, "Utility Theory," *Management Science*, Vol. 14, January 1968, p. 341.
[14] "Preference, Utility, and Subjective Probability," by R. Duncan Luce and Patrick Suppes, in *Handbook of Mathematical Psychology*, Vol. III, R. D. Luce et al., Eds., John Wiley & Sons, Inc., New York, 1965, p. 331. The authors give the following specific references: G. M. Becker, M. H. DeGroot, and J. Marschak, "Probabilities of

This presumption appears to be, as R. Duncan Luce and Howard Raiffa put it in an appendix to their book *Games and Decision* (in which they present a modification of utility theory) ". . . that people can neither discriminate perfectly between alternatives with respect to preferences nor between events with respect to likelihood."[15]

But even in the highly simplistic choice situation the assumption that inconsistencies are governed purely by randomizing mechanisms is not the only possible one. Luce and Suppes note that ". . . a number of authors believe that inconsistencies arise from the subject attending to different aspects of the choice situation. Were it possible to specify what it is that causes him to attend to one aspect rather than another aspect, a determinate model might very well be appropriate."[16] Perhaps, but certainly one would also need to be able to trace the choices to factors outside of the decision situation, otherwise the net result would still tend to be probabilistic utility. In any event, a rich field of further experiment is opened by this work.

A second type of test that would seem to present itself relates to the very large errors in the prediction of net payoffs that have been found even in fields where cost-benefit analysis has a long history—water resource development and military procurement. The general magnitudes of these errors are well known. They are cited in debates about the usefulness of cost-benefit analysis including the propriety of assumptions about interest rates;[17] they appear in reports on the relationship between

---

Choices among Very Similar Objects," *Behavioral Science,* 1963, No. 8, pp. 226–232; and H. D. Block and J. Marschak, "Random Orderings and Stochastic Theories of Response," in I. Olkin, S. Ghurye et al., Eds., *Contributions to Probability and Statistics,* Stanford University Press, 1960, pp. 97–132.

[15] *Games and Decisions, Introduction and Critical Survey,* John Wiley & Sons, Inc., New York, 1957, p. 373.

[16] Luce and Suppes, *op. cit.,* pp. 331–332.

[17] For a taste of the controversy, compare Arthur Smithies, *The Budgetary Process in the United States,* Committee for Economic Development Research Study, McGraw-Hill, New York, 1955, and Roland McKean, *Efficiency in Government Through Systems Analysis, with Emphasis on Water Resources Development,* John Wiley & Sons, Inc., New York, 1958, and Jack Hirshleifer, J. C. DeHaven, and J. W. Milliman, *Water Supply: Economics, Technology, and Policy,* University of Chicago Press, Chicago, Ill., 1961.

The criticism of the interest rate is exemplified in I. K. Fox and O. C. Herfindahl, "Attainment of Efficiency in Satisfying the Demands for Water Resources," *American Economic Review, Proceedings,* May 1964, p. 202. The authors reviewed 178 reports on water resource projects authorized in 1962. They found that interest charges of 2 5/8% was common. But if instead a 6% rate had been used, 64% of the projects would have had benefit-cost ratio of less than unity.

expected and actual results.[18] For our purposes the difficulties in these investigations is that they do not differentiate between error associated with the prediction of what will happen if a specific action is taken, and the error involved in the prediction of the utility that the outcome will generate. Obviously this is a very difficult distinction to embody in empirical evidence.

Probabilistic utility implies a three-dimensional, rather than a two-dimensional, decision matrix. The utility of a fully specified objective outcome can only be assigned in terms of its probability. Diagrammatically, probabilistic utility would plot on an orthogonal plane added to Exhibit 2-1. The additional dimension would take into account the various utilities expected to be associated, with specified probability, with each of the payoff cells (i.e., each of the primary outcomes of an act under each of the events considered).

Of course, the three-dimensional diagram can be converted to a sufficiently expanded two-dimensional one. All that is needed is to define each outcome in terms so precise as to describe uniquely each possible attribution of utility—terms, in other words, that conform to the classic description of an act-event conjunction. However, note the character of the additional descriptive items—the states of the world—which would need to be added. They would typically bear not on the external events that could influence primary outcomes but on the subjective states and values systems with which they are assessed: Are noncommensurables important to the value system? Is the collectives' approach well integrated? Do individuals feel vulnerable to criticism? Are the values that are generated (or threatened) growing in importance? How confi-

---

[18] In the field of defense expenditure, A. W. Marshall and W. H. Meckling made a comparison of expected and experienced achievements with respect to various objectives and this seemed to approach more specifically the matter of utilities. For example, how soon weapon systems will be ready to operate is an important value, and the authors calculated, for 10 different projects, the difference between early estimates of first operational dates and actual first operational dates. The slippage in years ranged from five years to one-third of a year, and averaged two years. This was an average slippage of one-half of the predicted time.

A further set of values is embodied in performance standards. The authors found that after large additional expenditures to correct deficiencies, weapons typically still failed to meet performance standards in one or more respects. Clearly these shortfalls affect utility but it is not clear whether the error lies in misjudging how a specified weapon would be valued, or whether the error lay in judging that weapons fully meeting the specifications could actually be produced and if so at what cost. "Predictability of the Costs Time, and Success of Development," in *The Rate and Direction of Inventive Activity: Economic and Social Factors,* a Conference of the Universities-National Bureau Committee for Economic Research, Princeton University Press, 1962, pp. 473 and 474.

dent are individuals of primary outcomes and how does this affect their developmental aspirations? The obvious way to deal with problems of this sort would seem to be to deal with them in terms of their essential character—problems in evaluation—rather than to force them into the analytic bed of questions about the objective things likely to take place under specified circumstances. Accordingly, it seems sensible to separate the inner from the outer states of the world and contemplate expectations with respect to each in terms of separate probabilistic assessments.

CHAPTER 6

Intendedly Rational Choice

The previous two chapters have sketched how actual decision agents differ from economic man who was the protagonist of Part One. They have suggested also the stuff of which reality judgments and value judgments are made in the actual world. How then should these decision makers proceed to make the best decisions that they can?

They must, it is clear, start with such constraints as their nature and the characteristics of the problem they confront place upon them. This is obvious in the same sense that the characteristics of a machine lathe are the necessary point of departure for designing a manufacturing schedule. In other words, *normative prescriptions must build upon description.*

Statistical decision theory actually does just this. Man is *described* for the purpose of the theory as a creature who can and always does behave perfectly if science points the way. Natural man on the other hand has no such capacities, nor can science always provide a correct answer to his decision problems.

ASPIRATION LEVEL FOR DECISION

Sometimes, however, actual situations conform closely to the conditions of statistical decision theory, and natural decision agents are in a position to behave very much as economic man would behave. At other times both decision collectives and the problems that they confront are very different indeed. Implied is the thought that diffuse decision situations, where decision collectives have poor control over the decision process and information concerning both reality and values is poor, *should* not be handled in the same fashion in which well-structured decision situations are handled by economic man. The level of finesse appropriate to a decision—its *aspiration level*—must vary with the decision situation.

Structural Attributes Profile

How then can the characteristics of diverse decision situations be schematized in order to exhibit their bearing on how decisions should be made? I suggest the following five attributes as a basis for a useful typology:

1. *Homogeneity:* Homogeneity versus divergence, dispersion, or lack of focus can apply to time (duration of the decision process), place (geographic spread of the collective), and constitution of the decision agent (complexity of the intrapersonal and interpersonal collectivity). Divergence exacerbates the problem of analyzing and achieving agreement about both reality and goals.

2. *Rational capacity:* Opportunity for highly rational behavior on the part of the collective contrasts with situations likely to make unrealistic demands on capacities to retain and process information and with situations likely to involve selective perception and developmental aspirations.

3. *Information bearing on outcomes:* This may range from rich and sharp to sparse and ambiguous information. The latter makes probabilistic, objective, reality judgments vague and even shifty.

4. *Clarity of utilities:* Goals and the utilities that they incorporate may be sharply delineated, quantified concisely and comprehensively, and associated with specific outcomes; or they may be difficult to stipulate, cover a range and thus be probabilistic, complex, vague, unstable, conflicting, and unpredictable.

5. *Seriability:* As indicated in Chapter 3, high seriability implies an actuarial basis for dealing with risk or uncertainty, in contrast to the nonseriable problem which cannot in whole or part be dealt with as a member of a series.

Every decision situation has necessarily each and all attributes which must be located at some point within its total range. The range may be viewed as a continuum stretching from the most contained and orderly end of the array at the left, situations in which a taut maximizing rule could be used (indexed 1), to the most vague and disorderly condition at the right which would foreclose any but perhaps the most nebulous judgmental decision (indexed 100).

To determine how choices can and should be made, each decision problem should be characterized in terms of each attribute. Diagrammatically, this implies a matrix in which each attribute, from 1 through 5, is listed along the vertical axis. The horizontal axis is the index marking the position of the attribute from 1 (left) to 100 (right). Each decision would be given a rating for each of the five attributes in terms of points on the index scale. A line connecting the five ratings may be thought of as the *attributes profile* for that particular decision situation.

For problems to which a simple Expected Value decision rule is completely appropriate, there will be a tendency for the attributes profile to look like a vertical straight line on the left-hand side of the page. The decision agent can then be thought of as *Homo economicus* (prescribed by the position of attributes 1 and 2). Information about probabilities of outcomes and utilities is rich (as per attributes 3 and 4). The problem is entirely seriable (attribute 5). Analogously the profile of the unique, complex, vague, and loosely judgmental group of decisions would tend toward a vertical line at the right of the page.

Profiles for the intermediate positions, which most decisions occupy, tend to be angular—some attributes being somewhat further to the left or right than others. Attribute 5, seriability, is particularly likely to locate independently of the other four, since many otherwise well-structured decisions cannot, and many poorly structured ones can, be dealt with on the basis of average rather than individual results.

Aspiration Level and Structural Attributes

When structural attributes cling to the left, decision procedures can be elegant. When they zigzag down the right, the aspiration level for decision must be lowered in just the same way that people adjust their personal and business ambitions to their abilities, resources, and individual histories, either explicitly or, as psychologists point out, implicitly.

The basis of the adjustments is suggested by the description of the attributes. The first two point to possible intracollective problems involving the capacity to function efficiently and rationally in arriving at decisions. The third and fourth, involving potential information problems, suggest wide ranges in the completeness with which questions concerning both objective processes and preferences can be analyzed and relevant factors adequately measured.

When the value system comprehends intangible and noncommensurable elements, and when information about process is imprecise and even spotty, it is unrealistic to aspire to a quantified judgment capable of applying to delicate choices. Benefit-cost analysis, for example, as ordinarily conceived, might be more misleading than helpful: the proportion of benefits subject to calibration may be small. Moreover, careful development of the measurable portion may do little to focus and toughen up the evaluation of the rest of the advantages or disadvantages.[1] Instead, aspirations should trade precision for comprehensiveness, calculation of judgment, and narrowly economic rationality for intuition.

When attribute 5, seriability, is high (a low index number), decisions, even if individually sloppy because of otherwise poor structure, can, on an average, approach an Expected Value providing no persistent *bias* is present. Low seriability, since it exposes the collective to each chance occurrence, tends to increase vulnerability to poor structure.

All of the attributes, via their bearing on the collective and the situation, have implications concerning the uncertainties which decision confronts and the costs they impose.

The first cost, reflected in the discounted values of a lottery ticket relative to receiving a sure reward, applies to all structural attributes profiles; but it would typically increase as the profile moves toward the right-hand side of the surface. At the extreme left, this is the only type of cost that uncertainty should imply, since the left straight-line profile completely fulfills the requirement of "rational" decision.

But as decision structures shift to the right, the costs of uncertainty tend to multiply. The uncertainty discount is likely to increase with respect to both predictions about what will happen and how one will like it if it does. In addition, the other two sources of uncertainty's costs—those reflecting confusion and externalities—intrude themselves and behavior deteriorates.

---

[1] These and other elements were included in a "usefulness test" for cost-benefit analysis in "Outdoor Recreation," Ruth P. Mack and Sumner Myers, in *Measuring Benefits of Government Investment*, Robert Dorfman, Ed., The Brookings Institution, Washington, 1965, p. 76.

ESSENTIALS COMMON TO CHOICE

I have developed a theme that decision processes need to vary in order to match the situations which they confront. Nevertheless, there are some common elements to any decision.

Decision Rule: Minimize the Cost of Uncertainty

Start with the assumption that if knowledge were complete, decisions could be and should be perfect. Under certainty no one should settle for less than a maximizing solution.

Uncertainty deteriorates choice. It involves costs having each of the three sources just referred to and defined in Chapter 1: (1) the uncertainty discount that is inherent in the nature of knowledge—the fact that a chance of winning a reward is less valuable than the reward for sure; (2) the tendency for people's behavior to be confused by the presence of uncertainty and therefore to deteriorate; (3) deterioration due to externalities, to inconsistency between individual and aggregate advantage.

Decision procedures should aim to minimize these costs of uncertainty. The word minimize is used in the common-sense way—simply to reduce "to the least of a set of numbers."[2] Remembering that certain knowledge implies perfect choice, the rule is equivalent to saying, *choose the act having the highest time-discounted expected net utility after all appropriate uncertainty discounts have been applied.*

I need not point out that this most certainly does not mean avoid uncertainty. High utility is often bought at great risk and whether the trade is worthwhile depends on the amounts involved. The Milquetoasts buy safety at an excessive cost in terms of potential utility. Thus *minimizing* the *cost* of uncertainty will often imply *increasing* the *amount* of uncertainty.

The decision rule as I have phrased it simply relaxes conventional optimizing rules when information is poor. Also, by focusing optimizing (inversely) on the cost of uncertainty, it aims to allow for differences in aspiration levels appropriate to various decision situations.

Six Decision Steps

Decision situations for which alternatives are given share not only the flexible decision rule just mentioned, but the steps that must be taken,

---

[2] *Webster's Seventh New Collegiate Dictionary,* G. & C. Merriam Co., 1963.

consciously, unconsciously, or by default, in the course of decision. The six steps are not necessarily taken in sequence since some or all can be part of a series of progressive approximations that roll the process back to an earlier step a number of times. They are performed with respect to each alternative act under consideration. Given the alternative acts, then, the steps are:

1. *Define utility* in the context of the decision problem: What purposes would a good solution promote? Whereof would it consist? What advantages would accrue and over what period of time? The answers will often be framed in terms of central values, secondary values, a weighting system, and constraints that delimit the character and extent of the utilities that may be sought. Ideally this step would simply reproduce the designation of goals (that is, utilities to be sought) that provided the basis for naming the acts to be considered.

2. *Assess the aspiration level appropriate to the decision situation.* This proceeds by picturing the attributes profile and judging matters such as those discussed in the previous section—control of the decision collective, degree to which purposes can be clarified and necessary information obtained, the extent to which a quantified approach is likely to be worthwhile, whether one must aim at a solution that encompasses all contingencies or whether a good average result will do.

3. *Lay out the strategy of decision.* On the basis of the tentative and general input of steps 1 and 2, (a) picture the range of possible primary outcomes and their probabilities of obtaining, (b) determine whether the whole range or selected focus outcomes should be analyzed, (c) determine whether choice should be total or stepwise.

4. *Describe the possible outcomes* (primary consequences) and their probabilities as completely as possible; if decision strategy prescribes selected foci, describe the focus outcomes in full objective terms.

5. *Estimate expected net utility of each outcome* under consideration (that is, arrive at evaluated consequences). Often an intermediate step is useful—the selection of an "objective function" and the constraints that need to be placed upon it.

6. *Compare the expected net utility of alternative acts* with a view to selecting the best.

I have schematized the difference among decision situations and then suggested the course that all decisions must somehow traverse. How then should the course be traveled under various types of decision situations?

It was evident in Part One that three major sorts of decision procedures or "rules" had been proposed. All of the variants of Expected

Value rules dealt with a complete distribution of act-event conjunctions; Shackle's model selected two such outcomes on which to focus; decision trees spread choice over time. As step 3 suggests, the same three approaches are usefully distinguished when natural man confronts choice among predelineated alternatives under the wide range of decision situations that have been sketched.

DECISIONS FOR WHICH DISTRIBUTIONS ARE COMPLETE

For situations in which act-event conjunctions can be described for a large set of relevant events, the decision situation will be well-structured in other respects also. In any event, assume this is the case.

Two-Dimensional Matrix

A well-trained student of a good business school will use decision matrices of the broad type described in Chapters 2 and 3. If he covers all of the benefits and costs that are material to the particular problem over the relevant time periods (including the cost of decision itself), if he can calibrate them with reasonable accuracy, and if each operationally completely-described outcome can be assigned a single-valued utility, he will choose the act having the highest time- and uncertainty-discounted expected net utility. For such decisions, then, properly schooled natural man simply does what statistical decision theory prescribes.

Probabilistic Utility and Three-Dimensional Matrix

When the utility of each primary consequence is not single-valued—and the previous chapter has urged that it seldom is—the decision matrix requires an additional dimension.

Exhibit 6-1 addresses itself to the case of an otherwise well-structured decision problem in which the expected utility of each possible outcome can only be probabilistically estimated.

The matrix incorporates the assumption that there are just two acts worth considering and three significant states of the world that may obtain. It differs from the matrices of Chapters 2 and 3 simply in that the utility expected to be generated (which for convenience we assume can be expressed in dollar figures) has a range, not a point, value. These values are shown in the three columns for each event (lines 3 and 7), and their respective probabilities are given (lines 4 and 8). These ranges for utilities represent the orthogonal plane of a three-di-

EXHIBIT 6-1 Decision Matrix with Probabilistic Utility

	Event 1			Event 2			Event 3			Expected Value $
1 Event number	1			2			3			
2 Event-probability	.3			.5			.2			1.0
Act I										
3 Dollar value	−10	0	+20	+35	+50	+70	+20	+35	+50	
4 Probability	.20	.50	.30	.35	.45	.20	.25	.50	.25	
5 Likelihood of obtaining (2 × 4)	.06	.15	.09	.175	.225	.10	.05	.10	.05	
6 Weighted dollar value (3 × 5)	−.6	0	1.8	6.13	11.25	7.0	1.0	3.5	2.5	32.58
Act II										
7 Dollar value	−100	−10	+20	+20	+35	+50	+100	+125	+150	
8 Probability	.35	.35	.30	.20	.50	.30	.30	.50	.20	
9 Likelihood of obtaining (2 × 8)	.105	.105	.09	.10	.25	.15	.06	.10	.04	
10 Weighted dollar value (7 × 9)	−10.5	−1.05	1.8	2.0	8.75	7.5	6.0	12.5	6.0	33.00

Summary

											Expected Value $
11 Array of dollar values	−100	−10	0	+20	+35	+50	+70	+100	+125	+150	
12 Likelihood under act I (5)	0	.06	.15	.14	.275	.275	.10	0	0	0	32.58
13 Likelihood under act II (9)	.105	.105	0	.19	.25	.15	0	.06	.10	.04	33.00

Most Likely Utilities

	Event 1	Event 2	Event 3	Expected Value $
Act I				
14 Dollar value (from 3)	0	+50	+35	
15 Weighted dollar value (14 × 2)	0	25.0	7.0	32.00
Act II				
16 Dollar value (from 7)	−10	+35	+125	
17 Weighted dollar value (16 × 2)	−3.00	17.5	25.0	39.50

mensional matrix in which acts and events with their probabilities occupy the other dimensions. The joint probability that each utility will actually be generated (lines 5 and 9) is a product of the probability that the event will obtain (line 2) *and* that the particular utility will be generated (lines 4 or 8). The Expected Value consists of the utilities weighted by these joint probabilities and summed (lines 6 and 10, last column). This procedure develops a single Expected Value for the three-dimensional matrix.

The figures present a set of arbitrary numbers which nevertheless tell a story about two hypothetical acts. Clearly, act I is the safer—there is only a small possibility of a small loss (first column for event 1), and the most likely event (second column for event 2) results in the best outcome. But in terms of an average result over a large number of trials, the two acts are virtually on a par—Expected Values are $32.58 for act I and $33.00 for act II. Comparisons of the range of outcomes is clearer if the payoffs are arranged from worst to best (line 11) and their probability under each act compared (lines 12 and 13). If the decision situation were highly seriable, the two acts should be considered of virtually equal promise, given the data as shown. But note that this would not have been the case if the acts had been believed to have single-valued expected utility (selected as the values having the highest probability in the table, lines 14 to 17).[3] Then, since the possibility of the large loss of $100 would not have been perceived, act II would have been the clear winner.

In any event, if the decision in question has low seriability, the three-dimensional matrix conveys information that needs to be considered in full. Act I could have a substantially lower Expected Value than act II and nevertheless be preferred because of its "fail-safe" quality. For act II, the 21 percent chance of loss (sum the first two figures in line 13) might more than overbalance the 20 percent chance of gain of $100 or more (sum the last three figures in line 13). For act I, probabilities are heavily concentrated at $35–$50 range values with little decision weight in the wings of the distribution.

The effect on decision will depend on the particulars of the formulation. If there is a tendency, as may well be the case, for the fear of undesirable results to assert itself more forcibly than the pleasure in the more desirable results, then the net effect would be to lower the

[3] The single-valued utility that would be thought to apply is assumed to be the utility in the range for each act-event conjuncture assigned the highest probability. However, for act II, event 1, the center value of the two utilities having equal probabilities was used.

Expected Value of evaluated consequences. Indeed, the awareness of probabilistic utility as here defined could be one aspect of "slanting" or of reacting to "ambiguity" as analyzed by William Fellner and Daniel Ellsberg.

The discussion is meant to bring out these ideas: if ranges for utility can be specified with probability weights, they can be embodied in a more or less conventional decision matrix without undue complexity. By applying the appropriate probability arithmetic to these figures, their relevance to decision can be clarified. Nonlinear relationships between objective functions and utility raise no serious problems. Manipulation along these lines does not necessarily produce the same recommendation as does manipulation in terms of single-valued utility estimates for each act-event conjuncture. Especially for decisions involving low seriability, the difference can be significant.

CHAPTER 7

Choice in Poorly Structured Situations

As the decision profile moves away from the highly structured side of the attributes table, it becomes intuitively clear that there is no possible way to consider a comprehensive set of states of the world. Instead it is necessary to select a few alternatives which seem to be of special interest.

DECISIONS BASED ON FOCUS OUTCOMES

Selection of a few possibilities on which to focus attention was the thrust of Shackle's model sketched in Chapter 3. However, his model, in addition to its use of the optimizing assumptions, presupposes that selection always lands on one good and one bad result; besides, the continuous preference function assumes profound appreciation of a wide range of other alternatives.

These assumptions may not be appropriate to decisions by natural man for whom concentration on selected outcomes is needed in many actual situations. It will be useful to rehearse how the six decision steps would be taken in this large class of real-world decision problems.

Laying Out the Problem

Step 1, the analysis of the value system and designation of utilities, has been sufficiently discussed in Chapter 5. Assume also that step 2 has been completed: in line with the realities of the problem as sketched in the attributes profile, it has been decided whether the choice must be made under conditions that make it useless to aim for a tight, quantitative evaluation, even for important elements of the total problem; also, thought has been given to whether the situation is one that should be viewed as a part of a series or dealt with largely on an individual basis.

The overview of possible outcomes and their expected utilities (step 3) will suggest whether the whole range can be dealt with; we assume for the purposes of this section that, on the one hand, it is clear that only selected outcomes can be envisioned and that, on the other hand, decisions will be made in one piece rather than stepwise.

These three steps clarify what one is trying to achieve and how in terms of the decision process itself, one should go about doing it.

Selecting and Describing Focus Outcomes

Step 4 demands that the focus outcomes be specified as fully as possible in objective, operational terms, and that their probabilities be estimated. Specification of the outcomes involves thinking through the causal relationships—the range suggested by the causal categories mentioned in Chapter 4.

The probability assignments pertain to the outcome as a whole, rather than to the complex of events which in combination bring it about. Say, for example, that the question concerns the replacement of an old machine with a new one. The outcome may be pictured in terms of the savings (relative to the status quo) that the purchase is expected to generate. All sorts of assumptions about events are implied in any estimate of savings—whether the machine will operate as promised by the machine tool salesman, how the labor force will accept it, how well they will operate and maintain it, whether materials will conform to specifications on which estimates of productivity are based, and the level and mix of customer demand. However, the basic notion of the focus outcome is that, having given some thought to these matters, attention brushes by them and focuses on a total complex result—the rate of return on the machine investment.

The earlier steps have indicated that the total distribution of relevant act-event conjunctures, or of outcomes, cannot be dealt with in full

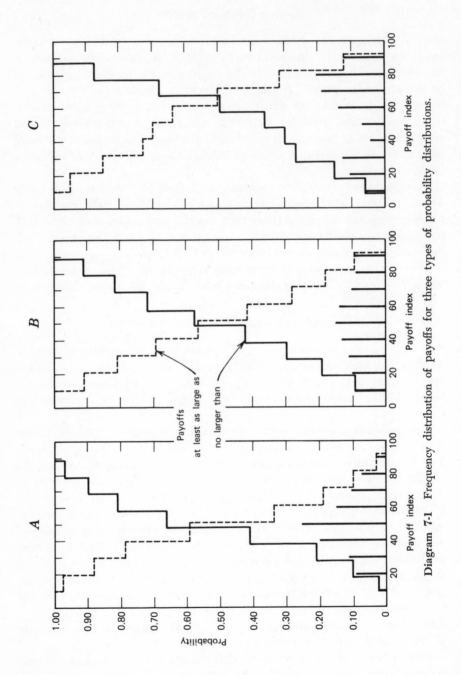

Diagram 7·1   Frequency distribution of payoffs for three types of probability distributions.

Payoffs
at least as large as

no larger than

98

and therefore it is necessary to select some particular outcome, or family of outcomes, on which to focus attention. Several kinds of considerations are relevant to the selection.

First, the underlying shape of the probability distribution needs to be envisioned. Is it peaked, flat, or bimodal? Diagram 7-1 sketches the alternatives assuming, to illustrate, that, for any act, ten outcomes having specified payoffs can be roughly envisioned and their probabilities assessed. The index numbers on the horizontal axis measure the relative size of expected payoff. The height of the bars shows for each its probability of obtaining. The difference between the three distributions is shown in a slightly different way by the cumulative diagrams—the probability that payoffs will be at least as large as (dotted lines) or no larger than (solid lines) a specified index value. For example, suppose the machine discussed a moment ago had been thoroughly tested and a prospective purchaser had a strong rising trend in sales. Then if the output of the machine was no greater than presently needed, the consequences of its installation might well be assumed to lie in a fairly narrow range, somewhat as in panel A—the peaked distribution of probabilities. If, on the other hand, the purchaser were a company for which the trend in sales was flat, and the machine had a capacity which would be adequate to meet boom levels of demand, then, if recession were to set in, the yield on investment in the machine would be much lower. Accordingly, distribution of payoffs is bimodal, somewhat as diagrammed in panel C. A bimodal distribution might also in election years characterize some public expenditure decisions—one lobe if the Democrats, the other if the Republicans, win. Panel B reflects the picture that anything can happen. It would apply if, for example, the machine combined new materials in a new way. Then it might be judged hard to say how it would stand up to protracted use and how the labor force would deal with it.

A second type of consideration affecting choice of focus is seriability. The difference in focus that these several situations call for is emphasized when the problem has low seriability. Theoretically, the consequences in the central portion of the probability distributions of either panels A or B would dominate if the act were repeated again and again, since the two distributions would have about the same Expected Value. However, if the situation is sensitive to individual outcomes it is clear that the peaked and diffuse situations need to be thought about differently.

For the well-tested machine and the rising sales trend, one could assume that the actual return on investments would not be very different from the expected return since the sales volume necessary to profitability can be reliably predicted. As drawn, 60 percent of the actual payoffs would tend to fall within something like the 60–40 index range. Thus for this sort of situation the tendency of many decision makers to disregard probability and think about a single result may not be too inappropriate.

On the other hand in nonseriable decision situations of the Panel *B* type where all of the possible outcomes are of significance, it is essential to picture some of the possibilities which could be seriously embarrassing or greatly advantageous.

This can be done in part by viewing wing-boundary outcomes. Thus one might select an outcome on the edge of the low-payoff part of the distribution the probability of which one cannot afford to ignore. For example, say one were willing to ignore a 20 percent chance of a result as depicted by Panel *B* which was worse than indicated by a payoff index of 20; the results would be as good or better than this in 80 percent of the possibilities (worse in 20 percent). Analogously, one might wish to picture the outcome having a payoff indexed at 70, since a result as good or better would occur about 20 percent of the time.

Another way to broaden the possibilities envisioned is to stretch out the focus on the most likely result to cover a family of results. Carried to the extreme, this type of conception has been developed by Herbert Simon in the "satisfying" model. He has proposed a "simple" payoff function with a "satisfying" criterion.[1] The decision maker visualizes the choice in terms of two evaluations—acceptable and unacceptable. He finds a possible set of outcomes all of which are satisfactory (acceptable) and then finds an act ("behavioral alternative") for which all of the outcomes are within the satisfactory set. Simon also finds the satisfactory-unsatisfactory dichotomy a "satisfactory approximation" of the full payoff function.[2] In other words, for two alternatives we focus on "satisfactory" outcomes only, and choose the act which has no unsatisfactory outcomes.

[1] "A Behavioral Model of Rational Choice," in *Models of Man*, John Wiley & Sons, Inc., New York, 1957, pp. 246–248.

[2] The rule also can be helpful, Simon points out, in connection with payoffs consisting of several noncommensurable values; for then, satisficing criteria can be applied to *each* of the noncommensurables individually. This avoids the difficulty of achieving a complete ordering by means of indifference curves (*ibid.*, pp. 251–252). Note, however, that it would debar as unsatisfactory some solutions which might meet the threshold level on the basis of indifference analysis; for then, a sufficient quantity of one utility, say, income, might compensate for a distinctly unsatisfactory quantity of some other utility, say, prestige. Thus it has further bias toward conservatism.

A decision rule of this sort is highly conservative. For one thing, it dwells entirely on the low-valued end of the probability distribution— the bad expected results which nevertheless may not be too bad to accept—and determines whether the act passes the satisfying test. The best expected result, or even the most likely one, does not seem to count. Simon's formulation requires that *all* of the possible consequences of an acceptable act must pass the satisfying test.[3]

Herbert Simon's notion can be modified to define satisfying to include the willingness to take a defined chance of getting a result that is unsatisfactory in some degree. If so, attention still focuses on the lower side of the distribution, but the bottom limit moves up somewhat. Moreover, the level of satisfying is not static. It rises with evidence that higher requirements are likely to be met and falls with evidence to the contrary.[4]

If decision situations are seriable, the conservative slant of the satisfying solution is disadvantageous. The values at the low end of the distribution are simply not correct decision criteria for such problems. For nonseriable situations on the other hand, the conservative tendency of the rule may reflect the actual way that people take account of a nonlinear relation between measured payoff and subjective utility. If so, all that can be said is: such is not the utility function of heroic man.

The modified satisfying model which accepts a specified chance of an unsatisfactory result can be combined with a bimodal focus. For example, James W. Angell found it usual for investors to formulate a "best guess" about what will happen if "things turn out well" (one boundary) and if "things turn out badly" (the second boundary). To make the investment, the investor must believe that if things turn out well the chances are about nine out of ten that the investment will yield, over the next ten years, capital gains of at least 25 percent plus an annual return of 6 percent. Concerning the level of the most likely loss outcome and its probability, generalization appears to be more diffi-

[3] The rule is stated thus: "(i) Search for a set of possible outcomes (a subset, S' in S) such that the pay-off is satisfactory ($V(s) = 1$) for all these possible outcomes (for all s in S'). (ii) Search for a behavior alternative (an a in A) whose possible outcomes all are in S' (such that a maps upon a set, S_a, that is contained in S')" (*ibid.*, p. 248).

[4] An example discussed by Simon in an appendix describes a man wishing to sell a house as having a price in mind that he believes he can surely get at the end of the period for which he is planning. However, "he will set his initial acceptance price quite high, watch the distribution of offers he receives, and gradually and approximately adjust his acceptance price downward or upward until he receives an offer he accepts . . ." (*ibid.*, p. 259).

cult.[5] Needless to say, the particular numbers will vary widely for particular problems; however, the question as formulated can have wide applicability. It is a variant of the questions we all ask ourselves constantly: What do I stand to gain, what do I risk, and what do I stand to lose? One asks also: What are the chances that things will turn out well and what are the chances that the poor results will materialize?

Assessing Utilities of Outcomes

Step 5 is a compound task. It requires first, that all the many significant utilities, positive or negative, inherent in each act are listed; second, that they are quantified (and I use the term broadly to cover even the vaguest sort of hefting); third, that several (often noncomparable) utilities are combined to represent the net expected advantage of the focus outcome as a whole (however, sometimes, as explained in connection with step 6, they are best carried through without being combined); and fourth, that the probability is evaluated that the specified utility will be generated if the outcome obtains. Since the expected utility of a particular outcome can ordinarily be assigned only as a range, not as a point estimate, the probability that a specified utility will materialize is a joint probability that the outcome will take place *and* have the particular utility. Exhibit 6-1 illustrated this joint probability, but it did so in terms of a situation in which the whole range of possible outcomes and their probabilities could be envisioned. For focus outcomes this is, by definition, not the case.

The probabilistic utility has to be assigned to the focus outcomes. There are a number of ways in which this could be conceptualized.[6]

---

[5] James W. Angell, "Uncertainty, Likelihoods and Investment Decisions," *The Quarterly Journal of Economics*, February 1960, pp. 1–28.

[6] One can visualize the assignment of probabilistic utility to a focus outcome in at least three ways. First, the range of utility which a specified outcome might imply could be dealt with in full, in which case the estimates of utility would include at least a few selected positions in the range. Second, the focus itself may be one part of the range of the utility only—that is, it may narrow the outcome down to one portion of the range of possible utilities, thereby narrowing the range of consequences on which attention actually focuses. Finally, the perception of range may be embodied in the evaluating procedure not by displaying it overtly but by discounting the estimates of utility for dispersion and ambiguity. I doubt that there is any objective evidence at the present time as to which of these conceptual paths tend to be followed. Accordingly, the statement in the text rejects the first alternative on the assumption that the whole structure of focus outcomes contrives to shortcut such precise and elaborate reckoning and emphasizes the second. However, I believe that the third is also present.

Perhaps the simplest is to assume that the focus is itself narrowed down to only one part of the range of utility that the outcome might be expected to generate.

How then is the focus outcome matched with an estimate of its expected utility? The process has a number of parts:

(a) *Assessment of utility to be generated.* The goals or utilities that are sought have been formulated and it remains to assess how the focus outcomes of each act under consideration will serve these purposes (create benefits, advantages), and in doing so what disadvantages—costs (monetary and in terms of opportunities foregone) and other undesired results—may ensue as a result of each act-event conjunction covered by the foci of attention. The list will tend to differ, at least around the fringes, for the several members of a collective. The list must include all substantial benefits, whether economic or otherwise, whether measurable or intangible, and whether comparable or noncomparable. There may be, for example: a central issue, such as how much potable water will be clearly and confidently needed at a target date; secondary issues, such as the values of insurance against less clearly envisioned requirements and hydrological variations; and further secondary issues, such as the disutility of foreclosing other uses of the basic water resource (recreation, ecological balance, and environmental beauty).

(b) *Surrogate consequences.* Quantification must eventually be stated in terms of expected utility, but an intermediate step is often taken: use of a surrogate, an objective function, capable of bridging the gap between the primary consequences, the objectively described outcome, and the utility in which it is expected to result, the evaluated consequences. The preferred unit is one with the highest generality and the greatest precision. Units of payoff will range in adequacy from money estimates based on competitive market prices, through other sorts of standardized physical units, to nothing more than the statement that the purpose will be served in some nonquantifiable fashion.

The objective function may have to recognize diverse noncomparable utilities. If so, these would be compared later in terms of indifference curves. What, for example, is the relationship between the utility of a given amount of highway expenditure with respect to a time saving of X^1 amount, accident reduction of X^2, creation of amenities in the amount of X^3, destruction of landscape (negative) in the amount of X^4? One approach is to convert, by hook or by crook, as many as possible of these units to money. It achieves generality through money's boundless convertibility; the extent to which it also achieves precision is often problematical. Another approach is to keep noncomparables separate and deal with the different classes of utilities separately in step 6, as we shall see. Inevitably, some advantages are likely to accept quantification in good grace and others are likely to disdain it. The analyst must be guided by what his ingenuity can *truly* accomplish and not beguile himself by providing form without content.

(c) *Nonlinearity in the payoff-utility function.* One source of nonlinearity is that future benefits are less desirable, and future costs less undesirable, than present ones, other things the same. This implies that advantages or disadvantages can only be compared if they are all converted to their value as of some particular moment of time. Calculation in terms of a futurity-discounted "present value" is one of several ways to make this adjustment. The appropriate discount rate to apply is a moot point. Note however our analysis requires that *the discount for futurity be made independently of the discount for uncertainty or risk.* The point is, I believe, absolutely essential to consistent analysis. Risk differs for the various benefits and for the various costs. Its incidence and patterns are quite different from those of futurity per se.[7]

A second adjustment in payoff-utility ratios should reflect possible asymmetry in the value to decision agents of losses relative to gains, and of expected large rewards or penalties relative to small and medium ones. Developmental aspirations, and interpersonal strategies that collective decision implies, seem likely to emphasize asymmetry of these sorts. As indicated in Chapter 3, such asymmetry tends to be more marked when decision situations are nonseriable than when they are seriable.

---

[7] That risk differs between benefits and costs (that is, for buyers or sellers) is familiar to price theory (see footnote 20 in Chapter 2). The point is developed specifically in the context of water resource analysis by Robert H. Haveman in *Water Resource Investment and the Public Interest, An Analysis of Federal Expenditures in Ten Southern States,* Vanderbilt University Press, Nashville, Tenn., 1965. Haveman advocates a futurity discount which incorporates an allowance for risk preference as well as for other costs. Because benefits are usually more uncertain than are costs, expected benefits should be discounted at a higher rate than are deferred costs (Appendix B, p. 171).

Our point is that risks differ also *among* benefits and *among* costs and need to be thought of separately from the discount for futurity. A discount for futurity is appropriate in a riskless situation as well as in a risky one and to deal with the two things together represents a confusion caused, no doubt, by the fact that risk often increases with time.

John Lintner arrives at aspects of this same conclusion by an altogether different route in "The Valuation of Risk Assets and the Selection of Risky Investments in Stock Portfolios and Capital Budgets," *Review of Economics and Statistics,* February 1965, pp. 13–34. He discusses the ". . . serious distortions inherently involved in the prevalent use of a risk-discount rate' or a company-risk-class,' 'the cost of capital' for project selection in capital budgeting . . ." (p. 34).

(d) *Discounts for uncertainty.* There is, of course, the routine discount that recognizes that a chance at a prize is less desirable than the prize for sure. The chanciness is partly a function of the probability that it will have the particular payoff or utility. This joint probability measures the routine uncertainty discount. But as explained, limited focus screens out some of the possible utilities that might be generated by a focus outcome (just as it screens out other outcomes).

Ambiguity of judgment, either about outcomes or their utilities, tends to reduce the expected utility of a given payoff. This may be subject to self-reinforcement within the decision-making collective. The feeling of one member of the decision collective that guesses about probabilities are themselves poorly founded, and subject to change without notice, may weaken his power to promote acceptance of the decision among other members of the collective. Such influences border on other sources of uncertainty's costs that ought to be kept at a minimum—the cost of befuddlement.[8]

Assigning Expected Utility to Acts

Step 6 requires a comparison between the total utility expected from alternative acts. The step is easy or difficult depending upon the extent to which addition (or subtraction) of measured quantities is possible. Addition is a touchy subject in decision theory.[9] A realistic approach, however, must be eclectic, varying with particular situations. Addition is, by wide margins, the easiest and cleanest way to summarize several advantages of an outcome and, with appropriate weights, of an act. But it is necessary to be aware of adding Cadillacs and donkeys.

Step 5 has resulted in estimates of each major sort of utility, positive or negative, expected to result from each focus outcome of each alternative act. It will be useful to assemble them in a decision matrix calculated to display the resistance of these figures to addition.

The problems can be conveniently explored by thinking in terms of two focus outcomes—a good and a bad result. Thus, if the advance

[8] A third source of uncertainty's costs, externalities and wide societal implications of a particular decision, can sometimes be reduced by appropriate structure of the decision collective itself. The externalities can be represented by members of the collective who are interested in matters somewhat external to the central issue of the decision situation. (See Chapter 13 item 5.6.)

[9] See for example Ward Edward's criticism of Shackle because he "doesn't seem to have a very good opinion of the mathematical operation of addition." "Note on Potential Surprise and Nonadditive Subjective Probabilities," in *Expectations, Uncertainty, and Business Behavior,* Mary Jean Bowman, Ed., Social Science Research Council, New York, 1958, p. 46.

EXHIBIT 7-1   Focus Consequences (Advantages Net of Disadvantages)

Act:	A_1 (Purchase of Tract A)			A_2 (Purchase of Tract B)			$A_1 - A_2$
Focus Outcomes: Probability of:	F_h P_h	F_j P_j	Com-bined	$F_{h'}$ $P_{h'}$	$F_{j'}$ $P_{j'}$	Com-bined	
	(1)	(2)	(3)	(4)	(5)	(6)	(7)
Type of Utility:							
Measured (M)	MC_{1h}	MC_{1j}	MC_1	$MC_{2h'}$	$MC_{2j'}$	MC_2	$MC_1 - MC_2$
Judged (J)	JC_{1h}	JC_{1j}	JC_1	$JC_{2h'}$	$MC_{2j'}$	MC_2	$MC_1 - MC_2$
Noncom-mensurable (N)	NC_{1h}	NC_{1j}	NC_1	$NC_{2h'}$	$NC_{2j'}$	NC_2	$NC_1 - NC_2$
Total	C_{1h}	C_{1j}	C_1	$C_{2h'}$	$C_{2j'}$	C_1	$C_1 - C_2$

acquisition by government of two tracts of land, tracts A and B, were under consideration, the good result, F_h might refer to the case where the acquisition was found to lie in the path of development, and the bad result, F_j might refer to the case where the area remains static.[10]

The probability that each of the two focus outcomes obtains is not necessarily the same for the two acts (unlike the probability of "events" as typically defined in statistical decision theory). This is shown by the superscript, prime, for the probabilities applying to the second act. Thus for advance acquisition, the contemplated acts, purchase of tracts A and B, would be in different locations for which the chances of development might differ. Of course, the probability of two (or more) foci would typically sum to well less than 1.0.

The rows (lines) of the matrix classify the various possible utilities, positive or negative, on the basis of their capacity to be measured and compared. The first row (or rows) consists of utilities which can be both well measured and readily compared. They are advantages or disadvantages for which payoff can be measured in a uniform unit having a systematic though not necessarily linear relationship to utility. Money

[10] References to advance land acquisition draws on a study by Donald C. Shoup and Ruth P. Mack, *Advance Land Acquisition by Local Governments, Benefit-Cost Analysis as an Aid to Policy*, Institute of Public Administration for the United States Department of Housing and Urban Development, Washington, D.C., U.S. Government Printing Office, 1968.

is the prototype, though not the only example of such a unit. Thus for advance acquisition of land for future park sites, the first row might estimate appreciation in land value forestalled by advance purchase and savings in the cost of demolishing new construction that might otherwise have been built. In the second row are utilities that can be compared to those in the measured row but can be only poorly measured, perhaps no more than in terms of a vague judgment—for example, the superior quality of a site due to a wider basis for selection when purchased in advance of development.

The third category of rows includes factors not directly comparable to others or among themselves. Such a utility in advance land acquisition of a park site is the support that it gives to the city-planning arm or the boost to a city's general development that a fine park can provide, or the negative utility, the opportunity cost, of preempting desirable sites on which people whose presence in the city would be particularly useful might locate. Utilities of this type proliferate in most poorly structured decision situations.

The figures in each box of the table are payoffs or evaluated consequences (C) (the products of step five classified as just explained), and are weighted by their probability of obtaining. Each net benefit has presumably been evaluated first, if possible, in terms of an expected payoff unit (the more general and more precise the better) and then in terms of the adjustment which attempts to draw closer to the utility, as the decision agent sees it. Ideally, they have been discounted for futurity, (perhaps expressed conventionally as "present value"). The uncertainty discount is expressed by the probability weights for each box. The types of rows will, of course, differ with respect to the terms in which utility is measured or broadly judged. Each type as listed may consist of several lines, particularly in the case of noncommensurables.[11] Costs may constitute different lines from benefits.

Columns 3 and 6 apply probability weights to the evaluated conse-

[11] The merit-weighted service unit provides another way of trying to deal with noncommensurables. For example, a number of noncommensurable values may be combined in conformity with performance criteria in a single measure of "merit-weighted user days" of outdoor recreation (see Mack and Myers, "Outdoor Recreation," in *Measuring Benefits of Government Investment*, Robert Dorfman, Ed., Brookings Institution, Washington, 1965. Since the criteria must then be made explicit, they are subject to public debate and, hopefully, progressive improvement. However, even such a measure is noncommensurable with the dollar measure of costs, and the two numeraires would need to be related in some fashion if a single net benefit estimate is to be achieved.

The merit-weighted service unit provides a method of in effect making Judged (J) or even Measured (M) lines out of Noncommensurable (N) lines.

quences under the good and bad outcomes. Thus they suggest some sort of expected value for an average result. But since only some of the possible happenings are evaluated, probabilities for the focus outcomes do not sum to 1.0. Nevertheless, a highly probable good result should obviously weigh more heavily than an off-chance bad result. Thus, if the good outcome or better was thought to have a 2-out-of-5 chance of taking place, and the bad one or worse a 1-out-of-5 chance, then the good result is twice as likely as the bad one and the decision weights are .67 and .33, respectively.[12] The application of the weights provides, in effect, an average value for the type of utility in the line. However, there are many times when one might wish to avoid or to supplement a summary of this sort. They will be considered presently, but for the moment assume that columns 3 and 6 contain acceptable figures.

The problem now is to achieve a consolidation of this information that makes it possible to choose among alternatives (including that of doing nothing). This requires not merely the horizontal summary just discussed but vertical summaries of the several sorts of net utilities. The bottom row, totals, would contain figures which ordinarily appear in a statistical decision matrix—the net benefit expected from a given act-event conjuncture. The corner boxes—the bottom rows for columns 3 and 6 give the probability-weighted expected value of each act.

Insofar as the payoffs are given in the same unit, and the utility-payoff relationship is systematic, all that is required is an adding machine. This would be the case for all measured utilities and all measured costs for which dollars were an adequate surrogate, whether or not an adjustment was required for a nonlinear surrogate-utility function. To add the noncommensurable items, indifference analysis (as structured by indifference curves or surfaces) is useful.[13] How much of one sort of value, say, strengthening the arm of city planning, is one willing to exchange for a given amount of another value, such as the prospect

[12] Of course, if none of the payoff-utility adjustments (except for futurity) have been made, then a trade-off function would be required along the lines described by Shackle. See p. 52 Note 9 above.

[13] Indifference analysis has been sketched earlier (p. 39). To review, chart prospective appreciation (in line M) vertically and aesthetic beauty (in line N) horizontally. Using any sort of unit of measurement for each, assume the following combinations of the two benefits are equally pleasing: 15 line-1-units and 5 of line n, 14 and 6, 13 and 8, 12 and 11, 11 and 15—such figures shape an indifference curve. (Similar ones for more pleasing combinations would lie above and for less pleasing ones, below it). The example illustrates exchange rates that differ depending on how much of each good is presently available; thus the incremental ratios are 1.0 at 15 line-1-units and 4.0 at 12 line-1-units.

of profit in land appreciation? The exchange rates ordinarily vary depending on the amount of each benefit one already has. The larger the level of one benefit, the more of it one will typically give up to acquire a unit of another benefit because the trade-off relations are structured by the indifference curve.

However, difficulties arise when the values that a decision agent is trying to apply are those which he attributes to the public or even to his boss. There can be conflicts among members of the collective; in addition there can be conflicts among the collective aspects of the agent. It is also possible that values in a noncommensurable, or judged, line may simply not be subject to a sufficient degree of quantification to enable even a well-focused decision collective to arrive at exchange ratios among different sorts of utilities. Thus, whether the trade-off relationships can be established depends on the circumstances. Fortunately, a consolidated figure is not necessary to sound choice. There are many possibilities.

One possibility is that the measurable portion of benefits is large and the measurable portion of costs is also large (at least the latter is often the case). Then acts can sometimes be compared by saying whether net *measured* benefits are large enough clearly to exceed the described (but unmeasured) other disadvantages less advantages. In other words, comparisons among acts are made primarily on the basis of columns 3 and 6 of Measured (M) lines with qualitative assessment of the rest of the advantages or disadvantages. Especially if one act is preferable with respect to most of the important utilities, there is little need for the missing totals.

But if choice is somewhat more problematical, *differences* between the entries in columns 3 and 6 can be examined selectively. These figures appear in column 7. Even if in each line only a plus or minus can be marked down in column 7, the pluses or minuses, respects in which act 1 is expected to be preferable (or inferior) to act 2, can be assigned weights that roughly assay the relative importance of each particular utility.

The difficulty with this crude difference-approach is that the two acts may really not be directly comparable. Then either costs or benefits need to be standardized for the two acts.

When costs are standardized, the method is known as *cost effectiveness* approach. It is natural to use this method when costs can be relatively well measured but benefits cannot be. Differences between costs for two or more acts are set equal to zero. The usual way to do this is to apply the assumption of proportionality. The ratio required to reduce the costs of the larger of the two projects to that of the smaller one is applied to the benefits of the more costly alternative. One can then ask, At the same cost, which of the alternatives would yield the most advantage? Which one, in other words, is most "cost effective"?

It is important in this approach to select the correct cost. The obvious and usual one is dollar cost. But often dollar costs are actually not the major constraint. Instead, it may be time (in military decisions); it can be qualified personnel, including talented ones.

These comparisons of benefits for a given expenditure are the stuff of which budgetary decisions are made—those of both consumers and governments. They have the advantage of great flexibility: the particulars of the focus outcomes, resulting from each of two acts which cost the same, can be presented in terms of quite highly structured measurements of advantage, or they can be presented only in terms of an orderly description of what is expected to take place.

The second approach reverses the previous one. The difference between the benefits of two or more *feasible* ways of accomplishing the same purpose are, in principle, set at zero and their costs compared. This method seems well suited to cases where the major benefits can be relatively well measured in a summary fashion. It is also useful when most of the noncomparable factors are common to the various acts. For example, it may be considered feasible and equally advantageous to accommodate a given number of families at a higher land-use density in eight-story apartments located in large open areas, or at lower density in two-family dwellings on quarter-acre lots. If so, the cost of each approach can be compared. In the field of the military, various ways of "hurting" the enemy to specified degrees can be proposed, or ways of providing a specified amount of deterrence. Cost of such alternatives can then be compared. Indeed, they can be compared in terms of more than one of the critical constraints. Here again, a chief precaution in the use of this formula is to make sure that the framework of the decision—the system that defines its bailiwick—is properly conceived. Otherwise, very important costs (and benefits), in the sense of elements actually affected by how the choice is made, may be disregarded (for example, if the cost of alternative bombs of a given destructiveness is compared without including the difference in the demand on aircraft needed to deliver the bombs).[14]

---

[14] See Malcolm W. Hoag, "Increasing Returns in Military Production Functions," in *Issues in Defense Economics*, Roland N. McKean, Ed., A Conference of the Universities—National Bureau Committee for Economic Research, New York, 1967, p. 7.

These cost-effectiveness and feasibility approaches can supplement one another. The literature in defense economics is particularly rich in illustrations of the need to circle in on difficult evaluations: first, cost can be equated and consequences compared, and then consequences can be equated and costs compared. No one set of comparisons or method of comparison is uniquely relevant to the delicate judgment about how best to destroy and to keep from being destroyed.[15]

Finally, I want to return to situations in which the horizontal summaries may seem awkward—the summary in column 3 of columns 1 and 2, line by line. This is the case in most poorly seriable situations. The same argument (sketched in Chapter 3) for needing to look at the range of consequences rather than (or in addition to) the Expected Value applies here. The fact that only selected spots on the range—those of the focus outcomes—have been described and evaluated changes nothing except which spots are examined. However, here evaluation must cope with the judgmental problems and the need to make a series of partial comparisons of noncommensurable values. The tactic is to *compare acts on the basis of first the good and then the bad outcomes* (columns 3 and 6 are avoided and comparisons are made on the basis of first 1 and 4, and second 2 and 5). In all other respects the analysis of this section can be applied without modification.

The previous analysis can likewise be applied when the probability distributions and the seriability of the decision situations imply that a single most probable outcome should be the center of attention. Also, the center focus can be augmented by supplementary ones—perhaps an upper and lower value at a selected point or by wing-boundary outcomes (discussed in connection with step 4).

Focus outcomes, then, provide a highly flexible analytic framework that can use all of the information available. At the same time the framework does not insist on rigor at the expense of realistic, sensitive, and, particularly, comprehensive analysis.

THE TIME DIMENSION IN CHOICE

We have been speaking as if decision is a unitary thing in the sense that a single conclusion is arrived at. However, *time* provides an impor-

[15] See Charles J. Hitch and Roland N. McKean, *The Economics of Defense in the Nuclear Age,* Harvard University Press, 1960, Chapter 7. And Malcolm W. Hoag, *op. cit.* And "The Structure of Choice Between Deterrence and Defense," by Martin C. McGuire, *Issues in Defense Economics,* Roland McKean, Ed., New York, 1967.

tant dimension that can be put to work in many actual situations. The compound and complex character of the acts among which choices are made means that to some degree the acts tend to be designed in the course of evaluating their worth. The collectivity of decision agents implies that a process of arriving at an agreement will necessarily introduce time into decision histories. The complex and developmental character of perception, aspiration, and even evaluation means that decision makers undergo change in the course of the decision process itself. Finally, the high cost of uncertainty underscores the need to collect information over time.

Decisions in Time-Space

Strategy of decision may require programming such aspects of its time dimension. A strategy is "the assignment, in advance of information, of specific actions to respond to the different messages that the decision maker may receive from an information source." Strategy for decision can also refer to a plan for arriving at consensus. I can only tiptoe into this range of problems and still maintain the assumption that acts are predelineated. Nevertheless, we cannot close the discussion of choice without projecting elements of the notion of the decision tree (sketched in Chapter 3) into the more realistic landscape viewed in these chapters. In Part Three, the tree, needless to say, becomes a forest.

Strategy can concern either the *programming of actions* or the *information* to be sought. The first, Jacob Marschak has called *sequential strategy*. It assigns a sequence of actions to each possible sequence of future messages. Not only probabilities of events but assignments of utilities may change as messages are received. Moreover, in highly unstructured decision situations, such as those considered in Part Three, both utilities and probabilities may change in response to *redesign*, on the basis of messages received, of the acts that are considered. Finally there is *information strategy* which attends chiefly to programming the flow of information to be used (and thus of questions to be asked).[16] The costs of obtaining and processing information must be weighed against expected benefits from increased payoffs.

The notion of strategy, even in the limited sense in which I introduce it here, implies that the outcomes on which attention can focus are partly designed in the course of the choosing process. In this sense

---

[16] Jacob Marschak, "Decision-Making: Economic Aspects" *International Encyclopedia of the Social Sciences* Vol. IV, Macmillan, New York, 1968, pp. 42–55.

acts have some fluidity. We move around on the goals pyramid fingering the interface of ends and means. The fluidity concerns particularly *how much* should be done (the basic economic notion of optimizing at the margin)—*when* it should be done (the staging of decision) and some *qualitative aspects of acts* which are subject to change within the compass of the decision itself.

One illustration will suffice to suggest how time can enter into even quite constrained choice.

An Underwriting Syndicate's Bid

The illustration concerns a bid for underwriting of a bond issue. It is taken from an article by Ernest Bloch, "Pricing a Corporate Bond Issue: A Look Behind the Scenes."[17] I have rearranged Bloch's running account in line with the decision steps previously outlined.

The decision collective was composed of two different parts, each consisting of many individuals—a large investment bank (the syndicate manager) and a syndicate of about 100 investment firms. The problem concerned what price to bid for a bond issue. The alternative acts were various bids which combined a price to be paid to the borrower and the coupon rate of the bond. The bid would be won or lost depending on whether the bids of this or of other investment syndicates were higher.

Step 1: The utility which the best act would generate is in the first instance to win the bid. In a more fundamental sense, it is, as usual, a compound of elements that differ somewhat for the several members of the collective.

For the investment bank, utility consisted of: (1) profit on the transaction; and (2) prestige, with its implication concerning future profits and power. The bank (one of about six large enough to swing large offerings) gains from winning "a fair share of the bidding competition" because this helps in managing future syndicates and in attracting "negotiated" financing.

For other members of the syndicate, utility consisted of: (1) profit on the transaction, and a large and safe margin of profit was particularly important to the smaller members; (2) maintaining independence of the syndicate manager, which was of special interest to the larger members.

Step 2: The aspiration level was very high. The bid had to be just

---

[17] In *Essays in Money and Credit,* Federal Reserve Bank of New York, December 1964, pp. 72–76.

right in terms of the several criteria previously mentioned. Moreover the calculations had to be very delicate; experience had shown that a winning bid could be a fraction of a cent per $1000 bond above the next contender.

Step 3: The basic layout of the decision process was set in terms of a stepwise process. The character of the process was determined by well-established practice. Indeed it is only because the procedure was so well established that the decision process can be thought of as dealing primarily with timing of predelineated alternatives in response to a flow of information. Were the choice of acts more open, consideration would have to wait for Part Three. The purpose of the decision procedure was to progressively narrow down alternatives in the light of information obtained from the outside and generated by the decision process itself.

Since these firms undertake any number of ventures of this sort, the situation is partly seriable. But most participants, particularly the smaller ones, were very unwilling to risk loss on this issue no matter how likely they would be to make it up on the next one. For the investment bank, on the other hand, the interest in building a long-term reputation may have caused the decision, in effect, to be regarded in a seriable framework.

Step 4: The outcome covers results in terms of win or lose the bid, the amount of the offering taken by each syndicate member, his profits, etc. The probability distribution of outcomes that the decision collective faced was a function of the act (particularized bid) selected, and the acts of other syndicates. The case illustrates a situation where it is virtually impossible to think about which are the most "interesting" outcomes of each act without at the same time thinking about which are the most "interesting" acts. The act, the precise bid, influences the outcome: winning with a low bid has a different outcome in terms of syndicate response and profits than would winning with a higher bid. The focus of attention must be the act-outcome most likely to be optimal in these multiple senses. The probability distribution is shaped like a flattened bell (low kurtosis) but covering a narrow dollar range.

Since the outcome will consist in part of what the members of the syndicate do (and its aggregate utility will thereby be vitally affected) it is important particularly for the bank to cause the decision process itself to narrow the range of the distribution, thereby closing in on a bid most likely both to win and to hold the syndicate together. Thus the probability distribution of outcomes must be made to become more peaked as the process proceeds. Strategy to this end is therefore an essential part of the decision's course.

The selection of act-outcomes most "interesting" in this rather subtle sense, was made in the light of a number of facts. Concerning the security issue: the bonds would have a triple-A rating (arguing for a lower yield); the size of the issue was large and call-protection small (arguing for a higher yield). Concerning the "feel of the market:" the market may be expected to be strong because the calendar of forthcoming quotations was light and dealer inventories (corporates *and* governments) was light (arguing for an "aggressive policy," i.e., the price offered the borrower should be high); general market rates, such as prime paper or the Federal Reserve Bank discount rates, were unlikely to change over the flotation period (arguing for the feasibility of a close judgment). Concerning the market for the issue: the "book" was reasonably strong—about half of the issue was covered by offers of purchase, though these offers are not finalized until the particulars of the bid are announced (this suggested that the syndicate members would be less likely to drop out). For the investment bank, these considerations seem to speak for an aggressive bid. Accordingly, the act-outcomes toward which their attention gravitated were at the higher price end, with a crucial problem being that of getting the syndicate to "go along."

These background considerations went some distance toward narrowing the acts and outcomes worth considering. But it was essential to narrow foci still further and the strategy to that end can be traced. There was a meeting three days before the bid date in which the fifteen senior officers of the managing investment bank agreed on some preliminary notions of what the bid should be. The next day about a hundred members of the syndicate went over the same question indicating at what price they would be willing to participate to a specified extent. At this point the bank officers could start to make some guesses about outcomes in terms of behavior of the syndicate members.

Step 5: Transformation of outcome into an objective function was a relatively minor part of this decision situation. The outcome in terms of win or lose, syndicate behavior, and prospective profits, can all be translated roughly into the objective function of dollar profits though it is deficient in omitting some important long-term considerations. To include these it is useful to make a distinction between the questions confronting the bank and confronting the other members of the syndicate.

The members of the syndicate are presented in the later stages of the process with one set of prices for the bid and coupon rate. Their choice is to go along or to drop out. If they go along, the bid may be won or lost.

In terms of the matrix of Exhibit 7-1, most of the consequences appear as measured payoffs in line 1—expected profits. For members of the winning syndicate, expected profits combine those on the underwriting and on the sale of the issue. This varies, other things the same, *inversely* with the price offered the borrower and *directly* with the coupon rate. However, the probability of winning the bid has the opposite association; it varies directly relative to the buying price and inversely relative to the coupon rate. Thus the payoff-utility function is nonlinear; the price that is just worthwhile accepting involves an indifference curve that exchanges risk for profit.

The leading bank deals with a more complex decision matrix. Its choice is not whether to go along or to drop out but what price to propose. Measured payoff—profits—are an important expectation, but so too are the items on other lines in the matrix in Exhibit 7-1: judged consequences involve the behavior of the syndicate; noncommensurables involve long-term prestige, etc. The range of alternative acts that are considered would narrow as the decision stages move on. At any given stage, the bank might be willing to push for a higher bid price even if it would cause some syndicate members to defect; the bank would pick up the drop-outs' commitments. In selecting the focus act-outcomes on which to concentrate, the bank's officers must weigh how far by way of increasing risks of defections and lowering profits they are willing to go in order to increase their chances of winning the bid.

The probability distribution of payoffs would start flat and grow more peaked later on. Attention will focus on a central value but also perhaps on a wing value, at least at the low end of the utility scale.[18] However, the judgment is complicated even with a single focus since it involves difficult guesses about facts and behavior external and internal to the syndicate; there is also a difficult problem of summing noncommensurable values. One thing is clear, and it will become increasingly clearer as we proceed, that if such judgments are made, and they must be made, they consist of little that can be set down on a page. They must be too swift and too subtle not to have a large component of intuitive wisdom. Note the corollary: the general ability of the person who makes the decision is a major variable in its quality.

The progress of the decision over time was a recursive repetition of steps 4, 5, and 6, in which syndicate members and the leading bank played their usual roles not without the spice of gamesmanship. The repetitions must have occurred from hour to hour during the next to last day, and from minute to minute in the final morning meeting.

---

[18] The bimodal structure would apply if there were a serious question whether there might be, for example, some change in Federal Reserve policy or some prior issue the offering price of which was not yet determined.

The meeting which would culminate in the final bid started behind locked doors with all members of the syndicate present. A bid was proposed by a vice-president of the bank and greeted by groans. A poll indicated that the membership's underwriting was cut by about a third. Private consultations ensued, followed by new proposals, interrupted by news flashes concerning the size of the book. In the course of this drama the range was narrowed. In response to each proposal, and such new information as was being generated, each member of the syndicate calculated his own advantage and embodied his conclusion in the expression of his willingness to pick up his allotment or drop out. The syndicate manager considered the further question of willingness to pick up the allotments of defectors (or of others that might occur as the negotiations proceeded) in exchange for improving the chances of winning the bid. Finally the end came. Agreement was reached, the doors were flung open, and the bid announced. Within thirty seconds it was known that the bid was lost. The winner had bid about $1 more per $1000 bond.

CHAPTER 8

Choice by Natural Man, Summary and Implications

It will be useful to review the course that the past four chapters have plotted. Thereafter we ask whether the reaction to uncertainty tends to bias choice among predelineated acts in an identifiable way.

SUMMARY

The Decision Agent and the Nature of Reality and Value Judgments

Decisions of many men of flesh-and-blood-and-complexes can scatter about a band for which *Homo economicus* plots a center line. Individual decisions are often not as wide of the mark as might be expected. Choices are sometimes easy, in that it is obvious which alternative is to be preferred. Moreover, men of judgment have the remarkable capacity to fetch up from their own totality delicate calculations of net advantage.

However there are three important elements which do cause systematic deflection from the line which *Homo economicus* would trace. The first two are selective perception and conditioned aspirations. These give a strongly developmental aspect to choice: understanding and events of the recent past condition those of today. As we shall see in Chapters 10 and 11, this social conditioning and ecological interplay are still more important in determining the alternatives among which choices are made. Third, the several complexities are extended in an additional dimension by the fact that even the individual decision maker is actually not a homogeneous entity but a collective, which adds further developmental aspects and perhaps a basic instability particularly to evaluative judgments.

How then does this composite and complex entity go about achieving deliberative choice among predelineated alternatives? The attribution of expected consequences to acts needs to be broken conceptually into two judgments: one that looks primarily outward toward what is expected to happen—the outcome; and the other looking inward toward how pleased one will be that it did—the utility assignment.

The first involves the large question of causality. I find it useful in my own thinking to visualize four major categories of things that need to be known in this connection. They are (1) intrinsic functional relationships, (2) external influences, (3) human elements and strategies, and (4) chance. Note that uncertainty is not simply a function of futurity as discussions often seem to suggest.

The second major source of uncertainty concerns the assignment of utility. How is utility defined and calculated by persons, indeed typically intrapersonal or interpersonal collectives, faced with saying, "this is preferable to that?"

I have sketched some of the methods of value identification implicit or explicit in the literature on consumer, business, and particularly government decision theory. These theories deal with the decision process as a whole but I have examined only what they say or imply about value systems.

For consumers, value is attributed by virtue of an internal feeling of desirability. The opportunity cost of the desired object—what one is willing and able to give up to possess it—constitutes a marvelously adaptive measure for calibrating expected utility.

In business, utility concerns in principle the long-term future of the organization as envisioned by the present incumbents of office—a protean decision collective. Expected profit (appropriately discounted for futurity and uncertainty) during some relevant period is the usual index of utility; but it often fails to reflect many important values and may reflect poorly those which it purports to cover. The unrepresented values, such as level of sales, access to finance, growth potential, prestige, and so on, are often noncomparable among themselves and with short-term profits. Likewise difficult to reconcile may be the goals of individuals relative to those of the organizations to which they belong.

For governments, the compound values of compound decision collectives are central. Political scientists feature the interpersonal aspect of the process; they consider how values arise, and how they are espoused and advocated in a complex, continuing, bargaining ritual. Voting mechanisms, partisan mutual adjustment, disjointed incrementalism, and heuristic decision processes not only solve problems but define them. In one sense the theories imply that those things that are espoused by the political processes are virtually by definition valuable for the society at the time. Economists typically look for sharper answers in terms of welfare functions, votes, or cost-benefit analysis. These are basically orderly, however incomplete, techniques for analyzing the elements of value assignments.

The several systems for defining and measuring utility in government are essentially supplementary, not competing concepts as the literature seems to suggest. To delineate objectives well, an individual should use all the tools of analysis and perception at his disposal; the process of advocacy, bargaining, and the like adds an additional dimension of problem definition to the economist's kit. Furthermore, as the notion of a goals-means pyramid seems to show, reality judgments are often prerequisites to value judgments.

The description of decision agents and the problems inherent in defining and measuring utility converge in the hypothesis that the expected utility of a specified outcome, however completely specified in physical terms, can at best typically be assigned as a range, rather than in terms of the single-valued estimate. The argument suggests the usefulness of thinking in terms of a three-dimensional matrix. Each outcome has a specified probability of obtaining, and if it does there is a specified probability that each of its possible utilities will result.

Decision Problems and Decision Processes

The description of decision agents and the reality and value judgments which they must make implies first and foremost that normative decision-making must build on this descriptive foundation. To this it is proper to add, people should try to do as well as they can.

How well they can do, and how to proceed, depends on the decision problem. Five structural attributes help to identify the problem with respect to decision procedures appropriate to it. The first two concern the ability of the decision collective to function efficiently—homogeneity and rational capacity. The third and fourth concern the informational basis for predicting objective outcomes (attribute 3) and their expected utility (attribute 4). The fifth, seriability, says whether average or particular results are of primary concern.

When a given decision situation is rated along the continuum which each attribute represents, an attributes profile appears which suggests a sensible "aspiration level" for deciding.

If the profile clings to the well-structured side—the left side of the continuum for each attribute—decisions can be made with the elegance and precision of statistical theory.

But as the attributes profile moves toward the right, aspirations must forfeit finesse to achieve comprehensiveness and relevance. The power of the collective to behave efficiently deteriorates; information becomes inadequate and shifty, and even to define objectives (as we saw all too clearly in Chapter 5) grows complex and elusive; vulnerability to the single instance is high. In consequence, quantification is likely to be poor and partial, only a few of the possible outcomes can be pictured and considered, and sometimes it seems wiser to delay and decide in stages rather than to push on toward a decision in one piece.

Is there, then, anything which decision procedures have in common under these diverse situations? I suggest that the rule "minimize the cost of uncertainty" provides a flexible objective.

Its application implies an adequate process of deciding. And to that end it is useful to identify six steps (which are not necessarily taken only once). The first three lay out the course of decision by defining utility, selecting the appropriate aspiration level, and designing the basic strategy, such as whether complete distributions of outcomes, focus outcomes, or a staged process should be used. The fourth describes in objective terms the outcomes that will be evaluated and their probabilities. The fifth determines their expected consequence first in terms of a surrogate and then in terms of desirability—utilities. The sixth compares the net expected utility of each act.

For well-structured decision situations—such as are frequently found in games of chance, production scheduling, and inventory or quality control—decision procedures discussed in Part One provide much of the answer. Where the utility of outcomes is itself probabilistic an additional dimension needs to be added to the matrix—it becomes a boxful of evaluated consequences rather than a surface of them. For nonseriable situations this model must be further modified to allow for more emphasis on extreme possibilities and for nonlinear relationships between utility and numerically measured payoffs.

But many decision situations are not capable of conceptualization in terms of a complete distribution of possibilities. For these, crucial information concerning both outcomes and utilities tends to be in short supply (whereas the subjective aspect of perception and aspirations tend to be in long supply). The mind must attach itself to outcomes which for one reason or another provide natural foci of attention. What these will be, I hypothesize, depends on necessarily vague sensing of the basic characteristics of the probability distribution of outcomes Is the distribution peaked, relatively flat, or bimodal? In the first case the mind tends to seek a most likely outcome; in the second, outcomes "this good or better" and "this bad or worse" (wing-boundary values) will be added to a central one; and in the last, central good and bad results are likely to be pictured with or without additional lower, and perhaps upper, boundary outcomes.

When decision situations require this focus-outcome approach, one discovers that decision processes can accommodate a great deal of flexibility.

For one thing, when intangible and noncommensurable values are important they should be exhibited as such in the decision matrix. By so doing they can be dealt with in one or more of a number of ways: Indifference analyses can compare unlike values thereby making it possible to sum the several sorts of expected utilities for a given focus outcome; noncomparable focus outcomes can be compared with respect to each of several sorts of utilities separately, and with any degree of precision or nothing more than a plus or minus rating. These comparisons can be made for matching outcomes of each act or for the act as a whole (after weighting outcomes by their probability relative to one another). Differences can be sharpened by forcing equality of either costs or benefits—the "cost-effectiveness" or "feasibility" approaches. The ways of arriving at useful judgments have the limits only of man's ingenuity and knowledge.

Finally, staging provides a way to integrate the acquisition of information with the decision process. When information is poor, staging can be desirable even at the cost of considerable efficiency. Of course the real value of deliberate staging of the decision process only becomes apparent when, in the chapters that follow, the field of vision is extended to include when and what to decide and which alternatives to consider.

THE COST OF UNCERTAINTY AND THE CONSERVATIVE BIAS

Decision rules for natural man necessarily carry no guarantee of optimization. We need, therefore, to scan these procedures for bias. Though there are a few biases that I want to point out, one deserves particular emphasis—a tendency to overestimate and overreact to uncertainty. This implies that less risky acts tend to be favored relative to more risky ones; the status quo especially tends to pull more than its proper weight. Uncertainty imparts, in other words, a conservative bias to behavior.

Excessive Costs Defined

The claim that there is a tendency to overestimate or overrespond to risk implies a standard from which behavior diverges. But the subjective view of probability holds that the utility inherent in a situation is described by the decision agent's view of it, rather than by any objective evaluation. This would seem to deny the notion of an objective standard. Is, then, reality irrelevant to decision? The question is theoretically troublesome. Certainly the subjective view can hardly license the decision of a psychotic based on his own sick visions.

Clearly, some boundaries are required to indicate when subjective evaluations depart sufficiently from reality to be unacceptable as a norm. Skirting the philosophical issue for the time being, it is useful to think of acceptable evaluations as those made in terms of *appropriate decision rules sensibly applied.* Sensible behavior is what well-trained people would agree lies within, not outside of, the area in which reasonable men might well differ. Reasonable men would take the whole situation, including their own limitations, into account—the situation as the structural attributes characterize it. *The situation, then, we accept as a given, and require that the collective make the most of it.*

Failure to meet these requirements can imply that the cost of uncertainty is too high. The sources of these costs can be of each of the three kinds we have outlined: the routine uncertainty discount; the tendency for uncertainty to confuse and obscure; and inconsistencies between the impact of uncertainty on individual and on societal well-being. The second and third costs are always "excessive" in that the objective of good deliberative procedures is to eliminate them.

The first cost—the routine discount—is legitimate and necessary. It is excessive only if it is unreasonably large in the sense just suggested. Another way to put it is that it expresses excessive "risk aversion."

Risk aversion does not apply to objective situations. For example, consequences in diffuse decision situations are by definition harder to foretell, and therefore larger uncertainty discounts are necessary to sensible choice. In addition, natural man is unable to gather or to utilize information fully, no matter how hard he tries. In consequence, the complement of knowledge, uncertainty, will necessarily be larger for him than for *Homo economicus*. The heightened uncertainty associated with these necessary shortcomings of decision agents and difficulty of decision situations is an unexceptionable fact of life.

Excessive risk aversion applies rather to the subjective scheme for evaluating outcomes. It refers to situations where a utility-payoff function is sensitive to risk *other things the same*. One "other thing" that is relevant is the degree of seriability. If seriability is low, it is appropriate for utility-payoff ratios to reflect the dispersion of outcomes believed to be present. However, in a perfectly seriable problem, and assuming that outcomes may be completely and correctly evaluated in terms of some payoff unit such as dollars, a utility-payoff ratio which decreases as dispersion increases may be evidence of excessive risk aversion.[1] In other words, the collective discounts the utility of a risky outcome by an amount which is greater than its probability of obtaining justifies.

The concept is related to that of slanting or ambiguity discussed in Chapter 2. However, I have emphasized the impact of risk aversion on the assignment of utility to an outcome (rather than on assessment of probability of the outcome). This deterioration of utility associated with uncertainty may tend to apply not only to expectations felt to be unstable and untrustworthy but also to those having wide dispersion in nonseriable situations.[2]

---

[1] For example, assume that an outcome has a payoff of 100 if sure; but since its probability of obtaining is .8 it has an uncertainty discount of 20 and an uncertainty-discounted expected payoff of 80. But risk aversion increases the desirability of the discount of 20 by the utility-payoff ratio of 1.25; thus the total subjective uncertainty-discounted utility is 75. If probability is lower, the impact of risk aversion increases. Thus if the probability of obtaining were .4 the uncertainty-discounted payoff is 40. But the payoff discount of 60 multiplied by the risk aversion ratio of 1.25 gives an uncertainty-discounted utility of 25 (i.e., $100 - [1.25 \times 60]$). Needless to say, the way in which utility is felt to be deteriorated by risk could follow all sorts of other patterns, depending on how evaluation and estimation takes place.

In all of this there appears to be a fascinating field for experimental study. The matter is more than academic, for if action is inhibited by ambiguity and doubt, it is encouraged by growing assurance. *The time patterns of behavior will be different if this sort of dynamics is at work than if it is not*—that is, if excessive risk aversion, originally present, had not declined.

[2] There is, so far as I know, little experimental evidence although it seems quite possible to provide it. For example, do people respond differently to risky bets compared with less risky bets in seriable compared with nonseriable situations? Is the size of the bet a further variable? For accounts of experiments that hit around these issues, but do not actually engage them, see John T. Lanzetta and Joan Sieber, "Predecisional Information Processes: Some Determinants of Information Acquisition Prior to Decision Making," in *Predecisional Processes in Decision Making: Proceedings of a Symposium*, D. P. Hunt and D. L. Zink, Eds., Behavioral Sciences

Sources of Excessive Costs

Costs of uncertainty are made "too" high in these senses, by faulty decision format. A bias in this direction (and we are only concerned with bias, not with random error) can result from a number of tendencies.

Unrecognized Seriability

Seriability, as I noted in the previous chapter, should decrease the uncertainty discount for dispersion and ambiguity. If best estimates are unbiased, then, in the long run, the results of repeated draws should average out, regardless of dispersion or ambitiuty. In consequence, the decision agent who fails to recognize a seriable situation and its implications is likely to make excessive discounts for uncertainty and therefore unduly upgrade the less risky of alternative ventures. This applies, though to a lesser extent, in situations where only partial seriability can be attained.

The tendency for unrecognized seriability to introduce a conservative bias is intensified when other sources of excessive discounts for uncertainty are present.

Excessive Risk Aversion

Excessive risk aversion, and the associated conservative bias, are a function of individual psychology, the collectivity of decision agents, and common management practices. I shall say a word concerning each.

Blurry and shifty knowledge is introspectively so obnoxious, and so commonly reported as such, that it seems reasonable to suppose that most people dislike it.[3] I might add, there is nothing inconsistent in feeling such distaste and nevertheless enjoying a gamble. For some, outright

---

Laboratory, Aerospace Medical Division, Air Force Systems Command, Wright-Patterson Air Force Base, Ohio, AMRL-TDR-64-77 (1964), pp. 125–173, and Emir H. Shuford, "Predecisional Processes Related to Psychophysical Judgment," *ibid.*, pp. 53–75. Shuford found that "Increasing the monetary payoffs given a subject for a correct judgment increases both the probability of a correct judgment and reaction time for a given pair of propositions" (p. 69). However, the experiments reported upon did not at the same time deal with either of the other variables I have mentioned. See also references supra Chapter 2, footnotes 16 and 17.

[3] Richard Cyert and James March, in *A Behavioral Theory of the Firm,* International Series in Management, Prentice-Hall, Englewood Cliffs, N.J., 1963, posit "uncertainty avoidance" as one of the four basic concepts on which their theory rests (p. 116). There are several discussions in the book of empirical investigations which the authors claim substantiate their theory. These contain many specific references to uncertainty avoidance.

gambling is a sport commanding a price, often a very high price. But it is a very different venture from trying to run a business or a government office or one's life in an effective manner.[4] This distaste for uncertainty itself is not a sensible part of evaluating the utility of alternative acts, and results in "excessive" uncertainty discounts.

Several other characteristics of natural man and of decision collectives cause deterioration in choice due to uncertainty avoidance: selective perception tends to screen out ambiguous evidence. The entrance fee for admission to the psychological field is lower for clean-cut evidence than for shadowy messy evidence. Because aspirations are conditioned by the past and by the concurrent behavior of others, the drive to push toward the limits of optimality may be replaced by "organizational slack."

The collectivity of decision agents further reinforces conservatism. It is usually easier for people to agree to let things stay as they are than to agree to institute some particular one of several possible changes.

Conservative Bias of Management

Perhaps most important, organizational practice often tends to discourage executives from choosing change. The "rule of exceptions," a device for disclosing items to which bosses shall attend, often makes mistakes more visible than good results. Efforts to make useful changes must overcome the viscous resistance of custom, break down walls of vested procedures, and bear the erosion of bargaining among interested parties. This implies that the optimization of utility for individuals in

---

[4] Kenneth Boulding shows what it takes to be a gambler by means of an indifference map with expected value and risk on the two axes (Fig. 55, p. 118). By comparing objective measures of risk with the gambler's subjective evaluation he shows that to explain professional gambling people must either "have an overweening opinion of their own good fortune and hence rate their chance of winning at more than the actuarial value" or have "a positive preference for risk." p. 120, *A Reconstruction of Economics,* Science Editions, Inc., New York, 1962. (First published, John Wiley, 1950.)

In contrast, businessmen with whom I have discussed policies about the purchasing of materials display a different syndrome. A common response to questions about the timing of buying is that of anger at the implication that they anticipate changes in prices and buy more materials when they think prices will rise. They assert that they are not "speculators" but responsible executives of a plant which manufactures goods. One of them actually said that when he wanted to gamble he went to Monte Carlo. I should add that many of these same men *actually do* buy more when prices are rising, but their attention is fixed on availability rather than price expectations. See R. P. Mack, *Information, Expectations, and Inventory Fluctuation, A Study of Materials Stock on Hand and on Order,* National Bureau of Economic Research, New York, 1967, pp. 42–44 and 272–276.

organizations is by no means necessarily identical to optimizing it for the organization itself. The ramifications of this tendency are a matter to which organizational theory has given a great deal of attention since Luther Gulick and Chester Barnard pointed it out long ago. My point here is simply that the uncertainty with which most evaluations are made supports the individual's hesitation to transcend organizational constraints. It thereby widens the difference between the individual's preference scheme, given the organizational framework, and the true preference scheme of the organization as a whole.[5]

In government administration, the pressures toward the do-nothing choice are far more powerful. The "howl meter," attuned to the noises made by the press, pressure groups, and the general public, is more sensitive to the shout occasioned by change than to the perennial low growl associated with customary incompetence.

Wing-Boundary Outcomes

A tendency to discredit risky alternatives also seems to reside in the use of wing-boundary outcomes unless they are adjusted to take this tendency into account.

I have discussed as part of normative procedures the use of focus values which stand at the boundary, rather than at the center, of the range of consequences which they represent (e.g., "this good result or better," and "this bad result or worse"). But the procedure has a tendency to penalize variance or ambiguity. To explain, I would like to compare two evaluations, one before and one after an increase in uncertainty (as viewed by the decision collective) concerning the utilities expected from a particular set of wing-boundary outcomes.

Start with the assumption that the wing-boundary values selected are acceptable. The good outcome has a minimum value accepted as good enough and sufficiently probable to be interesting—say consequences valued at 75 (on an index scale) at a probability of .60. If

---

[5] Cyert and March, op. cit., have made this widening of the difference a cornerstone in their Behavioral Theory of the Firm. The authors develop a model of behavior that includes all sorts of suboptimal (in the classic sense) behavior—"acceptable level decision rules"—in line with "quasi-resolution of conflict" with respect to goals; "problemistic search" which is "biased" and "simple-minded" (that is, it "proceeds on the basis of a simple model of causality until driven to a more complex one"), p. 121. (See also Chapter 6, "A Summary of Basic Concepts in the Behavioral Theory of the Firm.")

The authors do not derive their model from the fact of uncertainty alone, nor from the fact of uncertainty plus the characteristics of a world of decision and decision makers of the sort which I have described. However, it would be a fascinating exercise to see whether it could not in fact be so derived.

evaluation of this outcome later becomes unclear—perhaps its utility was thought to lie between 65 and 85—then an outcome ranging from 75 to 95 would be required to meet the 75 boundary or better (the standard originally set). An increase in uncertainty caused upgrading of the acceptably good focus outcome. For the poor result, added uncertainty works similarly. Say that a consequence valued at 25 or worse on an index scale was acceptable at a .20 probability level (i.e., no worse with a probability of .80). If this value came to be viewed as spread between 15 and 35, it would no longer be acceptable. A boundary outcome would have to carry utility ranging between 25 and 45 to fulfill the original standard. This source of conservative bias again plays into the hands of the status quo.

I mentioned earlier that the simplified satisficing decision rule had a conservative bias. Apparently, wing-boundary focus values have the same characteristic and for the same reasons, though to a lesser extent. Higher-valued outcomes do enter the calculation for wing boundary, although they do not for satisficing. Consequently, the selected act is not necessarily the one having the better of poor results; the better of good results can pull some countervailing weight.

But in spite of the conservative bias of wing-boundary values in the face of dispersion or ambiguity, I would nevertheless hold that their use may be included in normative decision procedures. Is it fail-safe? What do I stand to gain? These are questions that men do and really must ask in nonseriable decision situations; how these questions can be answered must be relevant to the expected utility of the outcomes. The fact that the questions tend to weight decision excessively in favor of the status quo or other low-risk situations can, if recognized, be partly counteracted by forcing particular attention and emphasis on most likely results (for other than clearly bimodal distributions).[6]

The Numbers Illusion

It seems likely that there is a qualitative bias in response to uncertainty: those strategies that have more advantages subject to quantification, particularly quantification in terms of money, are favored over those for which intangible and noncomparable values abound, other things the same. Intangibles and noncomparables are often not named as benefits, and if they are introduced they tend to be ignored. But even if there are real efforts to keep them in mind, measurable benefits may carry more weight than nonmeasurable ones of equal importance. This

---

[6] Even for bimodal distributions, wing-boundary values can be supplemented by most likely values for the wing—that is, the most likely good and bad results.

supposition rests on the notion that the sharpness of a number tends to transcend the fuzziness that may surround its meaning or its origin, thereby creating what may be termed a "numbers illusion."[7]

The selectivity generated by the *numbers illusion* is perhaps qualitative rather than conservative. But there may well be some tendency for more uncertain ventures to tend to involve difficult-to-quantify values. If so, a conservative bias, in the sense of overestimating and under-responding to uncertain values, would tend to emerge from it.

A further reason for expecting a conservative bias is a function of the fact that costs are typically far easier to quantify than benefits. This would at least set the status quo (to which few costs are attached) in a preferred position relative to new ventures.

Countervailing Influences

Excessive costs of uncertainty, and the conservative bias they imply, can be reduced by making use of available know-how about decision procedures, including methods of coping with uncertainty formulated in the closing chapter of this book.

Staging

One approach deserves particular attention: stepwise, staged decision decreases the bias if only because it decreases uncertainty itself. The example of the bond issue details how, even when staging takes place only within the course of a single decision procedure, the capacity that it provides to "learn while doing" makes it possible to grope toward a decision that truly represents the relevant value schemes under relatively well-understood objective circumstances. In that decision I see no evidence of a conservative bias over and above that imposed by the reasonable unwillingness of some syndicate members to accept a chance of a low profit (this unwilliigness being reflected in the routine uncertainty discount).

We shall see soon that when the entire decision process is examined in its full time dimension the importance of staged learning procedures is augmented in a number of startling ways.

[7] The term "numbers illusion" borrows from the standard economic notion of "money illusion" which has been used to explain why consumption patterns often appear to be more stable in terms of the dollar value of consumption goods than in terms of their value deflated to allow for changes in the purchasing power of money. This is actually one form of "numbers illusion"—dollars can be counted better than "real" value.

Uncertainty as an Aid to Conflict Resolution

A second major countervailing influence, a very important one, can actually make an asset rather than a liability out of uncertainty. It can in a few circumstances turn at least a part of uncertainty's impact from conservative to facilitating. Uncertainty can make coalitions possible which clarity would disrupt. The compound and partly conflicting value systems of a collective can coalesce in agreement on a proposition which is partly misinterpreted by each member to embody his own desires. If knowledge were more complete, differences would be sharper. In such cases, the attraction of the new venture may be strengthened.

Impact on Behavior

I have mentioned a number of reasons why decision agents tend to overestimate and overrespond to uncertainty. Just how does this reaction deteriorate choice?

First, it increases the cost of uncertainty by increasing the routine uncertainty discount, as the following figures illustrate:

	Act 1	*Act 2*
1. Utility under certainty	150	100
2. "Correct" discount for uncertainty	.50	.25
3. "Correct" Expected Value uncertainty-discounted utility (lines: $1 - [1 \times 2]$)	75	75
4. "Excessive" further discount for uncertainty	.20	.20
5. Total "subjective" Expected Value uncertainty-discounted utility (lines: $1 - [1 \times (2 + 4)]$)	45	55

The decision agent should be indifferent with respect to the two acts since they have the same uncertainty-discounted Expected Value (line 3). However, the "excessive discount" (even assuming it is no greater for the more than for the less uncertain outcome) erroneously causes act 2 to look better. The error would be emphasized if the rate of excessive discount increased with greater uncertainty, as it seems likely that it does, and therefore the discount in line 4 was larger for act 1 than act 2.

The bias toward playing safe has its sharpest impact in encouraging the selection of the alternative that consists of doing nothing. The reason is clear. Since there is usually considerable experience with the status quo, its future results can be predicted with less uncertainty than that of new departures. Accordingly, the uncertainty-discounted expected advantage of standing pat will tend to be elevated, other things the same (or even possibly other things considerably worse), than that of alternatives.

It is interesting, incidentally, that elevation of the status quo will be stronger in some societies than in others. A chief risk in doing nothing is that competitors will do something, and that this something will turn out to be effective. The risk depends in part on the competitive tone of the society. A low competitive tone is self-reinforcing in that it reduces one of the possible risks of doing nothing and thereby makes it even more popular than it would otherwise be.

In addition to increasing the routine uncertainty discount, the biases also obscure and befuddle. Choices are less than optimal because the responses of individuals and of organizations to uncertainty cause mistakes of a wide variety of kinds over and above an overevaluation of the virtues of security. These implications only become fully apparent in the context of an entire decision situation open to the whole range of ongoing deliberative procedures. But even in the choice among pre-delineated acts we see favoritism toward acts having measurable values, toward organizational structure that encourages individuals to favor acts deemed in line with what the "chief" expects, toward downgrading the possibility of gain from trying something new, and so forth. Such uncertainty-related behavior increases uncertainty's cost largely by deteriorating the potential utility of contemplated acts. If so, act 1 in the previous example would have been ruled out because, as chosen and put into effect under the befuddlement which uncertainty can engender, it would have an expected utility of at most, say, 130 instead of 150 (other lines of the table the same).

We have been speaking of impacts of uncertainty on individual decision collectives and on the organizations of which they are a part. Yet obviously the impacts do not stop there. They settle also on society as a whole, involving the further costs of inconsistencies in the impact of uncertainty on individual and on societal advantage. However, it will be well to wait to examine these matters until we are no longer encumbered by the assumption that choice is made only among prede-lineated alternatives.

It is now necessary to let time run free and view the decision as part of the ongoing history of deliberative-administrative processes.

PART THREE

Ongoing Deliberative
Processes

CHAPTER 9

Characteristics of the Deliberative Process

Decision itself, on which our attention has thus far focused, is only one incident in the life history of a deliberative process. That history starts with the events that bring some problem into focus and ends with the last efforts to correct and carry through on actions chosen. Uncertainty permeates the entire history, since knowledge is incomplete throughout. The task of this chapter is to examine the whole time-consuming process with a view to achieving an overview of the role that uncertainty plays in it, and what this implies about how to conceptualize the ongoing deliberative process.

A STAGED RECURSIVE PROCESS

Although any life history is continuous, it can sometimes be conveniently divided into stages. The life history of a man, for example, must somehow include an interuterine stage, a period of dependency, of maturity, and of progressive aging. Some of these stages have clear boundaries— conception and birth for the first, and death for the last. The life history of a decision cycle is seldom so clearly segmented or bounded; nevertheless, most analysts of the problem find it convenient to think in terms of stages. Decision among predelineated alternatives is only one of these stages. What are the others?

Five Stages

There are many ways of making the subdivisions, and it is perhaps not too important how the process is broken into parts so long as the totality of the deliberative process is kept in mind. Five stages can be usefully distinguished.

First, awareness of a problem must develop to a point where there is some readiness to start to formulate a solution. Second, contemplation must develop specific alternatives, which offer possibilities of improving the situation. Third, a choice among the alternatives must be made (the decision proper which the previous chapters have examined). Fourth, the decision must be put into effect, and this is likely to require a number of subsidiary determinations. Fifth, since uncertainty precludes a sure and perfect decision, it is typically necessary to correct and supplement the initial one. These five stages form a decision cycle.

The fourth and particularly the fifth stages imply that the history of most decision cycles merges with that of many others, some of which may parallel, and others supplement, the initial one; in any event, they succeed it. In other words, decision cycles are recursive:[1] they tend to spiral in developing series of partial approximations. Hence the five stages are themselves often only one phase of a broad deliberative-administrative process.

---

[1] A *recursive* deliberative process consists of repetitions of the staged decision cycles, in which some of the factors involved in previous cycles repeat themselves (though typically not in just the same form) and new elements may be present or old ones absent. *Recursive* was first defined in a general dictionary (Webster's Third International) as ". . . constituting a mathematical formula in which any element may be computed from one preceding it." The basic notion is that of a system in which current values of variables are based on linear functions of earlier ones. In recent econometric literature, nonlinear functions are sometimes specified and their coefficients may also sometimes be subject to change. I use the word in this broader sense and add that new variables may also spring into the system or old ones fade out.

EXHIBIT 9-1 Decision Cycle Stages

	A — Gore	B — Simon	C — Litchfield	D — Systems Analysis	E — Managerial Economics
1. Problem recognition	Recognition of strain; consideration of how far to open things up.	Awareness that present situation is no longer "satisfactory" in view of realistic aspirations	Definition of issues; analysis of existing situation	System studies	Planning
2. Specification of alternatives	Forming a response; delineating criteria.	Discovery and design of satisfactory possible courses of action.	Calculation and determination of alternatives	Focusing on a problem area; compiling or inventing and developing alternative systems to satisfy objectives.	Search activity
3. Choice (decision proper)	Focusing on something manageable, not too uncertain, and for which a coalition can be formed.	Evaluating alternatives and choosing in an "intendedly rational" fashion; the process differs for programmed and unprogrammed decisions.	Deliberation and choice	Detailed enumeration of consequences of each alternative and selection among them.	Decision
4. Effectuation	Mounting a response, reforming coalitions and generating actions		Programming and communicating	Making general objectives operational; communicating task to the engineers.	Engineering design
5. Correction and supplementation			Cycles of action: control and reappraisal	Final action phase: evaluation as long as system is in effect.	

Note. Sources are given in footnote 2.

Variety of Formulations

A great deal of very hard and productive work has gone into analysis of the decision process and a wide variety of formulations has emerged. A large part of the differences in these formulations derives from the variations of administrative situations on which they focus, rather than from disagreements as to the character of the deliberative process itself.

The descriptions range—to mention just a few—from the rational and orderly deliberative process pictured by managerial economics to the exploratory, remedial and nibbling process, "disjointed incrementalism," which Charles Lindblom and Braybrooke see as the nature of day-to-day decisions made by politicians, administrators, and executives. Between these views are many others. Systems analysis, for example, features a long and complicated process of circling in on a problem, beginning with study of the broad systemic context of an ongoing program. In their models of a process of delineating alternatives and choosing, Herbert Simon and Edward Litchfield accommodate the relationships among individuals and organizations and (particularly Litchfield) their environments. William Gore, often focusing on a legislative context, highlights the strategic interplay among individuals in a "heuristic" decision process of which the central dynamic is the inducement of shared conceptions. Insofar as these approaches define stages of the decision cycle paralleling those I have formulated, they are shown in Exhibit 9-1.[2]

---

[2] See, for example: Herbert A. Simon, *The New Science of Management Decision,* Ford Distinguished Lecture Series, Vol. 3, New York University, Harper Bros., New York, 1960, and "The Role of Expectations in an Adaptive or Behavioristic Model," in *Expectations, Uncertainty, and Business Behavior,* Mary Jean Bowman, Ed., Social Science Research Council, New York, 1958; Edward Litchfield, "Notes on a General Theory of Administration," *Administrative Science Quarterly,* Vol. 1, 1956, pp. 3–29; William Gore, *Administrative Decision-Making: A Heuristic Model,* John Wiley & Sons, New York, 1964, and "A Multidirectional Model of Heuristic Decision-Making," unpublished; David Braybrooke and Charles E. Lindblom, *A Strategy of Decision: Policy Evaluation as a Social Process,* Collier-Macmillan, London, 1963. The treatment of managerial economics is illustrated in most textbooks. Examples are: Neil E. Harlan, Charles J. Christenson, and Richard F. Vancil, *Managerial Economics,* Richard D. Irwin, Inc., Homewood, Ill., 1962; M. H. Spencer and L. Siegelman, *Managerial Economics,* Richard D. Irwin, Homewood, Ill., rev. ed., 1964; or David W. Miller and Martin K. Starr, *Executive Decision and Operations Research,* Prentice-Hall, Inc., Englewood Cliffs, N.J., 1960. *The Firm, Micro-Economic Planning and Action* (McGraw-Hill Book Company, Inc., New York, 1962) by Neil Chamberlain focuses the study of managerial behavior on planning activity. Original survey material was used in compiling the book. Nevertheless, it

Adequate *description* of deliberative-administrative processes must cover all of the aspects that are emphasized in these accounts. But what *normative* conclusions are implied? Do the descriptions indicate how things *should* be done? In the following chapters I indicate the conditions under which the answer to this question is *yes*.

THE IBM SYSTEM/360

We have been engaged thus far in abstractions and it will be useful to translate the five-stage decision process into a concrete example. The literature is lamentably thin in examples of how actual administrative decisions are made.[3] However there is a fortunate exception in *Fortune*

---

appears to be more usual for businessmen to describe how they make plans than how they remake or use them.

A good comprehensive display of the systems analysis approach is provided by Arthur D. Hall, *A Methodology for Systems Engineering*, D. Van Nostrand Co., Inc., Princeton, N.J., 1962. An interesting application of the general method is given by Thomas H. Marschak, "The Link Between Science and Invention: The Case of the Transistor," Universities National Bureau Committee for Economic Research, Conference, *The Rate and Direction of the Inventive Activity: Economic and Social Factors*, R. Nelson, Ed., Princeton University Press, 1962. The basic notion of the systems model has been applied to governments by David Easton, in *Systems Analysis of Political Life*, John Wiley & Sons, Inc., New York, 1965.

[3] The Inter-University Case Program in the field of political science has developed a large body of material, some of which has been embodied in case books such as those edited by Edwin A. Bock, "State and Local Government; a Case Book," University of Alabama, 1963; or Harold Stein, *American Civil Military Decisions*, University of Alabama, 1963, and *Public Administration and Policy Development*, Harcourt Brace, New York, 1962. But the accounts seem to emphasize the political aspects of the cases—how action was maneuvered—rather than how the participants decided what they *ought* to do or try to do. The large literature on cases in managerial economics tends to present substantive management questions rather than to describe how they were answered or how they came to be asked. Richard M. Cyert and his collaborators have published a few case studies of management decisions. See Richard M. Cyert, Herbert A. Simon, and Donald B. Trow, "Observation of a Business Decision," *Journal of Business*, 29, 1956; or R. M. Cyert and J. G. March, *A Behavioral Theory of the Firm*, Prentice-Hall, 1963. *The Rate and Direction of Inventive Activity: Economics and Social Factors*, R. R. Nelson, Ed. (A Conference of the Universities National Bureau Committee for Economic Research, Princeton, Princeton University Press, 1962), contains some excellent case studies, one of which, Thomas A. Marschak's account of the development of a micro-wave relay system, is discussed later in this chapter. Two other papers, one by Burton H. Klein and the other by Richard R. Nelson, are also replete with specific materials which are used in later chapters. Since they deal even more sharply with invention, their focus is somehow too specialized for our present purposes.

Footnote continues on page 140.

Magazine's account of the genesis of System/360 at International Business Machines Corporation.

The company is a venerable and highly management-conscious organization in which the notions of one man, Thomas Watson, Jr., are of outstanding importance. Accordingly, this may be as close to a rational decision as any organizational move of large scope is likely to be. Notwithstanding, it seems clear that the decision process did not want for strong elements of the gamesmanship and the interpersonal strategies that play such an important part in many government decisions.

The story is told by Thomas Wise, an editor of *Fortune Magazine,* in the September and October 1966 issues. I have rearranged the account in accordance with the stages of the decision process.

Stage 1: Deciding to Decide: Problem Recognition

Prior to early 1961, discontent seemed to be accumulating at the company with respect to the computer line and the organizational structure for designing new machines. Dissatisfactions with product line centered on: lack of an overall concept; overlap in the capabilities of different models; unavailability of some capabilities which competitors had developed or appeared to be on the verge of developing; too much supplementary equipment; and too great a demand on programming to meet the great variety of equipment and customer needs (a very important difficulty). Discontent concerning the organizational structure focused on: the relationship between the international and the U.S. divisions of the company; inefficiency resulting from the fact that innovation was spread in 15 to 20 engineering units; and difficulties with respect to headquarter's ordering and control of innovation and increased stress on programming.

Two sorts of external changes exacerbated the dissatisfactions. The

---

There are some generalized descriptions of business behavior based on case studies. For example, Robert Eisner, *Determinants of Capital Expenditures, An Interview Study,* Studies in Business Expectations and Planning, No. 2, Bureau of Business Research, University of Illinois, 1956; and Ruth P. Mack, *The Flow of Business Funds and Consumer Purchasing Power,* Columbia University Press, 1941. In the latter book, an analysis of how purchasing decisions were made was based on some ninety or more interviews with corporate officials. A number of these were conducted by selecting some particular new machine and trying to learn just how the decision came up and how it was dealt with. However, these discussions, though used as foundation material in the book, were never published as case studies.

scientific underpinnings and the basic technology of computer design were undergoing change. Some years earlier this had been recognized in a general way when, in 1956, Emanuel Piore, an outstanding scientist in the field, joined the company. Nevertheless, the product line was still fundamentally based on "first generation technology." Customer demand was also shifting. Broadly speaking, business requirements emphasize a large capacity to store information, whereas scientific needs are for large computational capacity. Now, however, a greater sophistication on the part of business users resulted in more interest in computational capacity.

Stage 2: Formulating Alternatives and Criteria

The formulation of alternatives, and criteria for an acceptable solution, were influenced by the history of previous events.

One set of events consisted of funeral services for a number of previous efforts. Program "STRETCH," for example, died in May 1961; this was a giant computer that never did better than about 70 percent of its promised performance and was dropped at a huge loss. A second corpse was a big computer program based on transistor technology, the 8000 series. A third corpse was a machine designed by the London World Trade Corporation called SCAMP which overlapped with the 7044.

The decisions to abandon individual products were partly based on interest in a more comprehensive plan—a computer line that would blanket the market. Accordingly, one division of the company started to work on the "New Product Line" (NPL). It is possible that the basic idea of the unified line had already been conceived and that some critically placed individuals felt their future to be identified with accomplishing its gestation and birth. If so, in reality the alternatives for the next few years were the unified product line versus the status quo. But this is conjecture.

Discontent culminated in the fall of 1961, in the appointment of a committee called "SPREAD" (an acronym for "systems programming, research, engineering, and development"). The committee included, among others, men who were prime movers in two of the abandoned previous efforts.

The group was closeted together for long intervals during the fall of 1961, and finally, in December, they brought in an 80-page report which made the following recommendations: A new line should be designed aimed at replacing the entire computer line. It should open up a whole new field of computer applications. Compatibility among the various new machines was essential; however, compatibility between a new machine and the comparable members of the old line was not important. The system must be useful for both business and scientific users. To meet this requirement, each new machine in the new line would be made available with core memories of varying sizes; in addition, the machines would provide a variety of technical and esoteric features such as "floating point arithmetic," "variable word length," and a "decimal instruction set" to handle both scientific and commercial assignments. "Information input and output equipment, and all other peripheral equipment, must have 'standard interface'—so that various types and sizes of peripheral equipment could be hitched to the main computer without missing a beat."[4]

In this decision, as is so often the case, only one alternative was sufficiently formulated to provide a challenge to the status quo.

Stage 3: Decision Proper

The decision proper was made at a meeting on January 4, 1962, at which the report of the SPREAD committee was presented. The top brass of the corporation was present. In the words of T. Vincent Learson, now president of the corporation, "There were all sorts of people up there and while it wasn't received too well, there were no real objections. So I said to them, 'All right, we'll do it.' " Learson continued with some statements that suggested the kind of evaluations that had taken place: "The problem was, they thought it was too grandiose. The report said we'd have to spend $125 million on programming the system at a time when we were spending only $10 million a year for programing. Everybody said you just couldn't spend that amount. The job just looked too big to the marketing people, the financial people, and the engineers. Everyone recognized it was a gigantic task that would mean all our resources were tied up in one project—and we knew that for a long time we wouldn't be getting anything out of it."[5]

In the light of the previous chapters of this book, it is interesting that the story does not report efforts at *numerical evaluation* of either the risk or payoff. There is no evidence of foreknowledge that approximately $5 billion would be spent on the program over a period of four years. But, of course, the decision of January 4 did not irrevocably commit anything like this sum. Had the next year's work proved clearly disappointing it would no doubt have been possible to retreat from the particulars of the commitment, and perhaps even from the general plan, at a cost, however huge, vastly less than the actual expenditure on the completed venture.

[4] *Fortune Magazine*, September 1966, p. 228.
[5] *Ibid.*, September 1966, p. 228.

Stage 4: Effectuation

The January 1962 decision was parent to a long line of development work. A number of engineering decisions were required. For example, monolithic circuits were abandoned in favor of a new sort of hybrid circuit. Late in 1962, it was determined that the new line would have operating systems by means of which computers schedule themselves without manual interruption.

A number of primarily managerial decisions were likewise part of the development work. In March, the company made a new departure when it determined to construct a plant to manufacture components; this involved the purchase of $100 million of automatic equipment. Late in 1963, it was determined to announce the whole 360 line at once, instead of sequentially as originally intended. Finally, in March, before announcing the model to the public, a "risk-assessment" session was held at which thirty top executives went over all of the details of the new program—patent protection, a policy on computer returns, and the company's ability to hire and train an enormous work force in the time allotted. Throughout March and April a sequence of pricing decisions took place. The production people figured a price at which a machine could be produced. The marketing men calculated the volume at the price, and at other prices, and then an additional "loop" was traversed to see whether, if the price were lower and the volume correspondingly higher, profit would increase. "We reviewed the competitive analysis for perhaps the fifteenth time. We had to take into consideration features that could be built in later with the turn of a screwdriver but that were not to be announced formally. We were pulling cost estimates out of a hat."[6]

On April 7, 1964, two-and-a-quarter years after the "we'll do it" decision, the new line was announced—six separate compatible computer machines, with their memories interchangeable so that a total of 90 different combinations would be available. Peripheral equipment provided 40 different input and output devices. Delivery would start in one year, April 1965.

Stage 5: Correction and Supplementation

Unforeseen events required some change in the IBM line. For example, in the fall of 1964, the Massachusetts Institute of Technology purchased one of the new General Electric 600 line of computers with time-sharing capability. Soon thereafter the Radio Corporation of America announced

[6] *Ibid.*, October 1966, p. 206.

that it would use the pure monolithic integrated circuitry in some models of its new Spectra 70 line. As a result of these and other challenges, IBM announced some additions to the 360 line in 1964 and 1965, which surrendered some of the insistence on full compatibility. The changes included addition of the model 390, a super computer-type designed to be competitive with Contral Data's 6800; the 344 model designed for special scientific purposes, the 367 model, a large time-sharing machine, and the 320 computer in the low end of the market.

By the fall of 1966, the new line offered nine central processes (six had been announced in 1964) and the supplementary devices had increased (from forty) to over seventy.

Recursive Cycles—Subsequent and Parallel

The printer's deadline for the October 1966 issue of *Fortune* may be thought of as the curtain on the first decision cycle. The sequence of decision cycles concerning the computer line included counterparts— some simultaneous and some subsequent—concerning programming and actual production. Programming appears to have produced mammoth difficulties—far larger than anticipated. The actual construction of the new line to meet delivery schedules strained every nerve in the company. Recursive cycles of related decisions will inevitably continue as long as the new line is on the market.

STAGING: DIFFERENCES AMONG PROBLEMS

The startling thing about the case history that has been told is that, although all the customary tenets of decision theory are relevant to it, they cover so little of what occurred. The case certainly involved a deliberative, ongoing, staged, recursive, administrative process in which all five stages were traversed.

Reflections on System/360

Stages 1 and 2 were important, yet one has the feeling that a very large part of the real stuff of problem recognition and the search among alternatives is invisible in the report. The reason may be that it took place inside of the top man's mind. Is it not reasonable to visualize a man, who senses in his blood the long history of the company, saying to himself, "the computer field is reaching the stage of maturation where many able competitors joust for the prize; what can Richard the Lion-Hearted do at his prime that others cannot do and will not be able to do for some time? The answer lies in taking advantage of the extraordinary mystique of the company, the vast marketing organization, the superb staff and the almost limitless financial resources" (over one-half of one percent of the gross national product of the U.S.A. was placed at risk). Whether or not any such musings ever occurred between dawn and breakfast in this case, they certainly often do. And if they antecede the right person's breakfast, the rest of "the decision process" can be simply a history of giving the idea substance and defending it against the status quo.

The second striking divergence in the IBM case was in stage 3—the calculation of expected payoffs and attendant risks. For one thing, many of the payoffs of the decision were peripheral to designing a product that would sell at a profit (a result described as "pretty breathtaking so far").[7] "The program has pushed IBM itself into feats of performance in manufacturing, technology, and communications that its own staff did not believe were possible when the project was undertaken."[8] IBM is now a major manufacturer rather than a company specializing in assembly, servicing, and marketing.[9] It is an integrated international manufacturing and sales company, whereas previously international subsidiaries specialized in marketing; there has been a fundamental shake-up in the major personnel of the company. A transatlantic line has been leased to facilitate constant communication between the United States and foreign offices; international communication reaches into the analyzing, correlating, and sorting of information and this may bypass the communications systems by common carriers.[10] It is, in general, a "more sophisticated and more thoroughly integrated organization than it was in 1962."[11]

Not only does the gross benefit, and its likelihood, appear to have eluded quantitative estimation but likewise the cost may have been impossible to prejudge. The account discusses calculations concerning programming and its large errors, but says little concerning the development and manufacture of the line itself. The actual cost of about $5 billion over four years appears to have represented on the order of two year's gross revenue from the general purpose computer program prior to the changeover, or about fourteen years' gross profits on that business. Of course this sum was put at risk incrementally as time passed and information accumulated. One view of the character of the gamble

[7] *Ibid.*, October 1966, pp. 211 and 212.
[8] *Ibid.*, October 1966, p. 212.
[9] *Ibid.*, September 1966, p. 121.
[10] *Ibid.*, October 1966, p. 142.
[11] *Ibid.*, October 1966, p. 212.

was perhaps adequately expressed by Bob Evans, the manager closest to the firing line. "We called this project 'You bet your company,'" but it was a "damn good risk, and a lot less risk than it would have been to do anything else, or to do nothing at all."[12]

The company may have been on the block as Evans said, but not in the usual sense. For the bet was really not *of* but *on* the company—on its power as an organization to bite hold of a gigantic conception and shape it slowly and strongly to its purpose. In any event, the moment of conventional "decision" seems to have been not much more than a day's meetingsmanship and a flamboyant gesture, "all right, we'll do it," by a man with a steel arm.

The IBM case, then, involved all five stages of the decision process, though much of the iceberg was submerged, particularly for stages 2 and 3. It was itself part of ongoing cycles of decision—there had been preceding, parallel, and subsequent decision processes, and there will be more to follow.

Comparison with Other Decision Problems

For other decision situations, the relative importance of the several stages differs widely. Take, for example, a question concerning whether state determination of poverty support standards should be replaced by some sort of national uniform minimum standards. Stage 1 is only partly deliberative. Rethinking of support programs has become an administrative and political necessity. Of course, questions concerning alternatives have not been insistently asked for a number of decades during which aid for dependent children has been in operation, and therefore to put the question is itself an important step. Insofar as the question is now asked, there is a clear departure from earlier practice, which for years has featured "disjointed incrementalism." The departure is less a function of a fresh decision to open things up than of a change in the external situation which has altered the nature of support problems and feasible ways of coping with them. Stage 2 has also developed as the result of diverse forces and interested parties, including scholars who have investigated one or more of the possible approaches (which range from better administration and state support of present programs, to federal jurisdiction via income tax or social insurance mechanisms). Stage 3 demands a careful and studied choice, well able to support sophisticated benefit-cost analysis in which the relative yields and costs (in terms of dollars and intangibles) of each alternate method of guaranteeing minimum living levels is weighed. Stage 4—the development and engi-

[12] *Ibid.*, September 1966, p. 118.

neering aspects—is also important. Adoption of a national standard would require extensive modifications of program administration. Finally, stage 5—auditing of the impact of the new devices—would be critical to the successful operation and improvement of the program. Of particular interest are the impacts that national standards might have on slowing migration to northern poverty areas in big cities or that guaranteed minimums might have on job seeking.

Consider now a case that is addressed to efficiency in running an office charged with administering welfare aid: Should interviewers' reports be greatly shortened? Although all the phases have some relevance, stages 2 and 3 are emphasized. Alternatives to simplifying reporting might include hiring a different sort of employee, introducing more automated equipment, streamlining methods, or even shifting the jurisdiction under which the work is conducted. Although these are not necessarily complete alternatives, they implicitly involve differences in the "system" in terms of which the problem is structured, such as that of a welfare department or of a larger human resources administration. Here again, stage 4—the technical problems of effectuating the programs—will necessarily influence not only the net results but the kinds of evaluations that are required to determine choice in stage 3. Stage 5 could very possibly feed back information that demanded reconsideration of the first cycle of decision.

An interesting rapid, recursive interplay between stages 2 to 5 characterizes the development of a microwave system by Bell Telephone Laboratories as described by Thomas Marschak.[13] Stage 1 was undertaken with the specific goal well defined—the development of a microwave relay system for the long-distance transmission of telephone conversations and signals having frequencies of about 6000 megacycles per second.

The specific alternatives considered consisted of a few of the innumerable ways of achieving capacity and other operational requirements within stipulated time and cost constraints (stage 2). Each selected "family" of methods is explored bit by bit. The exploration involved building experimental systems, so that back-and-forth recursive cycles through stages 2 through 5 took place as progressive development and narrowing of alternatives occurred. Some critical components may be "frozen" "after careful balancing of risks and gains." But a great deal of openness to change persisted over the six years that the project was evolving. "Until the final choice is made, flexibility is maintained. Com-

[13] "Strategy and Organization in a System Development Project," in *The Rate and Direction of Inventive Activity, op. cit.,* pp. 509–548.

mitments of personnel to specific tasks are made only for small periods, and it continues to be generally easy to drop one family [of techniques] or one way and shift effort to exploring another intensively."[14]

DOSRAP CHARACTERIZED

Decisions exemplified in the design of System/360 and the other cases briefly reviewed are highly various but share the fact that they are not in their entirety decisions in the sense discussed in the earlier parts of this book. *They are exercises in the perception of and solution of problems.*

More specifically, such a situation is basically *deliberative* in that thoughtful consideration and striving are presumably involved throughout. Moreover, since interpersonal strategies of a broadly political nature are often part of the process, "deliberative" must be broadly defined. The process is *ongoing* in that perception of and effort to solve one problem take time and, in addition, open up new problems; the continuousness often has a spatial as well as a time dimension. It is *staged* in that the process runs through the five stages identified. It is *recursive* since a five-stage sequence often starts over again, after a first go-round, in continuous cycles related to yet different from the first. It encompasses deliberative aspects of *administrative* activities closely intermeshed with most other aspects of administration. It will be handy to impound these adjectives in an acronym, DOSRAP, referring to the deliberative-administrative process in its full sense.

Needless to say, there is greater freedom in how DOSRAP can be conducted than is present in its third stage alone—decision among predelineated acts. Indeed, the process as a whole is open at its beginning, middle, and end. Whether a problem is perceived, recognized, and tackled is elective. How solutions are conceived and structured is subject to all sorts of determinations, including how much is undertaken in each decision stage, the length and timing of each cycle, the amount of information to be used or generated, and the sorts and amounts of inputs to be committed to the decision process. Finally, the termination of the deliberative sequence is also partially elective.

Obviously, the problems resulting from uncertainty that were reviewed in earlier chapters are vastly intensified when decision processes are viewed as a whole. To what extent is this difference in the degree of uncertainty also a difference in kind, and what are the implications concerning how to reduce the cost of uncertainty?

[14] *Ibid.*, p. 547

CHAPTER 10

The Possibility Shortfall

The whole deliberative process, DOSRAP, as well as decision proper, is aided by efforts to minimize the costs of uncertainty. For this purpose, however, the costs require clarification.

They can be defined as the difference between two time-discounted streams of expected net utility—one consisting of net benefits expected to result from some actual course of action, and the other consisting of net benefits resulting from the optimal course that the decision could take. For choice among predelineated acts, the instruction to minimize this cost means to choose the act having the highest time-discounted, expected net utility after all appropriate uncertainty discounts have been applied. The chosen act can be better than alternatives because the costs of uncertainty are lower, the utility higher, or both.

COSTS OF UNCERTAINTY AND THE POSSIBILITY VECTOR

For the ongoing deliberative situation, a strategy rather than an act is chosen. This must be the case, since the process as a whole is compound and there are many junctures at which the course of deliberations can branch and follow one road rather than another. In this process, the costs of uncertainty can be reduced in one or both of two ways: (1) reducing the uncertainty associated with the consequences of what is undertaken by reducing the *knowledge gap;* (2) causing what is undertaken to move toward the best possible strategy by reducing the *possibility shortfall.*

Reducing the possibility shortfall has uneven importance in various decision situations. For some, alternatives are necessarily standard and obvious and must be pursued in a routine fashion whereas for others, constraints of personnel, politics, or money may provide little leeway. However, in many situations there is a genuine potential to raise the sights on what is attempted.

The first approach, reducing the uncertainty discount associated with the information gap, has already been analyzed for decision proper. This lays groundwork for normative procedures applied to DOSRAP which are reexamined in the next chapter.

The second approach, reducing the possibility shortfall, requires avoiding the selection of acts for which utility is unnecessarily low. We have seen that inherent conservative biases tend to produce this sort of malselection. Here the emphasis is positive: What is the best possible strategy which theoretically might be undertaken, and how close to this ceiling is a collective able and willing to aim?

Possibility, in the context of an achievement to be sought, is a vector—it has direction and force, but cannot be even theoretically specified as a fixed point. What is possible is itself a function of how decisions are made, for, at a very general level, decision and possibility have a two-way association: *how decisions are made influences what is possible; what is deemed possible influences how decisions are made.* Jointly, the two-way relationship conditions how decisions *should* be made.

THE PROCLIVITY TO ADVANCE

Although no one can say what is possible, it seems clear that the *processes* whereby possibility may be invaded can be strengthened or weakened. They are weakened by traditionalism, diffidence, fear, and laziness. They are strengthened by imagination, confidence, commitment, energy, and, cumulatively, by the capacity and desire to learn.

A Personality Type

The characteristics that I have just listed are those commonly ascribed to Schumpeter's "entrepreneur," the phenomenon who is often credited with the major responsibility for rates of economic growth. More recently, Harvey Leibenstein has cited some of these forward-moving characteristics as "N-entrepreneurship" ("new type") in contrast to "routine entrepreneurship." Distinguishing features include a propensity to develop and evaluate new economic opportunities, to seek new information to provide leadership and risk bearing.[1] Entrepreneurial histories abound in resplendent examples of such individuals—individuals who appear to seek tensions and change, and whose behavior therefore demands explanation in developmental terms.

Foundations of developmental psychology are laid in the notion of built-in energy and a spontaneous need to change in a manner which fulfills and amplifies the individual. Gordon Allport identifies such "growth motives," in contrast to the familiar "deficit motives" which seek equilibrium. Such "Propriate striving confers unity upon personality, but it is never the unity of fulfillment, or repose, or of relieved tension. . . . its goals are, strictly speaking, unattainable."[2]

Altogether, this group of forward-moving characteristics—imagination, confidence, curiosity and interest in change, enterprise, commitment, creativity—can be called the *proclivity to advance*. Judgment should also be listed; though it is necessary to constructive behavior of any sort, it is particularly essential in connection with innovative behavior. "Proclivity" is meant to suggest that people do not simply either have these characteristics or not have them, but tend to possess and utilize them to different degrees.

The personality traits that constitute the proclivity to advance are action-oriented. Accordingly, their possession by individuals, singly and collectively, will result in *advancive behavior*, which might be manifest in anything people do, including their conduct of deliberative processes.

The proclivity to advance affects decision at any or all levels—it affects aspirations, the delineation of goals or values, and the development of means that can be enlisted. These levels can reinforce one another via the two-way causal association of means-end linkages. They reinforce one another from stage to stage of a decision process: the acceptance of an exciting problem invites comprehensive and imaginative search for ways to solve it and attention (in the light of well-devel-

[1] Harvey Leibenstein, "Entrepreneurship and Development," *American Economic Review, Papers and Proceedings*, May 1968, pp. 73–74.

[2] Gordon W. Allport, *Becoming: Basic Considerations for a Psychology of Personality*, Yale University Press, New Haven, 1955, pp. 66–68. The basic point of view has been developed by Charlotte Buhler, "Theoretical Observations about Life's Basic Tendencies," *American Journal of Psychotherapy*, Vol. 13, 1959, pp. 561–581.

oped information) to a forward-looking choice among alternatives. The snowball can roll on: a new cycle picks up where the old one stopped.

"The new management" as described by Rensis Likert, in a book for which he received three awards, discusses motivation in all its aspects. While including the "security motive" and "economic motive," it emphasizes "the motive of satisfying curiosity, creativity and the desire for new experience," and the "ego motives." The last include ". . . the desire for growth and significant achievement in terms of one's own values and goals, i.e., self-fulfillment, as well as the desire for status, recognition, approval, acceptance, and power and the desire to undertake significant and important tasks."[3]

Chris Argyris, in a study of motivation in the top management of a number of American corporations, focuses on the bearing on decision of the advancive characteristics, particularly those of commitment and the willingness to take chances. He arrives at the conclusion that "groups are valuable when they can maximize the unique contributions of each individual. Moreover, as each individual's contribution is enhanced his commitment to the resulting decision is increased and internalized." He felt, however, that the conditions which he found to prevail "rewarded the mediocre men but discouraged first-class executives."[4]

In short, there is a growing appreciation in the field of management of the value to the organization of creativity, motivation, commitment, and the willingness to take risks; accordingly, attention turns to how these characteristics can be identified and supported in the individuals who participate in the decision structure and other parts of business organizations. Though it may well be that only God can make a "N-entrepreneur," the arts of mangement can perhaps help the saplings grow.

Distribution in Culture

Although in any community or culture there must always be some individuals whose personality is characterized by a strong proclivity to advance, in some communities such individuals must, it would seem, be more numerous than in others. Communities in which advancive attitudes are common or increasing have been judged by a number of students to be those in which economic development tended to be high

---

[3] Rensis Likert, *New Patterns of Management*, McGraw-Hill Book Company, New York, 1961 (quotation from p. 98).

[4] Chris Argyris, "How Tomorrow's Executives will Make Decisions," *Think*, November-December 1967, pp. 118 and 120 (italics omitted).

or increasing. There are, for example, pieces of such linkages in Rostow's notion of "stages of development."[5] There are specific efforts to show an association between high rates of development and high rates of "need achievement" in the work of McClelland.[6] Everett Hagen suggests that development takes place under the influence of the "innovative personality" which, in turn, tends to appear where a particular sort of home environment and source of status and respect are found.[7]

One very interesting, entirely empirical link between advancive characteristics and development was forged in the course of statistical examination of how development potential could be identified. Irma Adelman and Cynthia Morris in an analysis of about thirty characteristics of the socioeconomic system, found that four variables jointly accounted for 97 percent of the overall variance in improvement in economic development in the seventy-three countries studied. The most important of the four was "the degree of modernization of outlook," and a second member

---

[5] Harvey Leibenstein has suggested that improved motivation increases efficiency. He moves from the N-entrepreneur to X-efficiency, one element of which corrects for the fact that "neither individuals nor firms work as hard, nor do they search for information as effectively, as they could" (intrafirm efficiency); motivations can also be boosted from outside one's self or one's organization ("external motivational efficiency"). Harvey Leibenstein, "Allocative Efficiency versus X-Efficiency," *American Economic Review,* June 1966, p. 407.

Walt W. Rostow pictures economic development as influenced by the motives, or what he calls "propensities," of people. He lists the relevant propensities: to develop fundamental science (physical and social), to apply science to economic ends, to accept innovation, to seek material advance, to consume, and to have children. *The Process of Economic Growth,* Oxford University Press, Toronto, Canada, 1960, p. 11, and *The Stages of Economic Growth, A Non-Communist Manifesto,* Cambridge University Press, Cambridge, England, 1961.

[6] McClelland attempts to frame ideas in a fashion in which they are subject to empirical tests. The motive of "need achievement" was defined by placing a group of young men in a situation which was believed to challenge them; he then studied the motives thereby aroused. To do so they were questioned about their fantasies. "There may be cultural differences, but the data to date point to major similarities—inducing achievement motivation increases in all types of subjects thoughts of doing well with respect to some standard of good performance, of being blocked in the attempt to achieve, of trying various means of achieving, and of reacting with joy or sadness to the result of one's efforts" (p. 43). Motives which stimulate such fantasies are intertwined with what I have called the proclivity to advance. Since McClelland found typical patterns of reaction which tended to cross cultural lines, it seems reasonable to describe his intercultural findings as an increased frequency of proclivities for need achievement (or alternatively for the proclivity to advance) in the "achieving societies." David C. McClelland, *The Achieving Society,* D. Van Nostrand Company, Inc., New York, 1961.

[7] Everett E. Hagen, *On the Theory of Social Change,* Dorsey Press, Homewood, Ill., 1962.

of the group of four was "leadership commitment to development." This is a striking indication of the relevance of advancive traits to cultural change.[8]

We have been speaking of a concentration of a group of personality traits in some individuals and a concentration of such individuals in some cultures. How an individual behaves depends, of course, on all sorts of things other than his personality. Indeed the *content*, in terms of his actual behavior which may be thought of as associated with the proclivity to advance is a function of his culture. Though this applies to almost every gesture, it seems to be especially pervasive and important in connection with decision processes.

THE "PRINCIPLE OF CIRCULAR AND CUMULATIVE CAUSATION"

The relationship between the proclivity to advance, advancive behavior, and the environment is easily overlooked because each man's roots lie so deep in his culture that he tends to be unaware of them.[9] Perhaps

[8] The four variables chosen by the procedures were improvement in effectiveness of financial institutions (F), rate of improvement of agricultural productivity (A), leadership commitment to development (L), and degree of modernization of outlook (M). The last was "a composite measure of the degree of modernization of outlook of educated urban groups and the extent to which programs of political and economic modernization have gained the support of both rural and urban populations" (p. 267). The statement in the text refers to the normalized form of the equation. $D_2^1 = 95.F + 139.M + 88L + 70A$ (p. 277). Irma Adelman and Cynthia Taft Morris, "Performance Criteria for Evaluating Economic Developmental Potential: An Operational Approach," *Quarterly Journal of Economics*, Vol. LXXXII, No. 2, May 1968, pp. 260–280.

The authors have in a later article tried to examine the relationship among variables. It is summarized in a model (Figure 1) which shows the directional interactions of 18 variables only 3 of which are exogenous. The determinations are based on stepwise regression analysis of the data for 74 countries. "An Econometric Model of Socio-Economic and Political Change in Underdeveloped Countries," *American Economic Review*, December 1968, p. 1202.

[9] A background for this line of thought, and development of it, is focused in the concept of "the image" as presented by Kenneth E. Boulding. The image is built up as a result of all the past experience of the possessor of the image. It consists of subjective knowledge of fact and value which comes from within and without, past and present. The image is changed by messages. *"The meaning of a message is the change which it produces in the image."* And a specific message can change it a lot or not at all. If it does change the image, the message can add to it, reorganize it, and, important in Boulding's scheme, make it clearer and more probable. A message changes the image, it alters behavior: ". . . behavior

the essence of the relationship can be seen best where environment may seem unimportant—in connection with invention. A. P. Usher's fascinating studies of the process of mechanical invention feature the critical influence of environment and learning. On the one hand, environment calls forth innovation: "all inventive accomplishment involves some special setting of the stage." The setting helps to reveal a gap that the innovator feels himself pushed to bridge. On the other hand, the environment, and its complement of available information about the past and present, provide the raw materials for extending the possibility vector: "Invention finds its distinctive feature in the constructive assimilation of pre-existing elements into new syntheses, new patterns, or new configurations of behavior."[10]

Invention, in other words, is influenced by the environment however much new it adds; it also influences the environment by providing a further item upon which to build. Involved is what Gunnar Myrdal has named "the principle of circular and cumulative causation."[11]

Social Learning

Edgar Dunn calls it "social learning" and explores it as a very general attribute of social processes, and indeed biological processes as well. His analysis provides a broad perspective for the argument of this chapter and I was most fortunate to have been able to read it in typescript. Social learning, Dunn demonstrates in the course of a most inventive and penetrating analysis, is pervasive in socioeconomic processes. It is generally under-understood and underemphasized in disciplines that define "scientific knowledge" primarily in terms of "machine systems." A learning system contrasts with a machine system because, among other things, it has the capacity "to reprogram itself through the action of internal sources of new behavioral ideas, *transformation motives* and *transformation behavior*."[12]

---

depends on the image." An adequate theory of behavior implies deeper understanding of ". . . the growth of images, both private and public, in individuals, in organizations, in society at large . . . ." Kenneth E. Boulding, *The Image: Knowledge in Life and Society*, University of Michigan Press, Ann Arbor, Mich., 1961 (copyright 1956) (quotations from pp. 6–18).

[10] Abbott Payson Usher, *History of Mechanical Invention*, rev. ed., Beacon Press, Boston, 1959 (quotations from pp. 18 and 11, respectively).

[11] Gunnar Myrdal, *Rich Lands and Poor, The Road to World Prosperity*, Harper & Row Publishers, New York, 1957.

[12] Edgar S. Dunn, Jr., *Economic and Social Development: A Process of Social Learning*, Published for Resources for the Future by Johns Hopkins Press, Baltimore, 1971, p. 21.

Certainly this description seems to fit the on-going deliberative process. Indeed, it is amusing to note how much more DOSRAP seems to have in common with the first compared with the second of the following quotations: "Living matter is dynamic, self-reproductive, and expansible. It is constantly seeking to embody itself in organic forms appropriate to the context of conditions in the external world."[13] Compare this with Bell's description "intelligent machines:" "A computer can always be programmed to carry out any productive process in which each step follows logically and unambiguously from previous results, and also to carry out an inductive process which can be expressed as a systematic extrapolation."[14] Even if one emphasizes the capacity of a computer to "learn" and reprogram itself (on the basis of some external criteria yielded by a broader program), typical deliberative processes do not resemble machine systems but comprehend inherent indeterminacy: "The essential step in innovation is to break away from the logically determined sequence or to jump over a missing step in the logical sequence and yet continue in a useful direction. . . ."[15]

Consider the many ways in which DOSRAP may multiply the impact of advancive behavior by the interaction of personal and social learning. We have noted how environments interact with personal characteristics in a geometry of cause and effect. There can also be a snowball effect whereby advancive behavior grows from step to step and among cycles of a particular decision process simply because of the interdependence of the steps. An analogous multiplier effect can amplify the advancive output of a decision collective and of organizations: two creative and committed people will tend to have more than double the impact of one such person on the course of DOSRAP; their impact will be far greater in an organization that invites creativity and commitment than in one that does not.

Ecological Interplay

The argument of the chapter thus far proposes that movement along the possibility vector is sensitive to the personality characteristics of individuals (both psychological and cultural components of these characteristics) and their distribution with respect to a collective, an organization, a culture. It is sensitive to the totality of influences and processes

[13] Amos H. Hawley, *Human Ecology, A Theory of Community Structure,* Ronald Press, New York, 1950, p. 31.

[14] D. A. Bell, *Intelligent Machines, An Introduction to Cybernatics,* Blaisdell Publishing Company, New York, 1962, p. 61.

[15] *Ibid.,* p. 67.

which, cumulatively, determine the environment. The interactive process, then, is cumulative in space and time.

It is important to appreciate the fact of this complex interaction. It would be still more desirable to be able to say something more specific about the dynamics of the process. Yet there seems to be few empirical materials and little analysis on which to build.

Some *conceptual* building blocks can be named: the frequency distribution of individuals with respect to a "proclivity to advance" (a proclivity rating which recognizes both their innate characteristics and the realities of particular decision situations); an objective set of relevant conditions; a cultural factor that influences the competitive key and attitudes toward changes; expectations about consequences. Actions of one decision unit, based on expectations, will influence the objective set of relevant conditions which enter into the expectations of other units (or subsequently of the same unit). The influence changes the external condition; or the influence may also be that of lessened uncertainty about previous expectations. The aggregate response will be greater as the changed situation becomes capable of influencing expectations and behavior of the many units (units located toward the center of a humped frequency distribution) having a more or less average proclivity to advance, than when it is only capable of activating the few (located toward one wing of the distribution) with an exceptionally high proclivity.

I have described a decision process which reflects an "interaction between living organisms and their environment"—an ecological process.[16] If these are in fact building blocks appropriate to the study of circular and cumulative processes, aggregate change is not likely to be well characterized by straight-line projections. Indeed, the growth histories of individual industries, or patterns whereby inventions are put to use, have been found to be more nearly S-shaped.[17]

[16] The definition of "ecology" in *Webster's Third International Dictionary.*

[17] More specifically the curves which have been fitted include the log-normal, logarithmic parabola and logistic curves. For mention of some of the empirical work see p. 51, note 13 in R. P. Mack, "Ecological Processes in Economic Change: Models, Measurement and Meaning," *American Economic Review, Papers and Proceedings,* May 1968, pp. 40–54. The article discusses ecological processes involved in inventory fluctuation and trends in education. A detailed study of why the interactive model is required to explain fluctuations in inventories appears in R. P. Mack, *Information, Expectations, and Inventory Fluctuation: A Study of Materials Stocks on Hand and on Order,* Chapter 13, Columbia University Press, New York, 1967. It is there noted that what seems to be called for is ". . . something more than the now familiar notion of analysis with a feedback from the environment. The character of the feedback is critical: it is one for which coefficients of reac-

Footnote continues on page 158.

A word of warning: I have spoken of cumulative processes as if they were always enlarging on *desirable advances*, and of course they are not. One could, for example, trace how traditional, hierarchical, and fearful attitudes spiral through decision processes, often gaining voltage and amperage as they go; circling also in wider rings as a result of ecological interplay with the environment. This is, in a sense, the negative side of the positive picture drawn here.

I have also spoken of progress along a possibility vector as if such progress was always a good thing. That this is not necessarily the case is a fact of which this generation is begrudgingly becoming aware. But needless to say, this type of normative issue cannot be considered here. One thing is clear: it puts a premium on wisdom and judgment.

ADVANCIVE BEHAVIOR AND ECONOMICS

In the past several pages I have been developing a hypothesis about elements that tend to cause deliberative behavior to push outward along the possibility vector. The personality traits that constitute the proclivity to advance will be possessed by some adults more than others and in some cultures more liberally than in others. Learning, the strong desire for which is a prime member of the advancive group of characteristics, involves an interplay among individuals and between individuals and the environment. The proclivity tends to produce behavior in deliberative decision processes which enhances the productivity of enterprises. This behavior, amplified by ecological interplay, enters the stream of history and provides the basis for further learning. By ratchet and thrust, then, productive activity is jacked outward along the possibility vector.

The analysis has implications about the normative conduct of economic decisions. But these in turn call into question some fundamental propositions in economics.

Nonscarce Resources

Other things the same, advancive behavior, exercised with good judgment, would tend to reduce the possibility shortfall and thereby reduce the cost of uncertainty. We have been speaking, in effect, of inputs

---

tion . . . themselves change. As far as I know, the aggregate implications of this sort of process have not been explored. Interestingly enough, the closest thing to it then has come to my attention is in the field of epidemiology—the Reed-Frost model" (p. 296; and footnote 23).

into a deliberative process. Theoretically these inputs could raise the *gross* value of the output of decision strategy and yet, because of high costs, fail to raise the *net* value. This is not likely to occur, however, for the simple reason that the inputs in question tend to be poorly priced by market mechanisms; indeed, they are often virtually free goods.

They are often not, in other words, scarce resources in the economist's sense. Their price is not set by "the principle governing the allocation of scarce means among competing ends when the objective is to maximize the attainment of the ends."[18] Creative personnel may well demand a higher price from a single enterprise, but at the present time, such capabilities are often not paid for because they are not appreciated.

But if they are not appreciated, they are not called forth, and this is another way in which they do not conform to the economist's notion of scarce resources. They have little "opportunity cost." If they are not used in one way, this does not free them for use in another way. The potential input simply continues to lie snug in the ground like unsurveyed ore.

Even for the economy as a whole, at a given time, there is not a fixed amount of innovative capacity, ambition, dedication, and the like. There must certainly be latent capacities which may be elicited by encouragement, need, praise or purchase. In this way the "resource" is, in a very real sense, created; it is mined. In addition, it can grow as a result of interactive cumulative processes.

Clearly these are not the characteristics of scarce resources in the economist's sense. Indeed, even for conventional resources there appears to be some question as to the applicability of classic scarcity notions.[19]

Equilibrium Tendencies and Chance

In economics the concept of an equilibrium path has a double function. It is a powerful conceptual tool for linking short-term and long-term

[18] George Stigler, *The Theory of Price*, Macmillan and Company, New York, 1946, p. 12.

[19] Harold Barnett and Chandler Morse found that the increasingly scarce resources of basic materials that economic theory has seemed to imply simply did not show up in the various tests they devised in the course of an empirical study of trends in the prices and use of resources. They concluded that, as viewed from the 20th century, "the process of growth . . . generates antidotes to a general increase of resource scarcity" (p. 240). The authors proposed a reformulation of the Ricardian hypothesis. "The 20th century's discovery of the uniformity of energy and matter has increased the possibilities of substitution to an unimaginable degree, and placed at man's disposal an indefinitely large number of alternatives from which to choose" (p. 244). Harold J. Barnett and Chandler Morse, *Scarcity and Growth: The Economics of Natural Resources Availability*, The Johns Hopkins Press, Baltimore, 1963.

analysis. It is also a normative concept which helps to determine not only what does, but also what should, happen. Both functions are performed under a set of restrictive assumptions regarding "rationality," economic structure, and information. The fact that actuality diverges from the assumptions (even when they are adjusted to envisage moving equilibria) means that the system can only approximate its ordained path. This limits, but does not destroy, the usefulness of the approach.

However, the line of thinking that has been set forth here introduces more fundamental difficulties: it suggests that an equilibrium path is theoretically (as well as actually) impossible. Further, it questions whether it would be desirable in any event:

First, the deep and pervasive uncertainty that permeates DOSRAP dilutes the notion of optimizing. Yet an optimizing tendency of some sort is essential to generating an equilibrium course.

Second, advancive inputs are, as we have just noted, poorly priced and thus do not properly belong within the constraints of the equilibrium system. Though they have some bearing on the shifts in moving equilibria, the laws which govern the shifts that they impose are not contained in equilibrium analysis, and certainly not in its normative implications.[20]

Third, the quantitative and qualitative uncertainties inherent in any decision situation, are magnified by social learning, and by ecological interplay between decision agents and the environment. Processes of these types, growing, as they may, according to factorial principles, resist interpretation in terms of equilibrium tendencies.[21]

[20] Advancive inputs can be thought of as agents causing changes in the "production function." And such changes can be covered in "dynamic" equilibrium models. The difficulty is that the nature of these shifts must be accepted on the basis of projections of past trends, or whatever. There is no internal criterion for optimizing the critical factors such as income distribution, labor versus leisure, war versus peace, or the extent and even directions of scientific progress.

Yet even ignoring these noneconomic elements, the part of the total trend in economic well-being (defined in terms simply of real national income) accounted for by more or less advancive inputs is huge. For example, Solow found that in the United States, 1909–1949, 87.5 percent of the increase in output per man hour was due to qualitative improvement in labor and capital; increase in capital accounted for the other 12.5 percent. Robert M. Solow, "Technical Change and the Aggregate Production Function," *Review of Economics and Statistics,* August 1957, p. 320.

[21] Assume that each new "component" of aggregate production, whether a new product, an industry, an innovation or whatever, tends to exhibit a sigmoidal principle of growth, other things the same. The pattern of aggregate economic growth would then depend on changes, period by period, in the number (and size) of components in each phase of their growth curves. A constant rate of growth for the economy

Fourth, behavior, in the light of these manifold uncertainties, is subject to partially elective evolution. Such elective elements are external to the forces compounded in equilibrium tendencies. Indeed, the process of social learning is subject to planning of a type yet to be delineated.

Finally, "mutations" can occur in the garb of pure chance in a society of large decision making units. Any decision can have a strong element of chance: the settlement of a long-standing feud among company directors which turns investment policy in one direction rather than another, a contract that was missed or won by a hair, the murder of a leader, a revolution just avoided or just carried off, or a four-to-five Supreme Court decision. Such events themselves, triggered by chance's forefinger, can turn out to be of large import for those immediately involved. However, when decision makers are small and competitive, the collective impact of such chance events may cancel out. But two factors can amplify the impact of random occurrences. First, many decision makers are huge corporations or governments, committing sizable hunks of resources in one episode. Second, the zigzag of ecological interaction on expectations, actions, and subsequent expectations will tend to magnify the influence of one chancy episode in the affairs of a government or "bellwether" firm. Let me give an example.

Would the fantastic development of office buildings in central New York City after World War II—a development that anyone would have been derided for predicting in 1940—have occurred had not Lever Brothers created a huge international central office in a building of exciting design shortly after the war? Certainly this step could not have failed to influence other companies.[22] The effect would cumulate geometrically. Yet whether the Lever Brothers building was located in New York or Boston may have hung on the chancy outcome of a battle of interests

---

as a whole could result in one of two ways: (1) The chances that the changes in the number of industries (weighted by size) in slow phases of growth were, over the years, accompanied by compensating changes in the number in a rapid phase. (2) A basic tendency for overcompensation in the latter terms, which was kept in check by some overall resource scarcity having a linear growth trend; man hours of work suggests itself as a candidate for the job.

It is difficult for me to see by what logic a time course of this sort could be thought of as having normative equilibrium qualities, even if one were to ignore the matter of noneconomic opportunity costs of economic progress.

[22] If Lever Brothers influenced two important new installations these in turn might influence four more and, continuing the assumption of a factor of two, these might influence eight more. Needless to say, there is no reason to predict a factor of two or indeed a constant factor of any size. For example, it would be quite possible that as the central office identity for the area developed, the influence of each building could shift upward.

among board members.[23] In the context of New York's history, what may be thought of as a random occurrence may have had an important influence on the development of the city.

SUMMARY

This chapter has explored one way in which the cost of uncertainty may be reduced—that of increasing the expected utility of the policy selected by reducing the possibility shortfall. Since there is no ceiling to benefits that might conceivably be achieved, the possibility shortfall— the difference between some hypothetical optimum and a course which is selected—can be reduced but not eliminated.

The potential of constraining the cost of uncertainty by reducing the possibility shortfall is emphasized when decision proper is placed in the broader context of the deliberative, ongoing, staged, recursive, ad- ministrative process (DOSRAP). Throughout its course this process is open to cognitive and motivational variables.

Promising policies relating to goals as well as means stretch outward in an endless sequence along what may be thought of as a possibility vector. Progress along this vector is accelerated by judicious advancive behavior.

Such behavior tends to be associated with personality characteristics and attitudes that include imagination, enterprise, confidence, restless curiosity, creativity, and commitment, as well as judgment.

It has also a strong cultural component with respect to a frequency distribution of these personality types, the content of advancive attitudes, and the actions towards which they may lead. The cultural component grows as the result of a circular and cumulative process of social learning in which there is intimate interaction between the particular situation and its environment—a societal counterpart of ecological interplay. Hitched to chance outcomes for large decision makers, these processes can imply a genuine indeterminacy in future developments. On the other hand there are all sorts of opportunities to raise the sights in deliberative processes (both with respect to goals and to ways to pursue them) by the exercise of good judgment.

We are speaking, in effect, of a selected group of inputs into delibera- tive situations. Far from being very costly, such inputs tend to be errati-

---

[23] The decision was itself, no doubt, significantly influenced by the elimination of slaughter houses along the East River and the creation of the United Nations complex.

cally priced, typically underpriced. Indeed, they are often not "scarce" at all, since they can be called into being by the demand for them.

But uncertainty about consequences, and their desirability, particularly for decisions with a long time reference, is increased by the very character of the learning processes that take place, and the contributions of inputs which conform only intermittently to efficient allocative principles. In consequence, the backbone of economic analysis, long-term equilibrium tendencies, turns to gristle, thereby increasing the difficulty of prediction.

At the same time, a direction of change once under way may grow more surely and rapidly. Part of the dynamics of the interactive cumulative learning process itself may be progressive reduction in uncertainty.

We are left, then, with "ashes and sparks." In the context of the full deliberative process, prophecy grows gray with uncertainty. Advancive behavior, on the other hand, magnified through societal learning, can lead to achievement capable of reducing the net cost of uncertainty. Obviously these thoughts affect how DOSRAP should be conducted.

They also offer food for thought of a more elementary sort: within the inner kernel of deliberative processes we find selective perception and developmental aspirations; we find circular and cumulative causation and social learning having the capacity to produce and utilize creative inputs; we find nonscarce resources; and we find inherent disequilibrium tendencies. If such are the *theoretical* (as well as circumstantial) stuff of many economic decisions, how relevant is analysis rooted in the notion of "rational" man optimizing scarce resources along equilibrium paths?

CHAPTER 11

Intendedly Rational Conduct of Deliberative Processes

The deliberative, ongoing, staged, recursive, administrative process (DOSRAP), then, is partly cognitive and partly behavioral. Problems must be perceived before efforts to solve them begin. Such efforts form an interrelated structure of aspirations, knowledge, and expectations about outcomes and their values. They concern strategies to deal with people, things, and information. They engage interrelated and dynamic forces causing multidirectional causality to build upon itself within and among decision situations. How can such a process be structured in the light of the uncertainty which permeates it?

THE GENERAL APPROACH

Coping with such problems is in part a matter of optimizing (under uncertainty) the output of a given set of resources. This is the standard issue of efficient allocation. Since perfect knowledge, properly utilized, implies perfect allocation of resources, minimizing the knowledge gap is crucial. Opportunities to do so arise throughout the five-stage decision cycle, not merely in stage 3, decision proper. However, there is the further problem of reducing the possibility shortfall by bringing the level of what is attempted closer to what is ideally possible.

Quasi-Optimizing and the Cost of Uncertainty

The notion of optimizing is not well adapted to this total process. Just what point may be "optimal" in tapping advancive potential cannot be stipulated for many reasons. To review: costs can often be only most inadequately determined and pricing mechanisms function poorly or not at all. Expected utility cannot be well stipulated, and values and knowledge of reality shift as a result of the learning embodied within and among decision situations; perception is selective and aspirations developmental. In addition to the heightened uncertainty which advancive behavior generates, the future has elements of genuine indeterminacy; possibility is open-ended; also, pure chance as it affects large decision makers can have a multiplicative influence on the future.

Moreover, in connection with efforts to reduce both possibility shortfall and the knowledge gap, there are the many familiar difficulties of a practical sort, such as inadequate information, constrained response, conflicting purposes within the decision collective, and the necessarily partial and unstable character of resolution of these conflicts.

Accordingly, a slack word—quasi-optimizing—is more suitable to refer to the goal of decision processes. It is intended to cover the pursuit of allocative efficiency as well as the judicious selection (and sometimes the virtual creation) of means and even purposes to be efficient with and about. *A quasi-optimal solution must have net expected consequences which are preferred to those of some other known solution. But the preference is never absolute* in the sense that the net expected consequence of some other possible solution might not be still more desirable.

A quasi-optimal solution becomes an optimal one when the best possible solution is or can be known, and this is often the case for well-structured problems constrained to choice proper. An optimizing solution can also be designed for subcategories of a problem; this constitutes suboptimizing as usually defined. The notion of optimizing remains a valuable analytic tool. Statistical decision theory, for example, underlies and contributes to the solution of even the most poorly structured decisions and ongoing deliberations of all sorts. Aspects of any problem can be lifted out of their real-world context and analyzed in an imposed optimizing framework. This can throw a great deal of light on the impact of selected elements in a total situation under the assumption of "other things the same." But of course *the problem must be returned to its wider setting before policy conclusions can be drawn.* The customary ceremonial bow to "the other things which may in fact not be the same" is not enough, particularly when, as is so often the case in learning situations, changes in the impounded "other things" are in fact linked to changes in the analyzed variables.

In order to structure normative approaches to DOSRAP, conceived in these quasi-optimal terms, the notion of minimizing the cost of uncertainty is useful here as for decision proper. But note that "minimize" takes on a more active meaning than for choice among predelineated alternatives. The dictionary meaning—reduce to a "minimum" which is the least of a set of numbers—now implies *finding a set containing a reasonable "minimum"* as a member. Again, by focusing optimizing (inversely) on the cost of uncertainty it recognizes aspiration levels appropriate to the situation.

For the five-stage process, expectations must of course refer to the result of a strategy of deliberative behavior as a whole. As explained at the start of the previous chapter, the cost of uncertainty is the difference between two time- and uncertainty-discounted streams of expected net utilities: (1) the expected value of some actual course of behavior, and (2) that which might be expected for some best possible course. Thus the difference, the cost of uncertainty, may be reduced, other things the same, if uncertainty (and thereby the discount) is reduced, if the utility of the actual course is increased, or both.[1] If uncertainty increases as utility increases, or vice versa, whether the cost of uncertainty

---

[1] The statement applies, of course, to probability-weighted evaluated consequences. For example, the second act in the following illustration would be thought of as more risky but aiming at a higher utility than the first. It would have a lower cost of uncertainty and be preferred to the first if the probabilities were judged to be as shown in the H columns but not as given in the L columns.

	Act I			Act II				
	Payoff	Proba-bility	Expected Value	Payoff	Proba-bility L	Expected Value L	Proba-bility H	Expected Value H
Event:								
1	20	.1	2	10	.5	5	.3	3
2	50	.4	20	50	.4	50	.4	20
3	100	.5	50	200	.1	20	.3	60
			72			45		83

increases or decreases depends on whether the positive or negative impacts are larger (that is, whether the larger expected utility, multiplied by the smaller probability coefficient, is larger than the smaller expected utility, multiplied by the larger probability coefficient).

The purpose of deliberative behavior is to contrive to keep the net cost as low as possible by whatever means are available. Each deliberative situation needs to be realistically and imaginatively examined from a background knowledge of the wide array of ways in which the cost of uncertainty can be reduced. Chapter 13 consists of a checklist of some fifty or more ways.

However, before such a shotgun approach can be fully useful there is work to be done with a rifle. Accordingly, this and the following chapter aims to develop criteria which suggest the "decision rules"—the basic deliberative strategy—appropriate to a given decision situation and provide some broad principles for their application.

Six Structural Attributes

Here as for decision proper it is essential to devise a strategy geared to the distinctive characteristics of the particular problem. To identify these characteristics, recourse to a structural attributes profile is a useful point of departure. Chapter 6 classified decisions for which alternatives had been predelineated in a fashion that suggested the decision procedures which were appropriate. Five structural attributes seemed to provide a useful basis of classification. The same five attributes are likewise applicable to the ongoing deliberative process and are here repeated; one further attribute is added:

1. *Homogeneity*. Homogeneity versus divergence, dispersion, or lack of focus, can apply to time (duration of the decision process), place (geographic spread of the collective), and constitution of the decision agent (complexity of the intrapersonal and interpersonal collectivity). Divergence exacerbates the problem of analyzing and achieving agreement about both reality and goals.

2. *Rational capacity*. Opportunity for highly rational behavior on the part of the collective contrasts with situations likely to make unrealistic demands on capacities to retain and process information and with situations likely to involve selective perception and developmental aspirations.

These two attributes refer, in effect, to the intrapersonal and intracollective control over the decision process, over and above difficulties associated with inadequate information about consequences or utilities. The difficulties can be situational (physical or temporal dispersion of the collective); conceptual (excessive demands on cognitive processes); or interpersonal (serious need to overcome inertia or to resolve disagreements and conflict). These difficulties call for resolution partly in terms of behavior which is broadly political in nature. Dealing with the first two stages of DOSRAP, deciding to decide and nominating alternatives, can emphasize each of these types of difficulties, particularly the interpersonal ones. However the process of deliberation can achieve improvement, and indeed must, if the outcome is not simply to resort to some least common denominator or the status quo.

3. *Information bearing on outcomes.* This may range from rich and sharp to sparse and ambiguous information. The latter makes probabilistic, objective, reality judgments vague and even shifty.

4. *Clarity of utilities.* Goals and the utilities which they incorporate may be sharply delineated, quantified concisely comprehensively, and associated with specific outcomes; or they may be difficult to stipulate, cover a range and thus be probabilistic, complex, vague, unstable, conflicting, and unpredictable.

Attributes 3 and 4 imply knowledge at decision stages 1 and 2 about matters *bearing on the final evaluated consequences* of DOSRAP. However at each stage such knowledge, and the probabilities associated with each consequence, need only be adequate to make it *worthwhile to proceed with the deliberative process.* Hence, if at an early stage information is felt to be inadequate to assess the desirability of the final outcome, part of the decision to continue the decision process must imply the belief that the requisite information will become available later. To make it available is then part of the strategy of the process.

5. *Seriability.* As indicated in Chapter 3, high seriability implies an actuarial basis for dealing with risk or uncertainty, in contrast to a totally nonseriable problem which cannot in whole or part be dealt with as a member of a series.

As indicated earlier, the averaging necessary to an actuarial basis can cover not only a number of identical acts but a number of very different ones providing the estimates of consequences are unbiased. But are not outcomes of long deliberations always biased in some degree by the characteristics of the individuals and organizations that are involved in the deliberative and indeed the effectuation processes? If so, this bias must be covered in the evaluations. To get results free of this bias, different organizations would need to pool their bets (as in commercial insurance).

6. *Potential for advancive behavior.* Advancive behavior raises the ceiling of achievement. It is explorative, experimental, and innovative, both with respect to improving goals and actions. Since high potential implies indeterminancy and therefore lack of structure in the decision problem, a high rating for attribute 6 tends to be associated with a low rating for the other attributes (mapping at the right of the attributes continuum).

The scope and implications of this attribute were covered in the previous chapter.

The structural attributes in the context of ongoing deliberative processes seem to make two sorts of contributions to how the process should be carried on.

The first follows the patterns cut in Chapters 6 and 7 for use of the profiles in guiding choice among predelineated acts, stage 3. Here too, in any given situation each structural attribute will apply in some degree which can be formalized on a scale from 1 (applying to perfect structure) to 100 (applying to extreme lack of structure). Here too, a well-structured deliberative situation may be visualized as presenting a profile in which all attributes have low index numbers (positioned toward the left margin of a page), and poorly structured as having high ratings (toward the right margin). However, the index positions for each attribute are not usually, and certainly not necessarily, stationary throughout the course of a deliberative process. This is a corollary of the time-extensive character of the process.

In situations for which all six attributes tend to cling to the well-structured side, from start to finish of DOSRAP, the progress of decision from stage to stage of the administrative processes as a whole can be guided by relatively highly rational and informed considerations in the classic economic sense of optimizing behavior. When the profile crowds the poorly structured side of the continuum, a highly judgmental, developmental approach is called for, one in which political behavior may virtually submerge task-oriented prescription. Indeed, at the farthest side, deliberative procedure, however loosely defined, may be quite impossible. However, most situations fall within the two extremes, with some attributes relatively well structured and others poorly structured. Then the broad strategy appropriate to the conduct of the ongoing decision process must depend on which attributes are well structured and which poorly structured, to what degree, and at what stages of the process as a whole.

Note, incidentally, that I have confined structural attributes to characteristics that tend to make the situation well structured or poorly structured. In consequence, many important attributes of decision situations themselves are not covered in the list but are dealt with later. These include the constraints of time, money, and talent.

The second type of impression which the attributes convey is that of the extent to which profiles are themselves a *product* of the deliberative process. The reasons are rooted in two salient characteristics of DOSRAP. First, politics, broadly defined, is clearly part of the material of deliberation. Second, the time-consuming character of the process means that the sequence as a whole is a history during which current situations, and expected outcomes, their utilities, and their probabilities change, sometimes fundamentally. Therefore, strategy *must continue to improve the structure* as decision proceeds; it must continue to facilitate learning. I shall now say a word on the subject of politics and then attempt to provide a model for the learning process.

Politics and Rational Behavior

Minimizing the cost of uncertainty involves people-oriented as well as object-oriented, or call it task-oriented, behavior. This fact has seeped into the unfolding analysis from many directions. That is why politics, broadly defined, enters into most deliberative-administrative problems.

It is helpful to distinguish the political ends from the task-oriented ends of a deliberative process. A purely political end is the desire to achieve power. Yet even winning political office is seldom entirely an effort to achieve power purely for its own sake. More usually, power is a necessary concomitant of achieving some more specific task, such as getting a bill through Congress, administering a welfare program well, or building an employees' lunchroom.

In any event, the focus of this book on administrative (in contrast to legislative) problems in business or government means that we concentrate on purposes which may be thought of as primarily task-oriented. Although political goals may play some part in the total purpose, politics enters primarily as a means of furthering the task.

In this capacity it plays an important part in deliberative policy. If "politics" is used broadly to refer to efforts to influence persons, then political behavior is essential to moving through most deliberative-administrative sequences from start to finish.

Political action endeavors to influence behavior in ways that can be classified, as Banfield does,[2] in terms of the types of behavior which

[2] E. C. Banfield, "Note on Conceptual Scheme," in. M. Meyerson and E. C. Banfield, *Politics, Planning and the Public Interest*, The Free Press, Glencoe, Ill., 1955.

result—e.g., cooperation, contention, accommodation, or dictation. It can be described in terms of the methods of influence that are used—threats, force, bribery, seduction, deception, bargaining, coalition, persuasion, etc. Considered in any of these ways, political action occurs in business as well as in government offices. Needless to say, it also occurs in legislatures, party offices, and the home, situations excluded by the terms of this book. In all cases, politics specializes in achieving the behavior necessary to further a purpose which in turn may be political or otherwise.

Purposive achievement, whether person-oriented or object-oriented, thrives on deliberative behavior. Thus cognition, evaluation, formation of expectations, and all other inputs to decision, including, particularly, the assembly and use of information, are required for political as well as for task-oriented purposes.

What of a political nature is worth considering may depend on all sorts of hard facts. How to induce a potential collective to act collectively can depend on a wide variety of information. The judgment concerning how best to influence others depends on knowledge of their past behavior and their current thinking (researchable subjects). Knowledge is itself a direct instrument for achieving agreement. A clear and convincing case that a problem needs to and can be dealt with, or that a particular course of action should be chosen, can typically (though not always) mobilize protagonists more effectively than can a cluster of question marks.

Finally, since deliberation is undertaken by collectives, and since the process typically takes time, person-oriented behavior tends to be required in order for the deliberative process itself to mature. Politics is necessary to afford cognition, investigation, and thought the opportunity to affect and effect what goes on. Political activity, as I have defined it, is capable of making the progress towards decision more efficient or even possible. It is capable of changing the consequences of a decision. (For example, it can improve the chances that workers will operate a machine properly and therefore that the equipment, if purchased, would have an acceptable earnings rate). It is capable of changing the appreciation of the results—the utility generated by the consequences of a decision.

Viewed, then, at each stage of the ongoing deliberative-administrative process, minimizing the cost of uncertainty requires that means be devised both for influencing and predicting person-oriented behavior and task-oriented behavior, though the degree of the duality varies among problems. Probabilistic knowledge is essential to both. The likelihood of a particular evaluated consequence is the conditional probability of a series of political and other results. The aspiration level that one may apply to the two directions of effort—person-oriented and task-oriented—may differ, but they belong to the same world.

A LEARNING MODEL

The past two-and-a-half chapters have been piling complications on top of complications. The time has come to simplify or smother. A schematic description of the conduct of DOSRAP is needed that will have prescriptive implications.

The deliberative process as a whole concerns learning because it is purposive and involves change. Learning models are the prose of ordinary behavior; people use them whether they know it or not. They "play it by ear"; "don't cross bridges until they come to them"; "try and try again." Only planners speak a special language.

Precedents

Yet when one looks about for a formal presentation of decision cast in the format of learning there appears to be no ready-made framework.

Economists have begun to essay "adaptive" models. But the work addresses the progressive striving toward an optimal solution assuming no change in what is deemed optimal or in how it may be achieved. On this point Kenneth Arrow, after reviewing the work available in 1958, concludes: "Learning is certainly one of the most important forms of behavior under uncertainty." Arrow remarks that adaptive behavior ". . . suggests that there is not the convergence to an optimum that we would ordinarily expect in economics," and "that equilibria may be different from those that we have predicted in our usual theory." He concludes with the comment: "such indications as have been received suggest strongly that motivational and cognitive factors, which do not originally enter into our economic theory, play a strong role, at least as far as the dynamics of the processes are concerned."[3]

In the years following Arrow's orderly and imaginative survey, work on learning has proliferated. But it appears to be primarily of two sorts: equipping machines to solve problems and thereby sharpening our knowledge of how problems are solved by men; and testing the components of learning by devising experiments capable of identifying and isolating them in the behavior of animals and men. These efforts, largely

[3] K. J. Arrow, "Utilities, Attitudes and Choices: A Review Note," *Econometrica*, January 1958, pp. 1–23. Quotations from pp. 13, 14, and 21 in sequence.

by psychologists, are building a base on which a model of policy decisions may some day find a solid scientific foundation. But as yet the work seems to promise only some small nuggets to set in the papier-mâché in which the deliberative process at a policy level must be modeled.

In the field of government, models have dealt more fully with the deliberative process as a whole. Learning is included but there is some question whether it is correct to call it purposive learning. An economist who studies these models, searching as usual for rationality, is offered something other: the logic of the political process, which is—like the logic of the unconscious—a special sort. Two examples will serve to illustrate the difficulty.[4]

Learning appears central to the Lindblom-Braybrooke strategy of disjointed incrementalism, which, proceeding by small steps, aims to surmount the difficulties of complex and inadequate information. At each successive step adverse consequences from previous steps can be corrected. "It is decision-making through small or incremental moves on particular problems . . . it takes the form of an indefinite sequence of policy moves. . . . it is exploratory in that the goals of policy-making continue to change as new experience with policy throws new light on what is possible and desirable. . . . it is policy-making that chooses those goals that draw policies forward in the light of what recent policy steps have shown to be probably realizable." "In the frequency with which past moves are found wanting and new moves debated, it reveals both man's limited capacities to understand and solve complex problems and an unsettled, shifting compromise of conflicting values."[5]

These phrases indubitably refer to ingredients of policy decisions.

[4] There are, of course, many other efforts to structure administrative or political decision making that do not share the dichotomous distinction between "rational" and "political" processes of the authors discussed below—e.g., the work of Downs, Buchanan or Maass previously mentioned. Other work of interest in this context is that of Fred W. Riggs who is deeply aware of the complex character of the structure of societies and the influences bearing upon them. His models, however, are more concerned with these matters than with decision making. Fred W. Riggs, "Models in the Comparative Study of Public Administration," in *Papers in Comparative Administration, Special Series No. 1*, American Society for Public Administration, Chicago, 1963, pp. 6–43. Another interesting model is that of William R. Dill, "Administrative Decision-Making," in *Concepts and Issues in Administrative Behavior*, Sidney Mailick and E. H. Van Ness, Eds., Prentice-Hall, Englewood Cliffs, N.J., 1962, pp. 29–48. See also J. D. Thompson and A. Tuden, "Strategies, Structures, and Processes of Organizational Decisions," in J. D. Thompson and others, *Comparative Studies in Administration*, University of Pittsburgh Press, Pittsburgh, 1959, pp. 195–216.

[5] David Braybrooke and Charles Lindblom, *A Strategy of Decision*, The Free Press of Glencoe, Collier-Macmillan Limited, London, 1963, p. 71.

But I am loath to think of them as providing a complete recipe for how policy is and should be made. Of course, the strategy of disjointed incrementalism applies to only some sorts of decision situations—those characterized by incremental change and low understanding.[6] However, while incremental decision can serve rational norms, it does not define them.

Somewhat more purposive in its plan is the "heuristic" decision model of William Gore.[7] "The essential function of the heuristic process is to induce a several-sided, commonly held set of understandings consisting of a shared conception of the world in general, the problem at hand, and the conditions under which the problem can be acceptably resolved from the jumble of concepts that constitute the normal state of affairs." However, much of the learning process with which Gore is concerned is internal: "through the heuristic process the private world of one individual is linked both to others and to the collectively constitute world which supports and nourishes individual existence." The process has elaborate political as well as personal channels of operation. However, Gore visualizes it as one of "two parallel and complementary systems of action" and believes that "our administrative doctrine will now have a permanent duality. The traditional and recently refurbished conception of organization as a rational system of action will coexist with a conception of organization as a social system or as a collective, heuristic strategy."[8]

In contrast, the basic thrust of our argument has been that it is irrational to fail to consider relevant political facts; and it is impolitic to

[6] Lindblom and Braybrooke identify four types of decision situations on the basis of a distinction between "large" or "small" changes (or "as it is sometimes put, between structural changes and changes within a given structure") and whether information is low or high. This gives four quadrants with a different analytic method appropriate to each:

Quadrant 1. High understanding and large change: "revolutionary and utopian decision-making"; analytic method—none.

Quadrant 2. High understanding and incremental change: "some administrative and technical decision-making"; analytic method—"synoptic" (something close to classic economic notions).

Quadrant 3. Incremental change and low understanding: "incremental politics"; analytic method—"disjointed incrementalism (among others)."

Quadrant 4. Low understanding and large change: "wars, revolutions, crises, and grand opportunities"; analytic method—"not formalized or well understood." *Op. cit.,* pp. 63, 78.

[7] William J. Gore, *Administrative Decision-Making: A Heuristic Model,* John Wiley & Sons, Inc., New York, 1964.

[8] *Ibid.,* pp. 12, 14 and 17.

fail to behave rationally. We need to devise a stereopticon viewer which can bring the two worlds into a single image.

Similarly a dichotomous distinction between decision situations to which statistical decision theory applies and all other situations (to which rational purposive behavior is inappropriate) is equally wall-eyed. A ground plan of the deliberative process as a whole must envisage the whole range of situations and suggest how each can be pursued as advantageously as circumstances permit. To draw such a plan at this stage is an impossible assignment. However, a beginning can be suggested.

The Diagram

We start with a diagram of an intendedly rational, time-consuming, purposive, progressive process in an uncertain world (Diagram 11-1). It undertakes to accommodate symbolically the major sorts of actors, inputs, and subprocesses which comprise, in varying degree, deliberative processes in business or government. The diagram aims to suggest the genus of which all deliberative-administrative efforts are species. However, to do so, it is forced to portray one species. The reader will, I trust, be able to distinguish the elements of the model that are always present from those that would be drawn differently for different problems.

The diagram concentrates on one decision cycle of an ongoing process. The time which the cycle requires, and its sequential stages appear along the horizontal dimension. The vertical dimension has a double meaning. The first represents action in behavioral space. The height indicates how many and diverse are the things considered or undertaken. The second reflects goals served, primary outcomes expected (uncertainly) to result from the final acts that are contemplated. Here again the vertical distance refers to the number and diversity of things expected (rather than, for example, to the amount of utility which they may be expected to generate). Expected consequences would be positioned at a later time than that covered by the diagram, a point representing the time at which consequences are expected to begin to accrue, that is, the point for which their "present value" would be calculated.

On the surfaces of the disks are the behavioral episodes that materialize during a subperiod of the DOSRAP cycle (diagrammed as slots and arrows on the first disk). Of course, behavior is continuous and therefore the disks are partly arbitrary sections of what would be more properly represented by an elongated solid shape. Each of the five stages is shown by one or more disks. (For stage 4—effectuation—disks are shown at

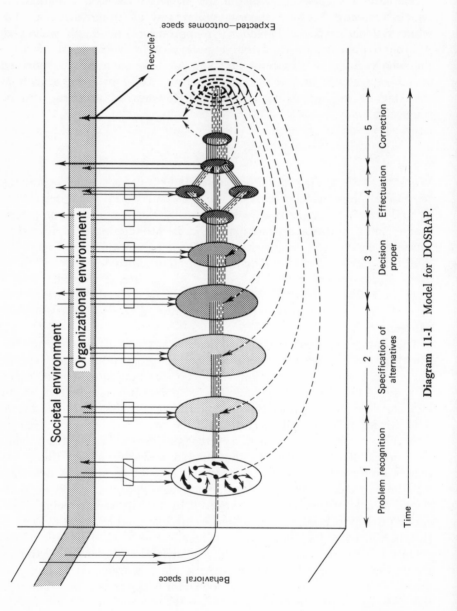

Diagram 11-1 Model for DOSRAP.

different levels to suggest the variety of problems which may need to be solved).

Any sort of behavior is encompassed—people-oriented or task-oriented as well as investigation or pure cerebration. Since goals and means are complexly interrelated, both the evaluative and problem-defining and problem-solving aspects of deliberation must be covered.

These various sorts of behavior may be undertaken by a variety of people at a variety of sites, a recognition of the conglomerate character of many decision collectives as discussed in Chapter 4. But particularly when attributes 1 and 2, which concern the collective, are poorly structured, the sites for which behavior is diagrammed on a particular disk may actually be geographically separated, as well as diverse in other ways; indeed in the early stages, collectivity may yet not have been achieved. Sites where decision work of any sort, by any one, is going on are shown as points on the first disk of the diagram (analogous ones would be present on all disks but are not shown).

Diffuseness of all types is shown diagrammatically by the size of the disk and its shading. Large size means that behavior covers a wide variety of forms and contemplates a wide variety of possibilities. Shading refers to the degree to which the units of the collective agree. (Dark shading signifies consensus.) Thus a single individual contemplating many aspects of a wide variety of possibilities would be shown by a large disk with dark shading.

Since it is always possible to convey information from one element of a collective to another, the surface of the disks may be thought of as a conductor of information. Specific interactor, or intersite, transmission during a specific period is exemplified by the small arrows on the first disk (they would appear on all disks but are not shown).

Information comes from and goes to the outside world. Deliberative situations do not exist in a vacuum. For one thing they draw heavily on a particular organizational environment in which the collective exists—the corporation, the government, or governmental complex. Likewise, they draw on the relevant knowledge, customs, values, etc., of the society at large. The two environments are shown as bands paralleling the decision space. Vertical arrows from these bands show messages moving from the organizational or total environment to the surface of the disks whence they are hypothetically conveyed to the relevant behavior sites.

Note, however, that each of these messages must pass through a box denoting the cognitive field, the screening apparatus associated with the selective and organizing characteristics of individual perception and learning. In reality these boxes would be particular to each actor so that the diagram simply calls attention to the fact that we are not dealing with economic man who knows everything there is to be known and its appropriate relationship to everything else. The boxes have some resemblance to "encoder" and "decoder" of information theory, which converts "messages" to "information." When messages and information are closely similar (the cognitive filter is inactive) the lines move straight through the box. When messages tend to be changed or ignored by the cognitive apparatus, the lines are shown as bent as they traverse the box (a characteristic shared at all stages but shown only at the first).[9]

A reverse flow of information—from the decision locale to the environments—is also indicated. This flow can be of critical importance after a deliberative situation has culminated in an action that may require observation, evaluation, and perhaps reevaluation. The diagram uses broad lines to suggest where the particular information paths are likely to be heavily traveled (note the arrows at the end of the effectuation and correction stages).

Finally, anything in process in one period can also receive information from and send it to earlier and later periods. This is diagrammed by the lines running through the center shaft. They may be visualized as a coaxial cable having vent points at each disk. New lines account for the progressively enlarging diameter of the cable.

Information flowing through the central shaft of the diagram is of several sorts—both information flowing into the decision locale from the left or away from it toward the right. First, it concerns the progress of the deliberative process itself. Second, it conveys expectations bearing on the intermediate and also the final outcomes of the process and their probabilities. Third, it bears on the values sought, their expected utilities, and the probabilities of each.

All three must profoundly affect how the decision process develops. The information about how things have gone in the past affects aspiration levels as well as the particulars of what it seems useful to do next. Likewise the last two types of messages, those that convey expectations about outcomes and, viewed in the light of the changing value system,

---

[9] Into this box crowds much of the work of psychologists on perception and cognition which has been and is still growing at a rapid pace. Fortunately, for our purposes the particulars of the screening, organizing, and motivational characteristics of the machinery in these boxes are of secondary importance, at least at the level of common denominators. Of critical importance, in the words of Norbert Wiener, is the fact that "these external messages are not taken *neat*, but through the internal transforming powers of the apparatus, whether it be alive or dead. The information is then turned into a new form available in the further stages of performance." Norbert Wiener, *The Human Use of Human Beings*, Houghton Mifflin, Boston, 1954, p. 26.

their consequences, can profoundly influence the step-by-step course of the deliberative process itself. This feedback of expectational material is shown by the dotted arrows returning from the goal area to the several decision stages or substages indicated by the disks.

The expected consequences are in the dotted coil at the right of the diagram. The several rings of the coil are, sequentially from the outside in, the result of the expectations generated at each stage and conveyed to the right. The rings become progressively smaller, thereby indicating how the course of deliberation narrows the possibilities which are expected to accrue. The narrowing is partly a function of the focusing of the actions that are contemplated and the utilities sought, and therefore of the consequences that may reasonably be expected; decreasing uncertainty (increasing peakedness of the probability distributions) also has this effect. The narrowing is partly a function also of aspirations that adjust to changing realities. Deepened shading suggests increased clarity—less diffusion and ambiguity about expected consequences.

Applications

The diagram is not a model in the sense that it portrays a theory of how learning takes place in deliberative situations. It aspires to comprehensiveness only in the sense of giving coherence to the wide differences among actual situations. Accordingly, it must accommodate any specific decision problem and suggest, partly by changing the particulars of the diagram, what is and is not characteristic of the problem at hand. Whether it achieves these acommodations and clarifications determines whether the model is useful.

Abortive and Short-Process Problems

Some problems never graduate from the first stage. This would be the case if attribute 1 is so poorly structured that the individuals in whose path a problem lies fail to achieve sufficient collectivity, consensus, or other sort of mobilization to proceed to a next step. For example, suppose that the perennial pressure to provide housing for the poor has drifted toward the need for a large new housing development. Nothing has as yet been proposed. There have been informal discussions in the Mayor's office, in the Department of Housing, in the Planning Council; there have been talks among individual members of the City Council. Each of these decision "sites," that is, points on a first disk, are aware of a mounting pressure in the city and of discrepancies between city and national performance. The information is likely to be partial, selective, and personal (information carried by the vertical arrows is bent as it traverses the cognitive filter).

Staff is put to studying the matter further; knowledge is sharpened at the individual decision points and information conveyed among decision sites (short arrows on the disks). But possible dollar and political costs and benefits are felt to cover a wide range, and it is difficult to say how probable is each contemplated result, or to rule out some of the more catastrophic ones. This ambiguity of expectations about consequences, shared at most of the decision points, does not help to energize work toward a meeting of minds or of interests. The arrows move palely from point to point on the disk without giving rise to convergence toward opinion or action to be conveyed through the central cable. As a result, the deliberative process aborts, at least for the time being. The diagram would consist of one moderately large and very pale disk, with spaced points and short arrows, heavy environment lines, and wide and pale outcomes circles.

At the other extreme is the routine decision which may be little more than effectuation (stage 4) of previous decisions or habit patterns. A household thermostat "decides" when to call for heat; but it, like the stock boy or a housewife buying staples, applies a rule which stipulates sharply when to turn it on and when to pass. Such decisions can edge back to stage 3 as discretion widens a bit.[10] The ever-broadened range of computer control mechanisms will tend progressively to move the dividing line backward toward earlier stages. But fundamentally, the "servomechanism," whether human or electronic, applies previous decisions which confine alternatives to a relatively narrow range of present alternatives. The real decision in connection with the thermostat is the earlier battle of the sexes which has set the temperature on the dial.

Here there are one or two very small dark discs with narrow goals rings very deeply shaded and strong information lines of all sorts.

Well Structured Throughout

Consider, now, the inventory decision in its standard textbook frame of reference. Although textbooks do not usually start with the point of deciding to decide, it is clear that a reevaluation of the inventory size formula must be specifically undertaken (diagrammed on the first disk). But this step should be readily accomplished since the decision is likely to involve the officers rather than the board of directors of a company and fall largely in the domain of the vice president in charge of operations. Such threats as the minor chieftains (other points on the disk's surface) may sense are resolved in line with power hierarchies,

[10] This process is beautifully set forth by Herbert Simon in "Application of Servomechanism Theory to Production Control," *Models of Man*, John Wiley & Sons, New York, 1957. Chapter 13.

influenced by the readily available factual information bearing on how present inventory practice is working. Information from outside sources (downward arrows on the diagram) suggests how the company's performance measures up to the state of the art. Assume that this relatively well-structured decision collective and the reasonably concise information results in a decision to look into the question of how procedures could be improved. Diagrammatically, information from the several points on a disk (which is relatively small) focuses in on a picture, however rangy, of possible benefits. This picture, charted as the outside ring in the outcomes area, gives rise to expectations that seem at least worth incurring more time and turmoil-costs to study further.

Moving now to the delineation of alternatives, I shall assume that vision is constrained within the framework of the usual variables—the cost of stock-outs, cost of money (the rate of return foregone), costs of storage, insurance, obsolescence, and lot-size ordering costs. Discussion concerns the size of some of these figures, and the appropriate distinctions to be made among various classes of stocks. The list implies that attribute 6 is well structured (advancive approaches are absent as the degree of routine is high). Consequences are measured in terms of average results, that is, the situation is seriable (attribute 5 is well structured). Similarly well structured are attributes 3 and 4. Information associated with outcomes is clear: changes of stocks are related to buying and selling in a fashion which is judged to be well controlled. The utility scheme, expressed largely in terms of dollar profits and the link between profits and stocks, is specified in terms of an inventory model which hypothetically incorporates the significant elements.

The well-defined alternatives and relatively sharp information imply that the formulas to be considered can be diagrammed on a single disk for stage 2, a relatively small and dark one. Deliberations involve primarily reviewing the various sorts of formulas in common use and considering their applicability. Arrows are numerous and stout; information from both environments is likewise plentiful and it passes without deflection through the cognitive filter. In selecting alternatives, it is possible that some methods are excluded on the basis of preliminary calculations. In any event the range of expectations narrows (they relate to a smaller dotted coil than previously) and sharpens (the color darkens). The process proceeds to stage 3, the next disk—of moderate size and quite dark. Here choice would be based on formal calculations using the statistical decision format. Since all attributes are well structured, the choice can probably utilize a matrix incorporating a complete probability distribution of consequences along lines described in Part One of this book (though there may be recognition of probabilistic utility as per Chapter

6, to cover some generally sensed failure of the formulas to take all relevant matters into account.) Information conveyed to the goal area becomes quite precise and the ring on the coil describing expectations small and darkly shaded.

Effectuation is a matter of issuing instructions. An information feedback which might lead to correction of some of the specific elements in the prescriptions may or may not be overtly sought.

This is the usual decision format. But note that the present discussion indicates that choices are made frequently in the course of the whole sequence of deliberations. The problem narrows and tightens. Probability distributions tend to become more peaked and less ambiguous as the process matures.

Advancive But Otherwise Well Structured

The example takes on some rather different characteristics if the nature of attribute 6 is changed by admitting advancive potentials. Suppose the decision to review inventory policy was to be based on doubts which go way beyond the conventional ideas embodied in efficient stock-management formulas, and this implies that attributes 3 and 4 are also poorly structured. There is a general idea that stocks are both costly themselves and, in addition, poorly integrated with broader business objectives. Discussions by top management cover a wide range of questions and information, about which the company chieftains differ as to particulars and relative significance. But discussions finally culminate in the selection of an operations-research team which is known to use a broad systems approach and to frame review to encompass what at the present time may be termed "advancive" considerations.

Note that the selection of an outside firm may be a way not only of filling the obvious need for expertise but also of getting around intercollective conflict (poor structure of attribute 1). Diagrammatically, the first disk is large and light. Information arrows are plentiful but slender.

Now assume the operations-research team starts with a wide-angle lens. Stage 2 opens on a disk which may even be larger than the previous one. It may progress to a still larger one, as the possibilities are enumerated and developed (heavy vertical down-arrows from the societal and organizational environment, long and numerous arrows on the disk which is pale).

The team spends some time reviewing the whole gamut of production, selling, and materials buying. The cost of stock-outs, the team finds, has not been properly assessed with an eye to the opportunity costs of salesforce effort; also, the negative impact of flexible production schedules on employee morale has been ignored. The cost assigned to money invested in stock (the same figure applied to investment in plant and equipment) is deemed too high (particularly at times when sales and profits are high, thereby providing cash suitable for short-term investment in stocks but unsuitable for long-term investment in capital improvements). The cost of stock associated with holding slow-moving items should be sharply distinguished from the cost of stock of equal size of well-selected and therefore fast-moving items; the potential advantage in purchasing which recognizes expected changes in delivery periods and raw materials prices has not been examined.[11] Thus the first part of delineating alternatives (stage 2) has to settle on a value system which clarifies the role of inventory in the business and determines what combination of conflicting objectives (such as low inventory costs, customer satisfaction, low marketing costs, and employment stability) should be sought. The closing-in process, which must carry company officials along, might be diagrammed by a second stage 2 disk, smaller and darker than the first, with strong vertical arrows to and from the organizational environment ending with well-delineated communications to the goals area.

Subsequent disks for stage 2 interpret a value system in terms of a few alternative inventory control systems (one or more smaller darker disks with many information channels—surface and vertical arrows). Preliminary calculations assess how the outcomes might stack up when projected to the outcomes area.

Decision itself and effectuation might be relatively routine and diagrammed on small, darkly shaded disks with the goal area showing a similar progression.

Stage 5 might involve the preparation of a monitoring system which would transmit to, and receive from, the organizational environment. This evidence alone, or in combination with information of other sorts, would feed into a subsequent decision cycle which would deterine whether to broaden the application of the broad-system approach or retreat to standard inventory procedures. The example is one in which the problem is clarified and structured as the deliberative process proceeds.

Advancive and Otherwise Poorly Structured

The IBM 360/System offers an engaging example to set in the diagram's frame. I shall leave the game to the playful reader, though he should remember that a precise fit is never possible and many assign-

---

[11] The complex of elements that are involved in inventory planning is discussed in Chapter 2, particularly Exhibit 1, pp. 34–35 in R. P. Mack, *Information, Expectations, and Inventory Behavior, Materials Stocks on Hand and in Order*, National Bureau of Economic Research, 1967.

ments are marginal. There were clearly many predecision disks as alternatives were weeded out and the contender groomed for the showdown. There were also many effectuation disks since action had to be designed at many levels, and tried and redesigned. Additional cycles of decision are evident in the last five years.

In a sense, the IBM unified line was less a decision than an invention. Any decision process in which alternatives are developed over its course shares elements of an inventive process, but the relative importance of these elements has a wide range. This structure tends to subdue the distinction between stage 2 and stage 3 (specification of alternatives and choice among them) and blend the two into, diagrammatically, a series of disks that gradually decrease in size and eventually darken as constant communication of all sorts takes place including to and from the goals area.

The development of the transistor at the Bell Telephone Laboratories is a further example of a highly inventive process.[12] The work lasted about five years. "At the start of the semiconductor research project there was considerable uncertainty whether an amplifier could be achieved at all. . . ." "Because of the great uncertainties involved, much of the research effort was directed toward learning rather than toward the achievement of a specific and well-defined result." ". . . the direction of research changed dramatically in response to what was learned." "There never seems to have been an attempt to list all research alternatives and to pick the best on the basis of some formal calculation. Rather, the *discovery* of new ideas and alternatives occurred often in the program." ". . . only toward the end of the project was the design which has proved most successful clearly perceived."[13]

A somewhat less open-ended innovative deliberative sequence is exemplified in the development of the microwave relay system at the Bell Laboratories which was mentioned at the close of Chapter 9. Thomas Marschak's "conclusion" seems to exemplify much of the process that we have been trying to formulate: the laboratory management picks a general goal area and a "maximum admissible" effort in achieving it.

Within the chosen region, an initial set of performance magnitudes is then chosen as system objectives. The number of ways of attaining them may be enormous and only a few can be explored. First are considered several 'families' of ways, each family defined by a set of system characteristics. Bit by bit, each family considered is narrowed, as the alternative component

[12] Richard Nelson, "The Link Between Science and Invention: The Case of the Transistor," in *The Rate and Direction of Inventive Activity*, R. Nelson, Ed.
[13] *Ibid.*, pp. 566–567.

specifications consistent with each family are explored and knowledge of their difficulty is gained (using parallel design approaches to them where there is much uncertainty). Gradually a choice of family and of one way (one set of component specifications) within that family is made.

Until the final choice is made, flexibility is maintained. Commitments of personnel to specific tasks are made only for small periods, and it continues to be generally easy to drop one family or one way and to shift effort to exploring another more intensively. (Commitments are kept particularly small while awaiting sharp jumps in knowledge, such as completion of 'breadboard' models may provide.) An exception are system-critical component specifications, which are 'frozen' somewhat before the complete system is specified (before the final way is chosen), but only after a careful balancing of the risks and the gains. In the background remains, until the final choice, the possibility of changing the system objectives or even the region of indifference aimed for. When the system is finally specified, a schedule for the remaining development tasks is drawn up (to choose a good one, for a complex system, may be quite difficult).[14]

Probabilistic Deliberative Process

The need to diagram DOSRAP in terms of a learning model has fundamental implications bearing on the problem of quasi-optimizing the consequences of the process. The model, as well as the examples just reviewed, reiterate the observation that there seems small basis for identifying an optimal or quasi-optimal solution to a problem.

This inability to point to a "correct answer" is implicit not only in the staged, time-consuming recursive character of the process, but also in the open-ended opportunities for innovation and resource-creation afforded by advancive behavior. It is implicit also in the fact that person-oriented, or broadly political, behavior must typically be sustained in parallel course with the wide variety of undertakings more directly related to the task at hand. It is implicit in the fact that typically the whole course of deliberation must narrow down toward a conclusion and to do so the structure of the problem must tighten (the profile for later stages must be coaxed toward the left hand side of the page).

The extent to which this can be achieved is, of course, the result of the purposive process that has been described involving contrivance at a person-oriented and task-oriented level. DOSRAP as a whole, in other words, may be viewed as the progressive design of a vehicle for clarifying and realizing its central purposes.

The result of this purposive process—how well the vehicle functions—

[14] Thomas A. Marschak, "Strategy and Organization in a System Development Project," *The Rate and Direction of Inventive Activity*, R. Nelson, Ed., pp. 546–547.

is itself a probabilistic affair. It can be predicted in terms of a range not a point.

Yet the good outcome is achieved via the good process. Therefore, how well DOSRAP functions will influence the probability of greater net advantage from its final outcomes—the consequences of the acts that are chosen. Accordingly, efforts to quasi-optimize the deliberative process itself provide a very important intermediate operation in the quasi-optimization of the task toward which deliberation aims.

There should be nothing especially difficult in thinking of the design of a quasi-optimal deliberative process as, in a sense, itself a goal, which in turn becomes a means to the final purpose of the deliberations. The need to deal with intermediate aims in a means-goals pyramid has appeared throughout our analysis. It is inherent in the DOSRAP model where intermediate ends must be achieved in order to progress to the next stage of deliberation. It is part of every man's daily doings: wake up to board a train, board a train to get to the office, get to the office to earn a living, earn a living to . . . .

What is perhaps less familiar, at least to economists, is to think in terms of optimizing a process—the deliberative process—rather than primarily in terms of optimizing the consequences of that process—the utility which it is expected to generate.

Yet there too, the difficulty may be more apparent than real. Classic formulations of economic theory speak of optimal outcomes, the maximized output of scarce resources. These outcomes are in fact the necessary result of an optimal process, one minutely described in terms of what *Homo economicus* does in a world of highly competitive markets. If the process (including its inherent conditions) conform to this prescription, the result is necessarily optimal. Conversely, if the results can be unequivocally identified as optimal, the process can be assumed to have conformed to the prescription.

Over the years, economists have recognized, some more willingly than others, divergences between the stereotype of the optimum-generating process and the actual processes (and conditions) of the real world. And the divergences imply imperfections in the optimality of the result. These imperfections invite correction. But in attempting to devise corrections, the emphasis seems typically to be placed on the nonoptimal result rather than on the nonoptimal process.

Of course, the emphasis can be placed in either spot so long as the process remains a near relative of the stereotype. But when the blood thins, trouble begins. One minor break in the line was occasioned by the appreciation that prediction is inherently probabilistic, not certain. Part One indicated some first principles of how this break has been mended.

The stereotype, optimum-generating process is now able to substitute probabilistically determinate outcomes for precisely determinate outcomes. The substitution was by no means simple. It has challenged the ingenuity of some remarkably capable people.

But if a precisely correct decision process (as stipulated by statistical theory) can achieve probabilistic optimality only on the average, what sort of a solution is generated by a decision process which itself is at best optimal only on the average? Perhaps the answer could be read in terms of conditional probabilities. However, the fact of the matter is that for a poorly structured deliberative process, nothing remotely approaching a useful probability distribution of the results (represented on the inner ring of the outcomes spiral in the diagram) could be stipulated at the beginning of stage 1. Indeed, at that stage, the results may be not probabilistically determinant at all, but genuinely indeterminant.

The point is that there are better and worse consequences of a deliberative process. Also, because of the vast discrepancy between the economic behavior-determining processes of the world of the late 20th century and those presumed by the classic competitive stereotype (or indeed any other stereotype with which I am familiar), it is safer and often more useful to consider the matter of better or worse consequences in terms of better or worse processes of generating consequences instead of directly in terms of the consequences themselves. So conceived, a good consequence is what a good deliberative process achieves. How then can this process be improved?

CHAPTER 12

Improving Deliberative Processes

The approach to how deliberative-administrative processes can be improved has been set forth. It focuses on reducing two costs of uncertainty—costs associated with knowledge gap and with possibility shortfall. A quasi-optimal solution must have net expected consequences
which are preferred to those of some other known solution. But the
preference is never absolute; the net expected consequences of some
other possible solution might be yet more desirable. It is often easier
to work toward this end by concentrating on the process whereby decision is achieved, in contrast to eyeing results, and in a sense working
backward. A good decision is what a good decision process generates.

How can one improve the likelihood that the deliberative process
will be well handled? The subject is discussed in the next two chapters.
In this chapter, the focus is selective. It deals with matters requiring

emphasis which lie at the core of deliberative procedure, subjects that correspond to those covered by decision rules in the context of well-structured choice. In the final chapter, the approach is comprehensive; it contains a checklist of a large number of ways to cope with uncertainty—some important and some unimportant.

BACKGROUND PROPOSITIONS

Purposive Learning and Progressive Design

The deliberative process runs a probabilistic course, thereby making the consequences of its ultimate outcome doubly unpredictable. One must predict the outcome of the process itself and the outcome of the actions eventually chosen. Consequently prediction, though essential, is often of limited worth. On the other hand, the essence of the process is susceptible to learning and to sensitive response in a purposive framework. Constructive learning must compensate for the partial impotence of prediction and its narrow range of application. Moreover, there are opportunities to plan desired results into existence.

There are a wide variety of points in the process as a whole at which learning is called for. Individual learning episodes build cumulatively into a complete DOSRAP cycle. Further decision cycles carry the learning on. Finally, these deliberative processes as a whole contribute to the "evolutionary experimentation" envisioned by Edgar Dunn: "Prediction as hypothesis, and planning as experimental design are the fundamental core of social learning."[1] The individual decision processes can contribute to the broader social learning. They affect it for good or ill, and are affected by it.

Hence, promoting "planning as experimental design" is a central point in coping with costs of uncertainty—costs due both to possibility shortfall and to knowledge gap. How this has been done must be gleaned, at the present state of the literature, from the few relevant descriptions of management structure in research and development, where learning is obviously of the essence. The Bell Telephone Laboratories are, no doubt, a prime example. We are fortunate in having two descriptions bearing on different problems.

Thomas Marschak develops "an ideal pattern, at which the formally designated leaders of TH [the group of departments primarily in charge of the development of the microwave system] seemed consciously to

[1] Edgar Dunn, Jr., *Economic and Social Development: A Process of Social Learning*, Johns Hopkins Press, Baltimore, 1971, p. 136.

have aimed. . . ." He speaks of the formal hierarchical and organizational characteristics; then he describes what followed after the executive group asked the "components group" to formulate goals. The components group starts to estimate the effort that is needed and reports:

It is, moreover, not only permitted but actively encouraged to tell the executive group as soon as it has evidence that a minor modification of its requirements . . . would significantly ease its task . . . This information . . . forms the basis for a series of 'parliamentary' conferences, presided over by the executive group, with members of the component groups and the systems analysis group as participants. . . . At all stages the executive group is easily accessible to the component groups. In the traditional informality of the Development Department (housed in a single building), conversations (face-to-face or by telephone) are generally as easy to arrange between members of different groups as between members of the same group. The members of the executive group, moreover, keep very well informed about the activities of the component and systems analysis groups, on occasion . . . working directly with them. . . . *The executives might better be thought of, in fact, as central storers of information than as makers of decisions.* Their knowledge of the status of all parts of the system is essential to decisions about changes in requirements, manpower allocations, and schedules, but the decisions are collectively made by the members of the parliamentary conferences (though formally issued, in memoranda or other documents, in the name of an executive).

Each component group is free to pursue its own ideas about the internal design of its component, exploring parallel approaches (or several approaches in sequence) if it wishes.

[Finally,] the relations between groups working on related components are very close. Each group can easily inform itself (and is kept informed through generally distributed memoranda) of the work of a related group; it does not need to proceed through the executive group in acquiring such information.[2]

Richard Nelson's description of the work on the transistor reveals a similar picture of an atmosphere calculated to produce easy supportive interaction. He discusses whether the work is an example of the fashionable emphasis on teamwork. He talks about ". . . what teamwork meant in the case of the transistor":

First of all, we have seen that it meant interaction and mutual stimulation and help. Shared intense interest in the general field, ease of communication, differences in the viewpoints and experience of different scientists—these elements naturally call for interaction and make interaction fruitful for scientific

[2] Thomas A. Marschak, "Strategy and Organization in a System Development Project," *The Rate and Direction of Inventive Activity*, R. Nelson, Ed., pp. 539–541, italics mine.

advance. The purpose of bringing together the people doing work in solid-state physics was to achieve this end, and from the history of the project it seems that the close interaction of several people definitely contributed to the advance achieved. But several people outside the team also interacted in an important way. . . .

Second, we have seen that teamwork in the case of the transistor did not mean a closely directed project with an assigned division of labor in the form of tasks and schedules for each of the team members. . . . The project was marked by flexibility—by the ability to shift directions and by the rather rapid focusing of attention by several people on problems and phenomena unearthed by others.

In general, Nelson concludes that the case of the transistor did not represent teamwork in the sense of ". . . a group of people whose work is closely coordinated and planned by a team leader." "The informality of the decision structure played a very important role in permitting speedy cooperative response to changing ideas and knowledge."[3] *The key fact appears to have been interaction.* "The major requirements for effective interaction seem to have been easy communication and the ability of individuals to drop what they were doing to help with problems their colleagues brought up, if these problems seemed interesting and important."[4]

In connection with inventions, it is natural to think in terms of an atmosphere conducive to free generation of ideas which can be worked through to practical outcomes. Yet our analysis suggests that the same recipe is widely applicable to dynamic decision processes of most sorts.

The DOSRAP model emphasized, however, that far more than direct task-related learning was required. Even in situations in which the person-related aspects of attributes 1 and 2 are well structured, (the collective's dispersion and capability for rationality), people need to be convinced that steps are wisely taken; they have to be moved from acquiescence to active commitment. Sir Geoffrey Vickers watched such a situation mature as a new general manager of a plant sought a plan for replacing obsolescent output. A long sequence of meetings was held with department managers and board members ". . . as the [proposed] product passed from sketch to model, from model to prototype, becoming at each stage more precisely defined. . . ." Vickers analyzed what appeared to have taken place, prior to the final decision, in the minds of the four participants. They "can all be described as learning, partly also as teach-

[3] Richard Nelson, "The Link Between Science and Invention: The Case of the Transistor," in *The Rate and Direction of Inventive Activity*, R. Nelson, Ed., pp. 578, 579.
[4] *Ibid.*, p. 567.

ing."[5] "The changes . . . altered the mental organization of all the parties to the debate . . . altered both the ways in which they were ready to see and value their situation (their appreciative setting) and the ways in which they were ready to respond to it (their instrumental system)."[6] But he emphasizes a further change which occurred "at the point of acceptance," at the point, that is, where "they identified the plan with themselves, assimilating its achievement into their personal standards of success." They became committed to it—"A potential fact had become a potential act."[7]

Sir Geoffrey is describing a type of learning, taking place around the table in the corporate directors' room, which Madame Montessori introduced into kindergartens decades ago. It is absolutely necessary to the conduct of business. On the DOSRAP diagram, it affects the load carried by the small arrows on the surface of the disks; the changing expectations and values carried by the dotted lines; and the darkening color, the increasing clarity, which develop as the new manager pursued his humanly, as well as technically, skilled work.

Another variety of learning which is built into the deliberative process involves the expert acquisition and use of information. Here, of course, there is a large expertise concerning both decision theory and information theory, as well as some aspects of systems analysis. Learning in this sense tends to minimize the cost of uncertainty by reducing the knowledge gap.

Psychologists likewise have worked prolifically on the subject of learning. Yet it would seem that the complex and subtle processes involved in purposive learning and policy decisions have not yet made contact with the experiments of psychologists concerning, for example, how people respond to clues of various sorts, whether they respond differently if given more time, if given higher rewards, if asked the same question repetitively, if the information is more rather than less sure, if more rather than less ambiguous, if other people are joining in a response situation, and so forth. Indeed even these seemingly elementary questions have not been answered to most people's satisfaction.[8]

[5] Vickers, The Art of Judgment, A Study of Policy Making, Chapman & Hall, London, 1965, p. 185.

[6] Ibid., p. 187.

[7] Ibid., p. 188.

[8] This work can be sampled in a number of compendiums: R. D. Luce, R. R. Bush, and E. Galanter, Readings in Mathematical Psychology, Vol. 1, Part II, "Learning and Stochastic Processes," John Wiley & Sons, Inc., New York, 1963; H. Raiffa and R. Schlaifer, Applied Statistical Decision Theory, Harvard Business School, Division of Research, Boston, 1961; R. D. Luce, R. R. Bush, and E. Galanter, Eds., Handbook of Mathematical Psychology, John Wiley & Sons, Inc., New York,

Moreover, even if one knew more about how people conceptualized and learned in a purposive fashion there is still a large void in knowledge which links cognition to action and certainly this link lies at the heart of deliberative-administrative behavior. One effort to bridge the gap has come to my attention and it seems to lay a foundation in individual psychology which has a most promising relation to the trend of our analysis. The book is *Plans and the Structure of Behavior* by George A. Miller, Eugene Galanter, and Karl H. Pribram.[9] Two notions are central to the analyses: the *image* is "all the accumulated, organized knowledge that the organism has about itself and its world" (including its values).[10] When faced with a problem, the image attempts to picture "what is and what ought to be and to focus on the gap between them." This is the "prediction paradigm."[11] The second notion is the *plan*—"any hierarchical process in the organism that can control the order in which a sequence of operations is to be performed."[12] When faced with a problem, the plan addresses the search for acceptable solutions (the "search paradigm").

If there are too many alternatives, then how to proceed depends on whether "the heart of the difficulty lies in the construction of a better Image or the elaboration of a better Plan."[13] One answer may lie in shortening the gaps which plans must bridge and integrating a sequence of plans into a single stream of behavior. In simplest form this means that a TOTE hierarchy (Test, Operate, Test, Exit) operates on itself, that is, plans must operate on plans as well as operate on information to guide motor behavior.[14] And certainly this repetitive self-censoring "search paradigm" has loomed ever larger in our own approach via the necessities of decision processes.

Another answer to difficulty in uniting image and plan, when it is the

---

1965; R. R. Bush and W. Estes, Eds., *Studies in Mathematical Learning Theory*, Stanford University Press, Stanford, Calif., 1959. See also H. M. Schroder, M. J. Driver and S. Streufert, *Human Information Processing*, Holt, Rinehart and Winston, New York, 1967.

A particularly interesting collection of papers appears in *Predecisional Processes in Decision Making: Proceedings of a Symposium*, D. P. Hunt and D. L. Zink, Eds., Behavioral Sciences Laboratory, Aerospace Medical Research Laboratories, Wright-Patterson Air Force Base, Ohio, AMRL-TDR-64-77, December 1964.

[9] George A. Miller, Eugene Galanter, and Karl H. Pribram, *Plans and the Structure of Behavior*, Holt, Rinehart and Winston, New York, 1960.

[10] *Ibid.*, pp. 17–18.

[11] *Ibid.*, p. 175.

[12] *Ibid.*, p. 16 (italics omitted).

[13] *Ibid.*, p. 175.

[14] *Ibid.*, p. 98.

image which chiefly is faulty, is to reenact a process rather than to try to predict its outcome. Reenactment, say the authors, which has been "the traditional approach of the artist . . . is emerging as a scientific alternative in its own right. The development of modern computing machines, more than anything else, has given scientists the tools required to reenact, or simulate, on a large scale, the processes they want to study."[15] Emphasis on reenactment of process, with a view to understanding where it leads and how to improve it, is certainly consonant with the emphasis on improving the deliberative process to which this study has lead. And it is reassuring to find this confluence of thinking from the direction of these pioneering psychological studies.

The emphasis on process and social learning likewise emerged in the work of Edgar Dunn, who traveled the route of phylogenesis and sociogenesis toward regional and national development. This further reinforces confidence in a notion toward which such diverse paths lead.

Learning, opened to widening horizons, implies creativity. Creativity has the capacity to reduce possibility shortfall. Its nature and genesis is being explored in a growing literature though it is not yet clear how much these studies will contribute to the improvement in deliberative procedures.[16]

Of course creativity in the deliberative process can be a threat as well as an opportunity. If anything which is theoretically possible ought to be thought of as a candidate for serious consideration, all of science fiction and poets' dreams might be appropriate grist for the decision mill. Imagine, for example, that a planner could realistically consider floating bedroom suburbs in the air, so that they could hover over the places of work during the day and places of play at other times. Obviously, the relative desirability of various public transport systems would be different from what they are if the bedroom suburb must stay securely fastened to the township of Scarsdale. However, possibilities that are separated from

---

[15] Ibid., p. 214. For a summary suggesting the potential of simulation see Simulation in Social Sciences, Reading, H. Guetzkow, Ed., Prentice-Hall, Englewood Cliffs, N.J., 1962; "Symposium on Simulation," American Economic Review, December 1960, pp. 893–932.

[16] A very useful compendium is Contemporary Approaches to Creative Thinking, Howard E. Gruber, G. Terrell and M. Wertheimer, Eds., Atherton Press, New York, 1963. It contains articles by people as diverse in their approaches as Jerome Bruner, Herbert Simon with his collaborators Allen Newell and J. C. Shaw, and Richard Crutchfield. Other works in which a notion of the scope of investigation can be judged are the annotated bibliography by Morris I. Stein and Shirley J. Heinze, Creativity and the Individual, Free Press, Glencoe, Illinois, 1960, and essays on Creativity and Its Cultivation, Harold D. Anderson, Ed., Harper Bros., New York, 1959.

the present by wide technological gaps must also carry very heavy un-certainty discounts. Furthermore, man's dreams do not venture thus fantastically; they haunt the edge of his waking day. These more proxi-mate advancive possibilities certainly provide competition to the well-understood choices. Their judicious introduction into the deliberative process is necessary to purposive learning.

One further necessity should be mentioned. When the deliberative process is viewed as dynamic and open ended, the purposes to be served may themselves not remain stationary. They are likely to change as a result of the deeper understanding of the problem which carrying through the deliberative process (at a person-oriented and task-oriented level) entails. They are likely to change as a result of interrelationships between ends and means (as suggested in the goals-means pyramid, of Chap-ter 5). But most significantly, they are, hopefully, likely to change because the purposes served undergo intentional clarification and devel-opment as part of the deliberative learning enterprise.

People and Organizations

Both the importance of advancive behavior and the complexity and subtlety of many deliberative processes imply, above all, that able people are required and that they must work in institutions in which their abilities can be utilized and enhanced. To develop this proposition, which is written between the lines of this book with increasing fre-quency as the argument progresses, would require another book. How-ever, let me stress a few assorted points.

With respect to people, *judgment* is an essential attribute in poorly structured situations. In this age of numbers and specialization, it is perhaps permissible to reassert the obvious: good judgment is a vital ingredient of deliberation. Judgment addresses reality and value. The first requires excellence in the capacity to imagine and to "assess the outcome of multiple, causal interactions, to apply appropriate time scales, to comprehend uncertainties, most of all perhaps to simplify without distorting by excluding the inessential."[17] The second, good judgment about values, is perhaps still more elusive. How much and what sort of movement toward the possible is benign? From whose point of view, and how should and can conflicting interest be combined? Selection of the appropriate time and spatial framework is a critical matter, and it may be that wise men characteristically set frames more broadly than others.

With respect to organizations, the DOSRAP diagram suggests the

[17] Vickers, *op. cit.*, p. 73.

kinds of policies that are needed. Clearly, for example, organizations will be better, other things the same, the *more frequent and the more frequented are channels of information.* The channels carry information within an organization; they carry information among organizations whose work has significant linkages. The sorts of information which must be assembled and joined are widely disparate. They concern know-how, facts, values, and people. An effective organization must facilitate the constant interrelating of information at these several levels. Theory and methods of collecting and utilizing information are the subject of a growing research emphasis.[18]

The process also, I suspect, implies waste—*redundancy.*[19] Only when questions and goals are precise is it possible to move efficiently in a straight line. An important application of the general point is in the notion of parallel R and D efforts which shows that staged duplication can actually be the efficient procedure.[20] But more broadly, the minute that experimentation enters, some experiments will be unpredictably more useful than others, and the organizational structure must provide for the duplication necessary to selection of the better result. The junk pile for ideas can be a good, not a bad, thing. Proponents of one course are encouraged to compete with those of another.

The model also has strong implications concerning the system of rewards that are required. The tendency to reward overconservatism and penalize judicious risk taking was noted in Chapter 8 as one of the reasons for conservative bias, and it appears again toward the end of this chapter. But from the standpoint of organizational structure, a more difficult problem is to *hitch a reward system to the pursuit of goals,* rather than to the proliferation of means (which empire building encourages). Experiment implies that there will be losers. The reward system should not force the losers to pretend, by hook or crook, to be winners; rather should they be moved, with appropriate reward, to the next problem.

[18] The launching pad for information theory was probably Norbert Wiener's *Cybernetics,* Massachusetts Institute of Technology, Boston, 1948 (revised 1961). For a fine summary statement see Jacob Marschak, "Economics of Inquiring, Communicating, Deciding," *American Economic Review,* Papers and Proceedings, May 1968, pp. 1–18.

[19] The point has been made by Yehezkel Dror in *Public Policymaking Reexamined,* Chandler Publishing Co., San Francisco, 1968. Dror selects nine very interesting "essential structural requirements for optimal policymaking," pp. 210–213.

[20] R. R. Nelson, *The Economics of Parallel R and D Efforts: A Sequential-Decision Analysis,* The Rand Corporation, RM2482, November 12, 1959, and Burton H. Klein, "The Decision Making Problem in Development," in *The Rate and Direction of Inventive Activity,* R. Nelson, Ed., Conference of the Universities National Bureau Committee, Princeton University Press, 1962.

The model has further implications bearing on the sort of *management information systems* that are required. The emphasis on the process means that how well the process is carried through ought to be visible to top management. There should be ways to reveal the amount and content of "bits" of information, the caliber of motivation and dedication. On the latter score, Rensis Likert is devising techniques for "human resource accounting" because measures of "intervening variables" in contrast to "end result variables" are needed to reflect the ". . . condition of the internal state of the organization, its loyalty, skills, motivation and capacity for effective interaction, communication and decision making."[21]

In the next chapter, the number five items on the checklist add some further ways of coping with uncertainty by "adapting the organization." However, the fundamental frustration remains: I have sketched deliberative procedures, the use of which is dependent, among other things, on an appropriate organizational structure, without being able to make more than a few random remarks on that large subject.

INTENDEDLY RATIONAL DELIBERATIVE PROCESS

In Chapters 6 and 7, we developed an approach to choice among predelineated acts which started by identifying the decision situation in terms of its attribute profile in order to judge the aspiration level appropriate to the decision process. Thereafter, one of three sorts of "decision rules" would be selected—a complete matrix of alternatives and their probabilities, focus outcomes, or a stepwise process, in which either of the other two rules are applied sequentially. A similar approach, appropriately adapted, has applications to various aspects of DOSRAP in whole or part.

Aspiration Level

Abjuring Decision

Whether a problem should be tackled at all depends on a judgment which compares the uncertainty- and time-discounted value of what might eventually be accomplished with an estimate of the cost of the decision process itself. Of course, this judgment may be reversed as

---

[21] Rensis Likert, *New Patterns of Management,* McGraw-Hill Book Company Inc., New York, 1961, p. 61. The University of Michigan Institute for Social Research is engaged in efforts to devise measures of intervening variables for the purpose of "human resource accounting."

deliberation proceeds, since estimates either of the expected value of the outcome or the cost of further deliberation may change.

The costs of deliberation include the direct expense of staffing, other expenses associated with the process and the outcome, and the opportunity costs of what individuals and resources so engaged would otherwise produce. There may be the further cost of good will that is foregone by raising unpopular questions. When only a limited number of questions can be raised, as is usually in some degree the case, there is the opportunity cost of other decisions that are foregone. Particularly in the political arena, efforts seem necessarily confined to only a few major directions at a given time; there are, in other words, popular-attention constraints analogous to the well-known budget constraints.[22] "Any given issue must compete with other issues for those scarce resources which determine the outcome: time, energy, attention, money, manpower, and goodwill. Where a given issue stands in priority affects not only the fight for resources but also the whole matter of its handling."[23]

A further cost of decision may be that of precluding a better decision later on when some of the uncertainties have diminished. I might add that there can likewise be a cost of avoiding a decision or of specifically deciding in favor of the status quo. The cost is intensified when the decision, or the failure to decide, tends to be irreversible. The foremost example of an irreversible positive decision is a declaration of war. A common example of the irreversible negative decision concerns preservation of recreation land—large tracts of land once built up tend to be, for all practical purposes, unavailable for reconversion to open space.

Attributes Profile

The attributes profile—indicating how well structured is the decision collective, how rich and clear the information, and how well confined the boundaries of the problem with which it deals—determines (as

---

[22] Luther Gulick tells a story from the early days of Franklin D. Roosevelt's administration. Braintrusters were advocating a course of action consisting of pushing a number of programs in combination; they billed their recommendations as capable of "optimizing the output of scarce resources." The President admitted that their solutions would no doubt optimize the output of scarce resources as they defined them. Nevertheless, they had the wrong answer. The critical scarce resource as he saw it was public attention.

[23] R. A. Bauer, I. de Sola Pool and L. A. Dexter, *American Business and Public Policy, The Politics of Foreign Trade*, Atherton Press, New York, 1963, p. 479. The research underlying the book consisted of surveys of 903 business leaders. The interviews "inquired into the sources from which these business leaders learned news in general and that of foreign-trade problems in particular . . . "; attitudes toward foreign trade and what businessmen did or did not do about it were studied, p. 6.

for decision proper) the finesse with which the deliberative-adminis-trative process may be carried through. However, there are important differences:

First, it is often possible to control, and thus to elect, how well struc-tured a deliberative problem is to be. The decision profile, for example, is likely to be affected by the "system" in the context of which a problem is to be considered. Broadening the system will often imply poor struc-ture for one or more attributes. nevertheless, some of the more dramatic results of operations-research teams have been achieved by changing, typically broadening, the conceptual framework in which a problem is set.

Second, the conduct of deliberations can be purposely arranged to *change* the attributes profile. Some improvement in its structure is vir-tually necessary to move toward a final outcome. However, a collective may aspire toward more or toward less improvement. For example, cost-benefit analysis can be used, as it unfortunately so often is, to develop information on a single alternative to the status quo; thereby, the need for information about other alternatives is ignored. In a more positive direction, skill in the conduct of deliberation achieved by virtue of ade-quate organization, personnel, and procedures can shift the attributes profile to the left as the process proceeds—sequential disks on the model contract and darken more markedly.

Constraints of Money, Personnel, Time, and Politics

Whereto one may usefully aspire, either in terms of the process of consideration or the act considered, depends on the resources that are at all likely to be available.

Perhaps the most obvious constraint is money. When budget strings are tightly drawn, all courses of action, including the conduct of decision itself, are confined to those that require a minimum of cash. A small business struggling to keep alive has few choices with respect to what problems to take on; there is one perennial problem: to have the cash in the bank required to pay the bills for rent, materials, and payroll City governments, with ten departments scrambling to capture each tax dollar, are spending at the level of proscriptive need, not of delib-erate choice. Developing nations are often heavily constrained by tight pursestrings—whether due to scarcity in liquid funds, in savings that can be drawn into new ventures, in foreign exchange, or in the inability to borrow at home or abroad.

Scarcity in the quantity of available personnel can produce close paral-lels to each of these cases. Although there are trade-offs between money and scarce personnel, the available hours of the day of people with necessary qualifications for accepting new responsibilities will often determine how effectively a problem can be dealt with or indeed whether it can be taken on at all.

The third constraint can be time. The decision process itself may need to yield a fast answer because the "time is ripe" for action and will soon grow overripe. Speed may also be required of the action selected. For example, the fact that executives tend to switch their jobs every few years has been cited as a chief reason why the building of well-motivated staff tends to be neglected—by the time the results of improved motivation appear, their creator may be elsewhere; he is better off using disciplinary methods that can get results while he is around. Thus aspirations to develop the best response to a problem are constrained by a very high time discount.

Finally, politics either in its narrow or broad meaning can severely limit how worthwhile it is to search for a good answer. What ought to be done (and technically and financially can be done) is often crystal clear; yet it may be politically quite out of reach. The required consensus and get-up-and-go could not be mobilized. This can apply to business as well as governmental problems.

Acceptable Levels of Risk

Finally, aspiration levels are affected by the capacities to tolerate uncertainty. In poorly seriable situations, particularly where constraints are tight, the exchange rates between risk and reward (as discussed in Chapter 3) reflect a rapidly rising risk discount as the constraint boundaries are approached. Opulence is valuable not only because it can purchase an ample prize but because it makes it possible to take a chance at a huge one. As Burton Klein has put it, "Economists have said a good deal about decision making under uncertainty, but very little about decision making when the responsible person is in the position to do something about the uncertainties facing him."[24] It may even at times make sense to pay a considerable price in terms of probable short-term payoff in order to reduce risk. If so, the deliberative process itself must be shaped to achieve more readily realizable results. An aspiration for a sophisticated canvas of all possibilities is replaced by an effort to produce a fail-safe answer.

Types of Deliberative Formats

Some one of the three types of decision "rules" developed in earlier chapters—complete distributions, focus outcomes, stepwise choice—

---

[24] Burton H. Klein, *Op. cit.*, p. 477.

apply by definition to stage 3 of DOSRAP, decision proper, although in many actual situations, as in the IBM case, the central choice among predelineated acts is a small part of the total deliberative process.

One of the three formats can likewise apply to the vast number of interstitial decisions that carry deliberations on to a conclusion: decisions at each turn which may concern person-oriented and task-oriented aspects of the process.

However, the three approaches, after appropriate adaptation, are also broadly applicable to DOSRAP as a whole. I shall now say a word on the first and third; the focus-outcome approach is discussed in the next section.

Complete Distributions and Stepwise Procedures

Deliberation that develops, in effect, a complete probability distribution (however sketchily supplied with numbers) can guide the deliberative-administrative process throughout. An illustration is the well-structured inventory problem mentioned in the previous chapter; there the need for reexamining the inventory formula, defining objectives to be sought, variables to be considered, and alternative functional relationships worth considering are all reasonably clear and subject to quantification in a probabilistic framework. The approach can even be extended to much of the broad-system inventory problem if utility itself is recognized as probabilistic (the three-dimensional matrix).

The third format, stepwise procedure, is obviously natural to DOSRAP as a whole and its individual steps can of course use the complete distribution or selective approach to deal with utilities or acts. Multiple, sequential elections are the essence of what occurs. Timing leeways occur within each stage as well as among them; they can be deliberately utilized to clarify values or ways to achieve them. Timing strategies can affect the relative importance of the five stages (particularly how much information feedback can be built into stages 4 and 5). They can, perhaps most important, affect the size of the bite into the problem that is made by each of the recursive cycles of decision. The election to use the short-jump, experimental method is partly an option in the time dimension. These matters are drawn into the horizontal dimension of the DOSRAP model.

But note that the decision tree applicable to DOSRAP differs in this comprehensive respect from those appropriate to choice among predelineated acts: the branchings are not necessarily known to start with, or at any later point. Thus, not only answers (the response to signals expected to be forthcoming) but also questions are developed in a stepwise fashion. The "decision tree" cannot be previewed; it must be grown as it is climbed.

Focus Outcomes and Focus Utilities

In connection with problems at the policy level, DOSRAP as a whole will typically be dealing with *multiple purposes and multiple means.* Thus, the same need to reduce outcomes to something with which the mind of man can cope, discussed in Chapter 7, applies also to purposes and utilities. I suggest that the focus approach can be used for the latter purpose as well as for the former. The collective decision maker selects one or more *bundles of utilities upon which to focus.* These are then interpreted in terms of the acts (often several acts), and focus outcomes for each act (or group of acts) are selected as previously described; evaluated, they provide the basis for judging the relative desirability of the alternatives.[25] But the final assessment is made in terms of the capacity to generate the *bundle of utilities chosen as a focus* of attention, rather than in terms of some comprehensive open-ended total utility system.

That purposes are typically compound was evident in the description of how utility is designated in Chapter 5. An example there given pertaining to water supply indicated that projects need to be consonant with multiple goals concerning potable water, recreation, conservation, etc. Further, some weighting of the several purposes is prerequisite to moving on to the selection of engineering proposals (the specific reservoir, flood skimming, desalination scheme, singly and in combination) that are worth costing out.

The DOSRAP model shows this process of defining and combining purposes as concentrated in stage 1, strong in stage 2, but continuing in terms of a back-and-forth ends-means dialogue throughout the process.

I have made the further point that multiple means (acts) are often needed to serve the purpose on which attention focuses. The point has

[25] The text describes what I take to be intendedly rational and typical procedure. Sometimes, however, it may be easier to get agreement among members of a collective with respect to an action to be taken than with respect to the purpose which that action will serve. Indeed, this sort of aid to consensus has been mentioned as one of the advantages of uncertain (incomplete) knowledge. Yet situations of this sort may perhaps be described not so much as never having arrived at focus utilities as having done so at a subcollective level; each member makes his own calculations about the purposes he wishes to serve and determines that the chances are acceptable that the act will do so to an acceptable extent. The act, in effect, is sufficiently versatile to pass the test on the basis of different examination questions.

been underscored by some very interesting work which shows that *compound* means are often needed for the optimal pursuit of a *single* end.

The notion contradicts the generally accepted idea that there is one best way to accomplish a specified purpose. If knowledge is complete, a one-to-one matching of "instruments" to "targets" is an efficient procedure.[26] But decision theorists have held to that instruction, even when the consequences of applying the instruments are probabilistic, by maintaining that "uncertainty equivalents" match targets and instruments on a one-to-one basis in an uncertain world.[27]

However, William Brainard in an important recent article has shown that this rule only applies when uncertainty is unrelated to the instrument (or means); when, in other words, it is simply an exogenous, random variable.[28] Brainard demonstrates that if there are a number of instruments which can help to further one policy target, the optimal course will tend to utilize all of them in a fashion which "combines the instruments so as to minimize the coefficient of variation of their combined impact." This implies "that in general all instruments available should be used in pursuing one target." Further, it follows that "the addition of an objective requires some sacrifice in performance vis-a-vis objectives already being considered."[29]

The questions and answers that William Brainard discusses move toward bridging a gap between guts judgment and the formal logic of decision theory. Every policy maker or, indeed, investor knows that it is usually foolish "to put all the eggs in one basket" and that important objectives must be closed in on by approaching from several sides.

[26] J. Tinbergen, *On the Theory of Economic Policy*, North-Holland Publishing Company, Amsterdam, 1952.

[27] See, for example, C. C. Holt, F. Modigliani, J. F. Muth, and H. A. Simon, *Planning Production, Inventories, and Workforce*, Prentice-Hall, New York, 1960, and Henry Theil, *Economic Forecasts and Policy*, North-Holland Publishing Company, Amsterdam, 1961.

[28] "Uncertainty and the Effectiveness of Policy," *American Economic Review*, Papers and Proceedings, May 1967, pp. 411–425. He points out that an exogenous random variable (u) is, of course, present in the effectiveness with which an instrument operates. However, there are uncertainties of other sorts associated with how a policy instrument will perform and Brainard consolidates them into one group— uncertainty about the effectiveness of the instrument (y). This uncertainty is measured by the variance of the coefficient, a, in $y = aP + u$ where P is performance and u the consolidated impact of exogenous variables. Brainard demonstrates that the utility generated by pursuing a given policy depends not only on the size of the coefficient, a, and of u, but also on the variance of a, and on its correlation with the variance of u. Positive covariance between the variance of a and u should cause the policy maker "to shoot for a lower value of $\bar{y}$ than otherwise; if negative, higher" (*ibid*, p. 416).

[29] Above quotes from *ibid.*, pp. 419 and 418.

The analysis clarifies the meaning of "an alternative." Typically it is a bundle of individual acts or approaches. And such a bundle, rather than individual items in it, is usually the best choice, even when the individual items have no capacity to reinforce one another in a cumulative fashion. When they do have this capacity, there is a further reason for considering compound courses of action.

If the question of compound purposes is raised, as it must be, the analysis suggests the desirability of finding bundles of acts which overlap with respect to the purposes they serve. For example, both cleaning up pollution in a river and confining the withdrawal of water to months when water levels are high (flood skimming) serve the purpose of providing potable water, improving recreation and perhaps ecological balance. However, no one of the purposes is served as well as it could be in isolation.[30]

In any event, the point that I want to make is that the focus-outcome approach, introduced by G. S. Shackle as a rigorous decision rule, has in the deliberative-administrative process as a whole progressively widening applications in terms of focus utilities as well as outcomes and their evolving interrelationships.

THE CONSERVATIVE BIAS REVISITED

The subjects discussed thus far in this chapter aim to point out a number of things to do in order to improve deliberative processes. In this last section I turn to things not to do—things which tend to produce the malady of overconservatism. That there is an underlying tendency for choice to result in costs of uncertainty that are too high was noted in Chapter 8. The costs there considered were associated with the knowledge gap and consisted of excessive routine uncertainty discounts and the befuddlement that uncertainty engenders. "Too high" a cost could

---

[30] Henry Wallich develops a case for compromise between two criterion in connection with economic advice to the heads of governments. He shows that an adviser can increase the likelihood that his advice will be followed if he recommends a policy which is somewhere between what his client thinks should be done and what the adviser thinks should be done. By so doing he sacrifices (relative to his first choice) expected value of the recommended act if it is undertaken, for a better chance that it will be undertaken; the trade is intended to increase the uncertainty discounted expected value of the final result. Henry C. Wallich, "The American Council of Economic Advisers and the German *Sachverstaendigenrat*, A Study in the Economics of Advice," *The Quarterly Journal of Economics*, August 1968, pp. 349–379. This article should be required reading.

be said to result if, given the realities of the decision situation (the characteristics of the collective and of the problem), the collective failed to make the most of its opportunities. Sources of bias causing excessive costs were discussed under the headings: unrecognized seriability, "excessive" risk aversion, a conservative bias of management, concentration on wing-boundary outcomes, and the "numbers illusion." The net result was a tendency for less risky alternatives to be favored relative to more risky ones; particularly, the do-nothing act tended to look too good.

Bias from the Point of View of the Decision-Making Unit

All of these costs operate with added force in the deliberative-administrative situation as a whole. The early decision stages, deciding to decide and designating alternatives, provide numerous opportunities for conservative biases to creep in. DOSRAP, in other words, is susceptible to excessive costs of uncertainty related to the knowledge gap. Moreover, there tends to be a further bias which manifests itself in undue possibility shortfall. For example, the excessive risk aversion and the conservative bias of management discussed in Chapter 8 can have the following further ramifications in the context of DOSRAP:

Ongoing deliberation offers many options concerning when decision is to be made and when consequences will accrue. These choices invite the bias of distorted time preference, if, as I judge is the case, it is common for people to discount for futurity more heavily than would truly serve their own long-range advantage.

Options concerning what to consider can benefit from a willingness to learn, to search for opportunities, to devise the human and physical means of achieving a contemplated objective. Yet these are scarce traits. We prefer "to bear those ills we have than fly to those we know not of." In addition, a greater responsibility somehow seems to attach to saying "yes" than to saying "no."

Organizations tend to reinforce these psychological foundations for abjuring risk and avoiding the activity of looking for problems to solve, or (as idiom perceives) "looking for trouble." Only a very rare president of a corporation seeks out and fires the executive who "no longer wants to take any risks."[31] In government, political costs are particularly likely to penalize action relative to inaction. The electorate and the press tend to ignore poor outcomes when they result from unchanged routines; but the alarm flashes when they result from ill-fated change. Rules of tenure and of promotion by seniority, whether overt or covert, stifle

---

[31] Lee S. Bickmore, President, Nabisco Company, "Lessons of Leadership: Making Decision-Makers," *Nation's Business*, October 1967 (Vol. 55, No. 10).

ambition. Paper work and red tape tie down action. The list is familiar. In government, such things tend to produce a standard image of the civil servant: a man who manages to remain unobtrusive, to play all the angles, and to accomplish the expected—no more and only a little less.

The conservative bias of management may have a further systematic source which involves considerations actually relevant to a course of action but lying outside the jurisdiction or perspectives of the deciding unit. These intraorganizational externalities may be fostered by a tendency for the management structure for *operations and control* to be generally narrower than that needed for *evaluation and decision*. In government, specialization and "home rule" may similarly be more suited to effective operation than to effective evaluation and planning.

These conservative biases limit the alternatives that are considered. They hide the sort of inaction which is so often a stubborn tenant of the institutional woodwork. They deteriorate the effectuation of whatever it is decided to undertake. Anticipation of such deterioration affects the judgments on which further decision rests. All of these depressants would, it would seem, tend to affect advancive possibilities more than those which are regarded as the standard things to talk about, such as what to do in order to keep one's "industry position" or to meet departmental or budget bureau standards. If so, advancive courses of action tend to be slighted.

Bias in Societal Behavior

Excessive costs of uncertainty which deteriorate the behavior of organizations in the ways that have been enumerated constitute a loss to society as a whole. The loss sums all of the losses due to less-than-quasi-optimal outcomes for each of the individual organizations. But there are further impacts on society which cause the total to be more than the sum of its parts—the possibility shortfall for society at large can amplify the shortfall for the individual decision units.

Externalities

Since uncertainty makes decisions more difficult yet does not by the same token make people smarter, it is clear that, on the average, decision problems in a world of uncertainty must be handled by people less able to cope with them. Individual organizations can escape from this dilemma by paying the price required to hire able people. But no such escape is provided for the community as a whole. Over time, the distribution of decisions, by difficulty, can be altered a bit so as to draw closer to the distribution of people, by capacity to cope. Likewise the capacity to cope can be improved. This is what training and the pursuit of technological advance attempts to achieve—advances in technology addressed to conceptual, managerial, and psychological as well as physical problems.

Scarcity of ability to cope with uncertainty has a qualitative dimension. There seems to be a complementarity of sorts between efficiency and imagination. In any case both are needed. G. L. S. Shackle observes that the manager is taught science; ". . . problem-solving is the bread and butter of life, and we shall starve without those who can do it. But besides those who can see ahead of them the one right answer we need those who can see around them a million possibilities. We need the radial, as well as the axial, type of mind."[32]

There are a number of further inconsistencies between the sum of individual advantage in coping with uncertainty and that of society as a whole. Thus the individual collective frames values, and determines probabilities within the compass of its own bailiwick (and often even there within too narrow a "system"). If a wider compass had been used, both values and probabilities might have differed. Thus, probabilities are often assessed in the context of a poorly seriable situation which, if the long-run welfare of society at large were the governing criterion, could have been shifted to a jurisdiction in terms of which a high order of seriability might have been achieved. Such is the role of insurance.[33] Society is, in effect, the super-Lloyd's of London; its profit depends on the net Expected Value of all risky ventures. Which individuals prosper and which succumb is, for the most part, quite immaterial to the total net result.

But the most important cost to society associated with failure to apply an appropriate systems framework results from the differences in *values* held at different levels of jurisdiction. The impact on the public at large of a power company optimizing its behavior in terms of its own interest is an illustration. The concerns of the municipality in which it is located include not only the electric power that the business generates and sells, but also the smoke that its chimneys generate and give away.

Time likewise may deserve different evaluation at wider levels of

---

[32] "Policy, Poetry and Success," *Economic Journal*, December 1966, p. 767.

[33] Though there is no reason to expect a bias against the use of insurance, its net effect on the totality of decision is unclear because of the "moral hazard"—the possibility that "the insurance policy might itself change incentives and therefore the probabilities upon which the insurance company has relied." (Kenneth J. Arrow, "Aspects of the Theory of Risk-Bearing," Yrjö Yahnssonia Säätiö, Helsinki, 1964, p. 55.)

jurisdiction. Should, for example, a national government, in the capacity of steward for ongoing national welfare, apply a time discount to expected benefits such as outdoor recreation and clean air for future generations?

There are, of course, many ways in which such costs of a too-limited value system can be reduced. Decisions at lower levels can be required to conform to criteria based on a wider reference. Specific aspects of lower-level problems can be dealt with by representatives of wider levels. Inducements or penalties may be invented which reward behavior of the desirable sort. Finally, there is the obvious expedient of transferring the entire problem to the organization having the more appropriate, the broader, value scheme. But such transfers may involve disadvantages on other counts—inefficient administration, concentration of power, loss of flexibility and of accountability, attrition of energy and will. It is the *net* advantage of transfer on all counts which should be sought.

The Interactive-Process Multiplier

The influence of these biases does not stop with the first impact. The losses are multiplied by piecemeal, interactive, recursive processes variously described as social learning, circular and cumulative causation, and ecological interaction. When change is cut back, a step is not taken which, had it been taken, would have provided a foothold for the next change, and this in turn for the next, and so on.

Obviously, implications of these sorts are very unevenly distributed among the decisions made in the course of a working day. However, it seems likely that the strength of the multiplier will be positively associated with the importance of the decision and with the extent to which it implies change.

Moreover, in a world of large organizations, making large-scale decisions, the particulars of virtually random events magnified by the interactive-process multiplier can place an imprint on the future.

The cumulating interactions take place in a number of dimensions and the basic arithmetic is multiplicative rather than additive: Values interact with means. Today interacts with yesterday and tomorrow. Decisions affecting one problem react upon other related problems. Places too are bound together by the complex interrelatedness of ideas and events.

In short, the conduct of private and public business in a world in which uncertainty abounds, appears subject to biases which cause deliberative-administrative processes to yield less by way of advantage than they would if uncertainty were dealt with in a more rational fashion. Society as a whole loses, in addition to the sum of these penalties to the organizations which comprise it, further penalties associated with a tendency to undertake decision under the aegis of too narrow a system —one which fails to exploit potential seriability, and the power to comprehend externalities, by restructuring the organizational or conceptual decision framework. Society loses from the initial impact of these several biases. But it loses far more as interactive processes build upon them. Deficiencies in risk assignments, in value system, in know-how, and indeed in the will to search and strive all cumulate to foreshorten societal achievement and progress.

The summary sections for each part of this book seem to rattle the conceptual bars that confine them. This final section is no exception.

When planning on uncertainty is opened to the creative aspects of ongoing administrative behavior and to the interaction among behavioral units throughout an economy, planning becomes open-ended. The role of prediction dwindles and the role of purpose grows. The personalistic view of consequences, reflecting subjective degrees of belief, seems strikingly inadequate when applied to values. One man's purposes, embodied in actions, far more routinely than the act itself, have externalities which circle outward. There is no escape from the large question of what values *should* be pursued.[34] "No past experience, however rich, and no historical research, however thorough, can save the living generation the creative task of finding their own answers and shaping their own future."[35]

I started this book by pointing out that uncertainty is a desirable attribute of life. The uncertainty of both joy and doom makes the first desirable and the second bearable. But the step-by-step argument has led to the further unexpected thought that uncertainty makes us all partners in our own and one another's fortune—the joy and the doom that lie ahead are partly of our own making. There is an operation-bootstrap at the core of things which presupposes faith and commitment: faith in adventure and seeking, faith that what lies ahead can be ever more attractive and attracting; commitment in the application of energy and cumulating expertise in seeing that what can and should be, is.

Our own tiny planet is itself an expanding universe. Contribution to the extent and manner of its growth is each man's burden and each man's enticing opportunity.

[34] It is particularly interesting to find the question asked in the context indicated by the title of C. West Churchman's book, *Prediction and Optimal Decision* (Prentice-Hall, Englewood Cliffs, N.J., 1961), by someone who has been a leader in the field of operations research. See particularly Chapter 8.
[35] Alexander Gerschenkron, *Economic Backwardness in Historic Perspective*, Harvard University Press, Cambridge, Mass., 1962, p. 6.

CHAPTER 13

Postscript: A List of Ways to Reduce Uncertainty's Costs

The previous chapters have been concerned with exploring broad approaches to improving the technology of the decision process in an uncertain world. If understanding of these broad approaches is to be of practical use, they must be convertible to the hard currency of specific things to do. Specifics tend to be myriad and best dealt with in terms of a number of case studies which are, of course, out of the question here. Nevertheless it should be useful at least to provide a checklist of the large number of ways in which the cost of uncertainty may be reduced. The major headings, if not the individual items, may be worth scanning.

The specifics group themselves along the course which the book has traveled and it is pertinent to reflect broadly on the basic trends of the argument.

AFTERTHOUGHTS ON THE INVESTIGATION'S EVOLUTION

Looking back, one is struck by the way in which subjects evolve into something else as they are examined under increasingly less restrictive assumptions. We started with decision as a sharply defined choice, and ended by almost losing decision in an active, potentially creative, persisting, administrative sequence whereby problems are formulated, semi-solutions engineered, values clarified and often changed, and new problems created.

We started with a choice, firmly anchored in a stabilized environment of givens. We have ended by finding that the active elements in DOSRAP come to include the need to influence the setting in which the process occurs—the conceptual context (the system, the organization, and time options) with their potential for purposive learning. Theories of decision, administration, and organization telescope into one another.

We started with the cost of uncertainty focused in the basically mathematical problem of dealing with probabilistic knowledge. We have ended by having to admit not only all sorts of strongly judgmental idiosyncratic, and nonquantitative elements into the calculation, but also, and far more striking, we have found that a major cost of uncertainty is the failure to seek a more useful target.

We started with ambiguity viewed as causing, in Leonard Savage's words, "unsurmountable difficulties" which beset laws of decision when opinion is very unsure. Fellner and Ellsberg ventured to legitimize the difficulty by recognizing the bias or "slanting" that ambiguity generates. This conservative bias takes on more breadth, depth, and variety when natural man and actual situations are substituted for the classic notion of economic rationality. Then bias can spread to the things that failed to be duly considered or considered at all.

In summary, we started with a result that could be recognized as optimal. But the characteristics of man, the interactive complexities of situations and the open-endedness of what may usefully be attempted required the substitution of quasi-optimal aims—relative rather than absolute criteria. Finally, as decisions stretch into ongoing, staged, recursive processes which need to be maneuvered as well as designed, it is the process rather than the result to which the criteria of quasi-optimization typically must refer.

These transformations are evolutionary. The broader formulations *contain* the narrower ones. Statistical decision theory generates solution of some deliberative administrative problems, contributes to parts of others, and provides at least the bone of the conceptual structure of others, though they are fleshed out less with the muscle of statistical information than with the soft tissue of judgment, politics, and imagination.

The diversity of problems demands, I have emphasized, differences in basic decision strategies and guidelines for matching these strategies to decision situations.

Moreover, the construction of a deliberative process requires, in addition to the basic decision strategy, a multiplicity of particular ways to deal with the fundamental technical problem—inadequate knowledge. Many of these particulars are listed below.

The list might be more confusing than helpful if each decision problem required explicit consideration of each item. But of course this is not the case. True, fairly broad applicability characterizes those points of a very general nature which call attention to what is virtually sound management of the deliberative aspects of administration. Reducing the cost of uncertainty is, in effect, one angle from which the whole of management behavior directed to formulating policy can be viewed. But points which deal more narrowly with the technical methods of coping with uncertainty apply to some problems and not to others, and the number applicable to a given problem is usually small. The fact that there are so many methods attests rather to the large diversity of problems.

A CHECKLIST

Although the many ways of reducing uncertainty's cost form part of an interlocking system, it is not one which submits to neat classification free of overlap and duplication. Items that are virtually omnipresent and general are mentioned in section 1. Next, in sections 2 and 3, are ways to improve the selection of the problems which are tackled and the alternatives considered, including, in section 3, ways to modify the problem in order to make it more tractable. Section 4 deals with information and imagination. Sections 5 and 6 turn to the setting of decision, first in the institution and then in the environment. Section 7 deals with the recursive aspects of decision sequences. Partial duplication occurs when warranted by differences in emphasis appropriate to the sections.

The purpose in providing the checklist is simply to indicate the very many ways in which these seven approaches to reducing uncertainty's cost may be pursued. In the course of the book, virtually all of them have been mentioned, and some developed at length. My intention here is to classify and itemize rather than to explain. For some items, mainly chosen among those less fully discussed in the book, footnotes suggest where I happen to have found some interesting discussions.

1. View purposive deliberation in appropriate basic ways, thereby improving the *process* of decision making.
    1.1 Think probabilistically and in terms of minimizing (reducing) uncertainty's cost.
    1.2 Recognize the time dimension of most deliberative processes. This will emphasize decision as learning, thereby involving search, communication, flexibility, and often, further decision cycles.
    1.3 Recognize a potential need for parallel lines of deliberative endeavor—person-oriented (political) as well as task-oriented.

1.4 View all meaningfully relevant matters, whether measurable, intangible, or noncommensurable, whether accessible to calculation, or only to judgment or even intuition.

    1.4.1 Use the notion of trade-off surfaces for comparing noncommensurables.

    1.4.2 Deal, when appropriate, with increments and differences, rather than with total aggregate results.

1.5 Match decision strategies to decision situations as typed, for example, by the attributes profile.

2. Choose and structure what to decide. These points apply mainly to stages 1 and 2, deciding to decide and selecting alternatives.

    2.1 Is the problem, considered probabilistically, ripe for deciding. Some relevant issues concern:

        2.1.1 Suitability for rational deliberation (versus "disjointed incrementalism," etc.).

        2.1.2 The costs of deciding (compared with the range of expected uncertainty-discounted benefits).

        2.1.3 Advantages or disadvantages of acting now rather than later.

        2.1.4 Should the problem be shifted to a different jurisdiction because of an inappropriate basis for action or inappropriate basis for value judgment (section 5.6, below).

    2.2 Clarify the values sought.

        2.2.1 Should purposes be conceived in terms of moving away from ills.

        2.2.2 Formulate of measures of merit.

        2.2.3 Be wary of uncritical use of "projections" (such as of population in a region, etc.) as, in effect, goals for planning.

    2.3 Select an appropriate frame of reference.

        2.3.1 The aspiration level—the finesse or crudity to which deliberations should aspire.[1]

        2.3.2 The appropriate context or "system" in terms of which the problem should be structured.

    2.4 Consider the internal timing of the decision process.

        2.4.1 The relative emphasis on each stage.

        2.4.2 The length of decision cycles as a whole in view, especially, of learning potential, see also section 3.4 below.

    2.5 Select alternative acts with special attention to:

---

[1] See discussion of structural attributes, Chapters 6 and 11. A particularly interesting discussion of what is worthwhile to try for is by Roland McKean in "Cost-Benefit Analysis and British Defense Expenditures," *Scottish Journal of Political Economy*, February 1963, Vol. X, No. 1. See particularly pp. 26, 32, and 35.

2.5.1 The true range of possibilities which ought to be developed to the point where they may be viewed as genuine alternatives.[2]

2.5.2 Multiple ways of pursuing a simple (to say nothing of a compound) purpose.

2.5.3 Constraints of time, money, and personnel on what may be usefully attempted.

2.5.4 Potential for building self-validating mechanisms into alternatives.

2.5.5 Productivity of advancive alternatives.

3. Modify the decision problem so as to reduce the uncertainty discount (without equivalent increase in other costs or decrease in utility). Stages 3 and, to a lesser extent, 2 and 4 are mainly concerned here.

3.1 Structure selection in terms of appropriate probabilistic notions (over and above the use of the proper analytic model).[3]

3.1.1 Find salient or dominant solutions, those best under all contingencies.[4]

3.1.2 Contingency analysis: consider how choice stands up if a selected element is assumed to change.

3.1.3 A fortiori analysis: consider two alternatives first with all uncertainties resolved in favor of the first and then in favor of the second alternative.[5]

---

[2] When alternatives need preliminary investigation there is sometimes a tendency for only one alternative to be developed in one effort at one time. See article by Roland N. McKean and Melvin Anshen in "Problems, Limitations and, Risks," in *Program Budgeting; Program Analysis and the Federal Budget,* D. Novick, Ed., Harvard University Press, Cambridge, Mass., 1965. The authors caution against the tendency for cost-utility analysis within an agency to become a "design study" rather than a study of alternatives. "When a cost-utility analysis is begun within an agency, participants and successive echelons of reviewers perceive that their superiors frown upon certain alternatives. It seems useless, perhaps even risky, to put the strongest case possible for the unpopular alternatives." Gradually they are dropped. They point to the fact that the presence of rival agencies helps to insure against this development (p. 297).

[3] For a fine exposition in the context of a water resource problem see Robert Dorfman, "Basic Economic and Technological Concepts: A General Statement," in *Design of Water Resource Systems,* Arthur Maass et al., Eds., Harvard University Press, Cambridge, Mass., 1966.

[4] Kenneth Boulding in *Conflict and Defense* (Harper, New York, 1961) discusses saliency in terms of some solution that is much more likely than other solutions to receive acceptance by both parties often without actual bargaining (p. 314). The point has an interesting bearing on the lure of the status quo, various aspects of which I have discussed.

[5] See discussion by Gene H. Fisher, "The Role of Cost-Utility Analysis in Program Budgeting," in *Program Budgeting, op. cit.,* p. 74.

3.1.4 Concentrate on some values and ignore others and "suboptimize the solution for these limited criteria."[6]

3.1.5 Reduce the difficulty of problems by factoring out parts capable of supporting well-structured analysis. These well-developed nuggets of information can then be set in the framework of the more judgmental aspects of the problem.[7]

3.1.6 Use Bayesian formulation of "prior" and "posterior" probabilities to improve capacity to deal with chains of probabilistic occurrences.[8]

3.1.7 Use "Sensitivity Analysis" to judge how sensitive consequences are to ranges in possible values of a few most critical variables. The calculations may be run through with, say, an optimistic, pessimistic, and most likely value.[9]

3.2 Increase seriability (or convert uncertainty to risk).

3.2.1 Buy insurance.

3.2.2 Achieve partial insurance by structuring decision in the organization so as to pool the impact (personal and financial) of many decisions. Pooling can feature interproblem pooling or that of similar problems over a longer span of time.

3.2.3 Achieve partial insurance by moving a problem to the jurisdiction of broader-based organization. The federal government is a prime example of an organization with power to pool risk spatially and temporarily.

3.3 Hedge.

---

[6] Charles Hitch discusses this method as appropriate to dealing at least at the lower level of military policy. He comments, "But at best, criteria selection is hard—harder in force composition than in operations problems, hardest in development problems. We have wrestled with criterion selection at Rand for eight years with at best moderate success. We have found negative rules—criteria to avoid—but few positive rules of general helpfulness. There is no substitute for good judgment, and no substitute for exercising it." "An Appreciation of Systems Analysis," *Journal of the Operations Research Society of America*, November 1955, p. 474.

[7] A common example is cost-benefit analysis of the conventional sort where costs and benefits are quantified in dollars but the net dollar benefit is finally viewed in the context of all other nonquantifiable advantages and disadvantages.

[8] For the basics of this approach see Irwin D. J. Bross, *Design for Decision* (Macmillan, New York, 1953), p. 81 ff, or William Fellner, *Probability and Profit* (Richard D. Irwin, Inc., 1965), pp. 48–56.

[9] Alain C. Enthoven has discussed the use of this method by the Department of Defense in "Decision Theory and Systems Analysis," in *The Armed Forces Comptroller*, March 1964, pp. 16–17. The procedure gets very tricky if, because there are several critical variables, sensitivity analysis is required for possible *combinations* of variation.

3.3.1 Use available formal institutions for hedging if such are available.

3.3.2 Accept a mixed solution, one that includes insurance against catastrophe at the expense of a less desirable most probable result.

3.4 Stage decision in the light of possibilities to improve information.

3.4.1 Buy time—the net advantage is the gain from better information minus the cost of delay.

3.4.2 Buy information which may add to 3.4.1 a further cost of acquiring the information.[10]

3.4.3 Parallel path development.[11]

3.4.4 Experimental trial run. When many small decisions and actions are administratively dispersed this method offers large opportunity. It has served well in the field of law and should do as well or better in the field of social planning.

3.4.5 Fracturing. Break a decision into parts which can be decided separately; the common economic notion of incremental decision is one form of fracturing—one based largely on quantitative considerations.

3.4.6 Flexible and sequential decision interspersed with learning. Divide the effort into subtargets and monitor the experience as a basis for correcting both preceding and subsequent steps.[12]

3.4.7 Sequential decision as formalized by the decision tree's capacity to summarize the impact of successive probabilistic occurrences.[13]

[10] Burton Klein gives a structured presentation of this procedure in "The Decision Making Problem in Development," in *The Rate and Direction of Inventive Activity* R. R. Nelson, Ed. (A Conference of the Universities-National Bureau Committee for Economic Research) Princeton University Press, 1962, pp. 485–6.

[11] There is a comprehensive statement of the notion by Richard R. Nelson in "Uncertainty, Learning, and the Economics of Parallel Research and Development Efforts," *Review of Economic Statistics*, November 1961, pp. 351–364. A provocative discussion of the approach appears in Joseph D. Cooper, *The Art of Decision Making*, Doubleday and Co., Garden City, New York, 1961, p. 139.

[12] The point constitutes a central theme of Part Two. It appears in less specific form in paragraphs 1.2 and 2.4 above. For a formal statement see Kenneth J. Arrow, "Utilities, Attitudes, Choices: A Review Note," *Econometrica*, January 1958, pp. 5–6. The importance of the "first move" in the context of keeping opportunities open is stressed by Franco Modigliani and Kalman J. Cohen in "The Role of Anticipations and Plans In Economic Behavior and Their Use in Economic Analysis and Forecasting," *Bureau of Economic and Business Research, University of Illinois Bulletin,* January 1961, p. 24.

[13] Decision trees are discussed in their usual sense and broadened to cover a

3.5 Devise effective strategies for achieving agreement (including the exploitation of uncertainty to encompass conflicting interpretations).[14]

4. Improve information concerning outcomes or their utilities. This applies to all stages of decision and should be thought of as an essential aspect of other methods of coping with uncertainty. Information is the basis of sound judgment as well as, if sufficiently rich, of explicit calculation.

4.1 Improve understanding by assembly and analysis of information bearing on goals, utilities, causality, alternatives (thereby exploring how to increase utility as well as reduce uncertainty). This instruction has underlaid many of the previous points. Though it can be pursued in sophisticated ways, it can also be highly productive when it takes the form of little more than careful thought and analysis. Often the cost of uncertainty can be substantially reduced simply by using information that is readily available—the literature, history and experience, the wisdom and know-how of people, observation of the customary roles that people or organizations play which makes their actions roughly predictable, and so on and on.

4.2 Promote communication thereby contributing to effective interpersonal aspects of the deliberative process with resultant potential improvement in many of the respects previously listed.

4.3 Use analytic techniques capable of reducing uncertainty. Sections 3.1 and 3.4 deal with this subject.

4.4 Devise reporting systems and their utilization. This is a basic aspect of stage 5, auditing. Our analysis has emphasized the value of the informal sorts of communication as well as those more

---

decision "strategy." In the latter sense they merge with the previous point (3.4.6) in the checklist. Under the name of "partition tree" the concept is featured by Karl-Olof Faxén in *Monetary and Fiscal Policy under Uncertainty*, Stockholm Economic Studies, New Series 1, Almqvist and Wiksell, Stockholm, 1957.

[14] Strategy of achieving agreement features in the person-oriented aspect of DOSRAP. It is developed in the large and growing literature on conflict resolution, e.g., *Conflict and Defense, A General Theory* by Kenneth E. Boulding and *The Strategy of Conflict*, by Thomas C. Schelling (Harvard University Press, Cambridge, 1960). An ongoing series of papers appear in *The Journal of Conflict Resolution*. For a very different approach see Bertram M. Gross' discussion of drafting a bill in a fashion likely to facilitate agreement, *The Legislative Struggle, A Study in Social Combat*, McGraw-Hill Book Co., New York, 1953, p. 216. In some sense, the point is illustrated in most case studies of political behavior. Anthony Downs in *An Economic Theory of Democracy* (Harper and Row, 1957) suggests that political parties will often find it advantageous to cloud their platforms in uncertainty (see particularly pp. 135–38).

commonly called reporting systems. The approach has a high potential usefulness but to achieve it, several capabilities must be exploited:

4.4.1 Design of auditing as part of the administrative decision procedure;

4.4.2 Design of ways to bring information rapidly into use, as well as to collect it (very important and very easily overlooked);

4.4.3 Consideration not merely of questions concerning how successful a program may be, but, very especially, of how it may be improved. Improvement may involve definition of objectives as well as how to achieve them.

4.5 Improve information bearing on the staging of decisions. See item 3.4 above.

4.6 Judicious neglect of information (see also item 3.1.4).

4.6.1 Select important variables and neglect the rest.[15]

4.6.2 Use a "rule of thumb" as a basis of decision.[16]

4.7 Beware of biased evaluation such as:

4.7.1 The use of unadjusted "wing-boundary" values particularly in the context of "satisficing" constructions.

4.7.2 The trap of the "numbers illusion."

4.8 Imitate the behavior of a successful colleague or competitor. This sharply reduces the need for information.[17]

5. Adapt the organization to the needs of improved deliberative procedures including those related to reducing the cost of uncertainty both by decreasing the possibility shortfall and the knowledge gap. The point here emphasized is that many of the ways to cope with uncertainty listed above can be fostered by building them into organizational structure, procedures, and customs.

5.1 Build a personnel capable of creative and well-motivated (as well as efficient) work. The emphasis here is on reducing the cost of

---

[15] The subject is discussed in a particularly persuasive way by Aaron Wildavsky in *Politics of the Budgetary Process* (Little Brown & Co., Boston, 1965) in terms of a zone of indifference which it is unnecessary (and confusing) to try to penetrate (p. 154) and the value of neglecting information which could in any event not be dealt with (p. 160). Automatic devices for indicating what can be neglected are discussed by Herbert Simon in "Application of Servomechanism Theory to Production Control," Chapter 13 in *Models of Man,* John Wiley & Sons, Inc., New York, 1957.

[16] Management literature (as well as practice) is rich in such rules. For applications in the political sphere see Wildavsky, *op. cit.,* pp. 151–152.

[17] Some of the broad implications of this procedure are developed in a most interesting fashion by A. Alchian, "Uncertainty, Evolution, and Economic Theory," *Journal of Political Economy,* Vol. 58, No. 3, June 1950, p. 217.

uncertainty by improving the targets considered (reducing the possibility shortfall),

5.2 Employ "uncertainty bearers," people with a talent for absorbing uncertainty and arriving at sound judgments.[18]

5.3 Build a set of relationships and procedures which aim to reduce unpredictability of behavior.

    5.3.1 Use the wide variety of methods such as information systems, checks and balances, standards, etc., including the organizational aspects of those discussed in section 4. above.

    5.3.2 Build the basis for stable expectations about attitudes and relationships in the organization itself.

5.4 Foster channels and customs of communication in the organization. This is a major requirement of effective deliberation as the diagram of Chapter 11 emphasizes. It is capable of reducing uncertainty's costs in terms both of possibility shortfall and a knowledge gap. (See the further development in paragraph 4.4 above.)

5.5 Create a reward system that tends to reduce disparity between personal and organizational interests:

    5.5.1 Correct the usual nonsymmetrical reward for playing safe vs. taking a sensible chance

    5.5.2 Assign personnel to a purpose rather than to a project so that individuals are not personally penalized if their evaluation of the project recommends drastic change, curtailment or elimination.

    5.5.3 Build review, self-evaluation, and change into the routines of management.

5.6 Explicit shift of the locale of decision to a different organization can be the appropriate way to "improve the organization." Such shifts can affect the purposes sought, as well as the costs of uncertainty in pursuing a given purpose.

    5.6.1 Shift to broader jurisdiction to increase seriability thereby fostering experiment or reducing uncertainty discount by causing consequences to depend on average rather than particluar results (paragraph 3.2).

    5.6.2 Shift to a broader jurisdiction can internalize externalities thereby introducing a more appropriate value scheme.

    5.6.3 Shift the locale only to the extent of having the broader juris-

---

[18] A. C. Pigou introduced this point in an important chapter in his *Economics of Welfare*, Macmillan & Co., New York, 1920; Frank H. Knight likewise emphasized it in *Risk, Uncertainty and Profit*, Houghton Mifflin Co., Boston, 1921, see particularly p. 239 ff.

dictions subsidize values external to the narrower jurisdiction (where decision itself continues to be located).

6. Improve the behavior of the relevant environment.

6.1 Strategy to define goals and form reactions. This can be valuable if it is explicit rather than hidden in "projections" which are validated by actions based on them (as when a high estimate of "need" for water is validated by supplying it at a give-away price). Much broad social and regional planning is deeply dependent on shaping desires, and particularly behavior, in fashions prescribed by the plan. The methods that can be used are endless. I select a few at random.

6.1.1 Use of methods that weight individual decisions in a way favorable to the plan, e.g., prices, taxes, and regulation.[19]

6.1.2 Elicit broad participation in planning.

6.1.3 Roles and games believed to have capacity to stabilize behavior.[20]

6.2 Strategy to control other's behavior in connection with the decision process itself where environmental reaction is important, as in the public sphere.

6.3 Built-in correctives.[21]

6.4 Law. In the words of Justice Holmes, ". . . the tendency of the law must always be to narrow the field of uncertainty."[22]

7. Follow through. This is primarily directed to stage 5 and carrying through on the need for additional cycles of decision as they evolve during earlier stages. To underscore the recursive aspect of the process I assemble the chief points mentioned earlier in the checklist and add a matter of further emphasis.

[19] The impact of most of these methods, however multitudinous, are perhaps obvious; though far from obvious is how they can be combined to bear on particular objectives. For an example of one not so obvious method see Judge Henry J. Friendly's suggestion that if administrative agencies would define their values and rules more sharply it would decrease the force of special influence. *The Federal Administrative Agencies, The Need for Better Definition of Standards* Harvard University Press, Cambridge, Mass., 1962.

[20] See Norton E. Long, *The Polity* (Chapter 10, "The Local Community as an Ecology of Games") Rand McNally, Chicago, 1962; Thomas Schelling, *op. cit.,* develops analogous notions, pp. 168 and 188.

[21] Response to decreasing marginal utility illustrates automatic correction for excessive development of one sort of public service vis a vis others. Such correction can also be introduced directly into a system of shadow prices implied in a merit-weighting scheme for the multiple purposes which a single public service performs. (See Mack and Myers, "Outdoor Recreation," in *Measuring Benefits of Public Investment,* Brookings Institution, 1965, pp. 94 to 97.)

[22] *The Common Law,* 127 (1881).

7.1 Regard decision as potentially an experimental learning process and emphasize, accordingly, how its time-dimension and recursive capacity can be put to use (paragraph 1.2).

7.2 Select alternatives in the light of timing options concerning the staging and scope of each decision cycle as a whole (paragraph 2.4.2).

7.3 Modify the problem of choice by staging and cycling decision in the light of possibilities to improve information (paragraph 3.4).

7.4 Improve information by devising reporting systems and their utilization (paragraph 4.4).

7.5 Adapt the organization by creating a system of rewards which aim to encourage and routinize a process of self-audit, revision, and re-cycling. The problem is to reward rather than to penalize participants in decision to attach their ego's to the *purposes* of the work, and thus to elicit commitment to audit and revise (paragraph 5.5).

7.6 Implement the auditing and redecision steps in every way which ingenuity and determination can devise. I refer to the difference between recognizing that a possibility is "out there" and realizing that it is a close-in reality on which achievement depends. The need for explicit emphasis is perhaps strongest, since it is most easily overlooked, in three contexts:

7.6.1 Strategies directed to influencing the environment or other elements external to the immediate decision.

7.6.2 Strategies directed specifically to enhancing, as a part of the total strategy of staging and recursive cycling, the learning process internal to decision.

7.6.3 Strategies directed to developing and clarifying the values and more specific utilities which are sought.

8. Define "improvement." Because of the large uncertainty about what will happen of its own accord, and the wide range to which determination and ingenuity can shape the course of events, uncertainty about the future can be decreased by intentional design. This point has threaded in and out of earlier paragraphs and is central to paragraph 6.

It remains to point out that to reduce uncertainty by molding future events *is only a normative instruction if these events are desirable.* Wherever value systems are at issue (and we have noted that this is the case far more often than at first seems apparent) there is no avoiding the responsibility of considering in what directions, in terms of what processes and institutions, and toward what sorts of value enhancement social betterment lies.

Index